To Samuel,

Rom 11:26!

[signature]

#047

They say that imitation is the ultimate form of flattery, and by this standard I should be highly grateful that my dear friend and constant debating partner, Dr. Michael Brown, is now publishing his new book, *The Real Kosher Jesus*, modeled on my original *Kosher Jesus*. But Mike and I have so much history in religious, historical, and social values debate that we have gone beyond being only respectful public adversaries—which will certainly continue until he renounces his adopted faith to return to the Judaism into which he was born—to being friends with deep affection between us, even as we disagree passionately on the issues. Mike wants to serve G-d. I don't doubt that. The proper way for a Christian to serve G-d is within his faith. And the proper way for a Jew to do so is within his. In this book Mike fights back against my *Kosher Jesus* book. And while his arguments are utterly futile against my intellectual onslaught, you have to give him credit for trying. And yes, I say this both seriously and tongue-in-cheek. G-d bless you, Mike, and I look forward to many more debates.

—RABBI SHMULEY BOTEACH
AUTHOR OF *KOSHER JESUS*

Michael Brown is a compelling voice in the critically important debate over the true identity of Jesus of Nazareth.

—LEE STROBEL
NEW YORK TIMES BEST-SELLING AUTHOR OF *THE CASE FOR CHRIST*

Jesus acceptable as a Jew and through Jewish eyes? Isn't that a contradiction? *The Real Kosher Jesus* explains with real clarity how Jesus as a Jew makes sense—biblically, historically, and theologically. It is a pleasure to recommend this work for any who are just curious about him and his relationship to Judaism.

—DARRELL BOCK, PhD
RESEARCH PROFESSOR OF NEW TESTAMENT STUDIES,
DALLAS THEOLOGICAL SEMINARY
AUTHOR OF *BLASPHEMY AND EXALTATION IN JUDAISM*

Any Jew or Gentile who wants to know who the real Jesus is need look no further than the spectacular and brilliant Dr. Michael Brown. So what are you waiting for?

—ERIC METAXAS
NEW YORK TIMES BEST-SELLING AUTHOR OF *BONHOEFFER: PASTOR, MARTYR, PROPHET, SPY*

Michael Brown excels as a true scholar as well as an apologist; his answers to objections are carefully thought out, honest, and well researched.

—CRAIG KEENER
AUTHOR OF *THE HISTORICAL JESUS OF THE GOSPELS*

Will the real kosher Jesus please stand up? Is he a great Jewish rabbi? Or is he the Son of God? Now we know the truth thanks to this groundbreaking book by Dr. Michael Brown.

—SID ROTH
HOST, *IT'S SUPERNATURAL!*

I am grateful that Rabbi Shmuley Boteach wrote the book *Kosher Jesus*, if for no other reason than it prompted my dear friend and colleague Mike Brown to write this incredible new book *The Real Kosher Jesus*. I am especially pleased that over the years Chosen People Ministries, the ministry I lead, has had the privilege of sponsoring a dozen debates between Mike and Shmuley, which has resulted in more light than heat—including a recent debate in New York City addressing the very issues included in Dr. Brown's book.

The real, kosher Jesus—as Dr. Brown explains with painstaking detail—is not a radical Jewish revolutionary whose goal in life was to overthrow Rome. He indeed was a revolutionary and even a radical, but not in the way Rabbi Boteach suggested. He claimed to be the Messiah, in fulfillment of the words of the prophets, especially Isaiah 53.

Dr. Brown powerfully details why Yeshua is the Messiah, who came to die for our sins and rise from the dead to provide the gift of forgiveness of sin and eternal life to both Jews and Gentiles. Mike argues his point from both Testaments, bolstering his arguments by the extensive use of Jewish sources, both modern and Rabbinic. This book is a must-read for all those who care about God's chosen people.

—MITCH GLASER, PHD
PRESIDENT, CHOSEN PEOPLE MINISTRIES

Michael Brown has established himself as the foremost messianic apologist in the world.

—BARRY R. LEVENTHAL
PROVOST AND DISTINGUISHED PROFESSOR OF CHURCH MINISTRY AND
MISSIONS, SOUTHERN EVANGELICAL SEMINARY

Other Books by the Same Author

To contact the author, visit his website at AskDrBrown.org, or write:

Michael L. Brown
P. O. Box 5546
Concord, NC 28027

the

REAL
Kosher
JESUS

MICHAEL L. BROWN, PhD

FRONT
LINE

Most CHARISMA HOUSE BOOK GROUP products are available at special quantity discounts for bulk purchase for sales promotions, premiums, fund-raising, and educational needs. For details, write Charisma House Book Group, 600 Rinehart Road, Lake Mary, Florida 32746, or telephone (407) 333-0600.

THE REAL KOSHER JESUS by Michael L. Brown, PhD
Published by FrontLine
Charisma Media/Charisma House Book Group
600 Rinehart Road
Lake Mary, Florida 32746
www.charismahouse.com

Scripture quotations marked THE MESSAGE are from *The Message: The Bible in Contemporary English*, copyright © 1993, 1994, 1995, 1996, 2000, 2001, 2002. Used by permission of NavPress Publishing Group.

Cover design by Justin Evans
Design Director: Bill Johnson

Visit the author's website at www.askdrbrown.org.

This book has not been prepared, approved, or licensed by any entity that created or produced the book *The Kosher Jesus* by Shmuley Boteach

AUTHOR'S NOTE: I wish to thank Gefen Publishing for their permission to quote from *Kosher Jesus* by Shmuley Boteach, ISBN 978-9652295781, copyright © 2012 by Gefen Publishing, www.gefenpublishing.com.

Portions of this book have been adapted from Michael L. Brown, *Answering Jewish Objections to Jesus*, vols. 1 and 2 (Grand Rapids, MI: Baker Academic, a division of Baker Publishing Group, 2000). Used by permission.

Library of Congress Cataloging-in-Publication Data:
An application to register this book for cataloging has been submitted to the Library of Congress.
International Standard Book Number: 978-1-62136-007-0 (trade paper)
                                                            978-1-62136-008-7 (hardcover)
E-book ISBN: 978-1-62136-009-4

While the author has made every effort to provide accurate telephone numbers and Internet addresses at the time of publication, neither the publisher nor the author assumes any responsibility for errors or for changes that occur after publication.

First edition

12 13 14 15 16 — 9 8 7 6 5 4 3 2 1
Printed in the United States of America

CONTENTS

PREFACE

A LITTLE MORE THAN forty years ago I made the greatest discovery of my life: Jesus was the Jewish Messiah! The radical transformation that took place at that time (in late 1971) and the amazing things I have experienced since then are a testimony to the mercy and grace of God.

Once I came to faith, my dad wanted me to talk with the local rabbi, who quickly became a good friend, challenging me respectfully and also introducing me to many more rabbis, some of them very religious. They all told me that my spirituality, however sincere, was deeply misguided, reminding me at every turn that I didn't know Hebrew. How, then, could I tell these men they were wrong in their beliefs and interpretations? They had been studying Hebrew long before I was born!

It was this challenge that prompted me to start studying Hebrew in college, as well as learning with different rabbis when possible, ultimately leading to a PhD in Semitic languages from New York University. I was determined to deal with the key texts in their original languages without having to rely on someone else's position. And from my first days of dialogue with the rabbis, I had a firm conviction: if my beliefs were true, they could withstand all the criticism and testing that my Jewish community could offer.

Over the years I exposed myself to every objection I could find, from the rabbinic community (especially from the "counter-missionary" rabbis) and from atheistic or skeptical professors in college and grad school. But the more I studied and tackled objections and earnestly sought the Lord, the clearer it became to me that the things I believed were real and true. I can testify firsthand that faith in Jesus can withstand the most intense scrutiny, both intellectually and experientially.

Because of my interaction with so many rabbis, and as a result of my academic studies, I became somewhat of a specialist in answering Jewish objections to Jesus (called by some "Messianic Jewish apologetics," meaning, the defense of the faith), leading to many public debates with Jewish leaders, most frequently with a man who has become a dear friend in the process, Rabbi Shmuley Boteach. And this leads to the writing of the book you now hold in your hands (or read in digital form).

Just days before Shmuley's new book *Kosher Jesus* was about to be released (meaning, in mid-January of 2012), I suddenly felt compelled to write my own book in which I would put together decades of study and reflection and practical experience while also interacting with the novel theories put forth in his volume. The odd thing is that I had received a digital copy of *Kosher Jesus* months earlier in order to write an endorsement for it, yet I didn't have the slightest thought about writing my own version of who the real kosher Jesus was (plus, I had other projects I was working on and other writing deadlines). But now in the third week of January 2012, less than two months before our first debate about his book was scheduled (specifically, March 13, in New York City), I felt deeply moved to write—and to get the book published immediately (meaning, within a month or so of our first debate).

But how would this be possible? It takes months or years to write a book and then, after that, a good nine to twelve months to get it published. How in the world could a serious book be written and published in less than four months total? The obvious answer was that it couldn't.

Readers of the Bible, however, will be familiar with phrases such as "With God, all things are possible," and once again, I have experienced this reality for myself. I wrote the first words of this book on January 19, and I made first contact with Steve Strang of Charisma Media and FrontLine one week later on January 26. *Less than two and a half months from the day I felt stirred to write, the book was scheduled to be released* (meaning in early April). In all my years of writing, I have never experienced anything close to this, and I am duly humbled by the process.

I express my deep appreciation to the wonder-working publishing team put together by Steve, including Tessie DeVore, Debbie Marrie, Deborah Moss, Woodley Auguste, Susan Simcox, Bill Johnson, and others. From the bottom of my heart, I thank Steve and each of you for recognizing the timeliness of this project and for working with such an incredible combination of excellence and speed. (And yes, I'm tired too!)

I am also indebted to my ministry team and staff, along with our supporters and friends who prayed for me during this time in order to get this important project completed at breakneck speed. We will share in the rewards together.

I also want to thank Rabbi Shmuley for his friendship and collegiality—despite our profound differences—and for his kind acknowledgment in the back of his book (after attacking my writings, of course, throughout *Kosher Jesus,* but what else could I expect, since he's an Orthodox rabbi and I'm a committed Messianic Jew, which makes our friendship so unique).

My appreciation is also extended to Gefen Publishing in Israel for allowing me to cite several passages from *Kosher Jesus,* as well as to Baker Books, publishers of four of my five volumes devoted to answering Jewish objections to Jesus, for allowing me to adapt some of my earlier material in several of the later chapters of this book.

Most of all, and with all my heart, I express my deep love and appreciation to Nancy, my Jewish bride of thirty-six years, my very best friend, and my soul mate. She allowed me to focus on getting this book written and edited (in the midst of an already intense ministry schedule), even when it meant writing until 5:00 a.m. She is an incredible gift from God to me, as well as to our two wonderful daughters, our two terrific sons-in-law, and our four indescribably special grandchildren. Nancy and I owe everything we are or could ever be to the one who died for us and brought us from darkness to light (Nancy was a committed atheist when we met in 1974, both nineteen years old), forgiving our sins and giving us a new heart. We joyfully give all that we have to him!

It is my heartfelt prayer that you will make the discovery of a lifetime as you read the pages that follow, and if I can help you on your spiritual journey, please contact me and my team through the AskDrBrown.org website. And remember: God has promised that all those who earnestly seek him will find him. Are you ready?

—Michael L. Brown
February 22, 2012

Note on the citations and endnotes: Because this book is not intended to be a technical, academic volume for scholars only, I have not tried to cite every relevant study in the endnotes, since that would require a book many times longer than the present one. I did cite leading scholarly studies by highly respected specialists in their areas of expertise, and those references in turn will point toward other relevant studies. When citing rabbinic literature, I used the standard abbreviations, with m. denoting Mishnah, t. denoting Tosefta, b. denoting the Babylonian Talmud, and y. denoting the Jerusalem Talmud.

Introduction

SO, WHEN DID JESUS
BECOME CATHOLIC?

I WAS ABOUT TWELVE years old when I first learned that Jesus was Jewish. It was definitely before I was thirteen because I distinctly remember talking with my friends about this one afternoon before our pre–Bar Mitzvah Hebrew classes. Had they heard about this too? Was it true?

The question actually stirred up a lively discussion, as some had heard the same thing—they were pretty sure that Jesus was Jewish—while others weren't so confident. Jesus, Jewish?

True to form, I came up with what I thought was a very clever quip: "So, when did Jesus become Catholic? After he rose from the dead?"

Born into a Conservative Jewish home in New York City and raised on Long Island, I actually had a good number of Gentile friends, but we never really talked religion, and Jesus—who was sometimes called "JC" among my Jewish friends and relatives—was basically "for them," meaning the Catholics, the Christians, the Gentiles. (During another one of our brilliant, pre–Hebrew school discussions, we concluded that the words *Catholic*, *Christian*, and *Gentile* were all synonymous.)

When I was a boy, my father and I would often ride the New York City subways together, and there was one station where the words "Jesus saves" were scrawled on a wall. I saw it many times but didn't have the foggiest idea what it meant. Jesus saves?

Years later I was told of a Jewish bumper sticker carrying the caption "Jesus Saves, Moses Invests." Not to be outdone, some Boston Bruin hockey fans made up their own bumper sticker: "Jesus Saves, Esposito

Scores on the Rebound" (speaking of hockey great Phil Esposito). Jesus saves? What does it mean?

A South African Jewish friend named Geoff Cohen first discovered that Jesus was Jewish when he was twenty-two. He told me that he once passed a truck on the road with the words "Jesus Saves" painted on the back. He actually thought they ran out of paint and weren't able to finish the sentence. Jesus saves who from what?

Another Jewish friend, Jeffrey Bernstein, told me that he used to think that Jesus was the son of Mr. and Mrs. Christ. (I've heard this many times over the years.) After all, Jeff Bernstein was the son of Mr. and Mrs. Bernstein, and so Jesus Christ was the son of Mr. and Mrs. Christ, right?[1]

Little did we know that Jesus' original name was Yeshua, that Christ was the Greek way of saying Messiah (in other words, "Jesus Christ" was "Yeshua the Messiah"), that his mother's name was not Mary but Miriam, that his followers had names like Ya'akov and Yehudah, and that Saint John the Baptist was actually Rabbi Yochanan the Immerser.

Yeshua the Messiah, Miriam's boy? Rabbi Yochanan the Immerser? Really?

I can honestly say, though, that as a kid I didn't have any animosity toward Jesus. He was just some emaciated guy with long hair who hung on a cross and who was the god of the Catholic church. And in the early days of the hippie movement, when my cousin Andy grew shoulder-length hair and a beard, we dubbed him "JC."

The childhood experience of my dear friend and debating partner, Rabbi Shmuley Boteach, was quite different. Growing up in an Orthodox Jewish household, he "held great antipathy toward Jesus." "The very name," Shmuley explained, "reminded me of the suffering [that] Christians laid upon Jewish communities for two thousand years: persecutions, forced conversions, expulsions, inquisitions, false accusations, degradations, economic exile, taxation, pogroms, stereotyping, ghettoization, and systematic extermination. . . . In my neighborhood, we did not even mention his name. We said 'Yoshke,' a Hebrew play on his name, or some children learned to say 'cheese and crust' in place of 'Jesus Christ.'"[2]

He continues: "Fundamentally, we understood Jesus as a foreign deity, a man worshipped by people. The Torah instructs us never to mention the names of other gods, as no other god exists except God. We also understood Jesus to be as anti-Jewish as his followers. Was he not the Jew who had rebelled against his people? Was he not the one who instructed his followers to hate the Jews as he did, instigating countless cruelties against those with whom God had established an everlasting covenant? Was he not also the man who had abrogated the Law and said that the Torah is now mostly abolished? In truth, Jesus was not that man."[3]

After years of study, Shmuley now believes that "we can see in the Christian Bible one of our rabbis, Jesus, ever our brother."[4] And Shmuley is so passionate about getting this message out that he wrote a major book on the subject entitled *Kosher Jesus*, a book that I joyfully endorsed, at Shmuley's request, albeit with my profound differences clearly expressed.

Shmuley tells readers of *Kosher Jesus* that, "based on ancient Hebrew sources as well as Christian scripture, you will discover the authentic story of Jesus of Nazareth."[5] And he writes that, "It is time to build on these overtures of peace and address the first and last sticking point in the relationship between Christians and Jews: their common claim on Jesus,"[6] a most praiseworthy goal, for sure. And by reclaiming Yeshua as a fellow Jew and rabbi, Shmuley has taken a very major and truly wonderful step in the right direction.

It is my contention, however, that along the way he has taken some very serious missteps, ultimately creating a fictional Jesus who cannot save or transform or bring redemption to the world, revising much of the New Testament in the process.

Prompted by the occasion of the publishing of *Kosher Jesus,* but not simply as a response to *Kosher Jesus,* I have written this book, which reflects forty years of continuous dialogue with my fellow Jews (including many fine rabbis and learned professors) and decades of serious academic study.

The dialogue began at the end of 1971 when, to my shock, I discovered who Jesus really was, and although I was a headstrong, sixteen-year-old hippie, playing drums in a rock band, full of rebellion, smoking pot, using LSD, and shooting drugs—a product of the sixties counterculture revolution—my life was transformed overnight when I recognized Yeshua as our Savior, truly repented (to repent means to turn away from sin and to turn to God), and gave my life to our heavenly Father. I have never looked back since.

Join me, then, on a journey that covers thousands of years, a journey with many amazing discoveries and delightful surprises, a journey that is sometimes painful but that ends with joy, a journey through which you will learn the real story of this man named Yeshua: the most famous Jew of all time, the Jewish nation's greatest prophet, the most illustrious rabbi ever, the light of the nations—and Israel's hidden Messiah.

Shall we begin?

Section I

YESHUA-JESUS-YESHU: WHO IS HE?

1

"MAY HIS NAME AND MEMORY
BE BLOTTED OUT!"

O N WEDNESDAY EVENING, November 9, 1938, the Holocaust began as Nazi troops destroyed or set on fire Jewish homes and synagogues, smashed the windows of Jewish places of business (looting them too), and killed or wounded scores of Jews. This was *Kristallnacht*, the Night of Broken Glass, a vicious Nazi response to the November 7 murder of a German diplomat in France by a seventeen-year-old German Jewish refugee named Herschel Grynszpan.

Kristallnacht also served as a test run for the Nazis. What would the German people do when the Jews were attacked? Nothing.

In typical Nazi fashion, a detailed report of the atrocities was submitted by Reinhard Heydrich (second in command of the SS after Heinrich Himmler) stating that "815 shops [were] destroyed, 171 dwelling houses set on fire or destroyed...119 synagogues were set on fire, and another 76 completely destroyed...20,000 Jews were arrested, 36 deaths were reported and those seriously injured were also numbered at 36..."[1]

To the delight of some German pastors, the fires were still burning on November 10, the birthday of the famed German Christian leader Martin Luther, the father of the Protestant Reformation, who was born in 1483. Author Daniel Jonah Goldhagen noted:

One leading Protestant churchman, Bishop Martin Sasse of Thuringia, published a compendium of Martin Luther's anti-semitic vitriol shortly after *Kristallnacht's* orgy of anti-Jewish violence. In the foreword to the volume, he applauded the burning of the synagogues and the coincidence of the day: "On November 10, 1938, on Luther's birthday, the synagogues are burning in Germany." The German people, he urged, ought to heed these words "of the greatest antisemite of his time, the warner of his people against the Jews."[2]

Martin Luther, the greatest anti-Semite of his time?

THE LUTHER-HITLER CONNECTION

During the post–World War II Nuremberg trials for war criminals, Julius Streicher, one of Hitler's top henchmen and publisher of the anti-Semitic *Der Sturmer*, was asked if there were any other publications in Germany that treated the Jewish question in an anti-Semitic way. Streicher put it well:

> Dr. Martin Luther would very probably sit in my place in the defendants' dock today, if this book had been taken into consideration by the Prosecution. In the book "The Jews and Their Lies," Dr. Martin Luther writes that the Jews are a serpent's brood and one should burn down their synagogues and destroy them...[3]

Luther wrote those dreadful words in 1543, but just twenty years earlier, he had struck a very different tone in his booklet *That Jesus Christ Was Born a Jew*. In it he spoke scornfully of the terrible way the Catholic church had treated the Jews until that time.

> If the apostles, who also were Jews, had dealt with us Gentiles as we Gentiles deal with the Jews, there would never have been a Christian among the Gentiles.... [W]e in our turn ought to treat the Jews in a brotherly manner in order that we might convert some of them.... [W]e are but Gentiles, while the Jews

are of the lineage of Christ. We are aliens and in-laws; they are blood relatives, cousins, and brothers of our Lord.[4]

Twenty years later, now old and sick, disappointed with his lack of success in "converting" the Jews, watching some of his own parishioners express an interest in Judaism, and, worst of all, being exposed to some shameful, vulgar anti-Jesus literature penned by some Jewish leaders in reaction to years of church-sponsored persecution, Luther lashed out with venom:

> A Jew or a Jewish heart is as hard as stone and iron and cannot be moved by any means.... In sum, they are the devil's children damned to hell.[5]

For Luther, the Jews were the worst enemy of all, "devils and nothing more":

> Verily, a hopeless, wicked, venomous and devilish thing is the existence of these Jews, who for fourteen hundred years have been, and still are, our pest, torment and misfortune. They are just devils and nothing more.[6]

> Know, Christian, that next to the devil thou hast no enemy more cruel, more venomous and violent than a true Jew.[7]

What then was his counsel to the local German princes for dealing with the Jews?

> First, to set fire to their synagogues or schools.... Second, I advise that their houses also be razed and destroyed.... Instead they might be lodged under a roof or in a barn, like the gypsies.... Third, I advise that all their prayer books and Talmudic writings, in which such idolatry, lies, cursing, and blasphemy are taught, be taken from them. Fourth, I advise that their rabbis be forbidden to teach henceforth on pain of loss of life and limb. Fifth, I advise that safe-conduct on the highways be abolished completely for the Jews.... Sixth, I advise that usury

[charging interest] be prohibited to them, and that all cash and treasure of silver and gold be taken from them and put aside for safekeeping....Seventh, I recommend putting a flail, an ax, a hoe, a spade, a distaff, or a spindle into the hands of young, strong Jews and Jewesses and letting them earn their bread in the sweat of their brow...

Summing up this horrific "Christian" counsel, Luther wrote:

In brief, dear princes and lords, those of you who have Jews under your rule: if my counsel does not please you, find better advice, so that you and we all can be rid of the unbearable, devilish burden of the Jews...[8]

No wonder that Luther has been called "the John the Baptist of Adolf Hitler," since it was Hitler who resurrected Luther's anti-Semitic writings and followed his counsel to a tee before going far beyond anything Luther would have imagined or approved.[9]

How tragic and shameful it is that Bible colleges and seminaries everywhere teach exhaustive courses on church history and whole courses on Martin Luther without mentioning a word about his horrific anti-Semitic writings (of which *Concerning the Jews and Their Lies* does not stand alone).[10]

In the words of Father Edward Flannery, a respected Catholic historian:

The vast majority of Christians, even well educated, are all but totally ignorant of what happened to Jews in history and of the culpable involvement of the Church....It is little exaggeration to state that those pages of history Jews have committed to memory are the very ones that have been torn from Christian (and secular) history books.[11]

But the story doesn't begin with Luther. In 1961, Holocaust historian Raul Hilberg published his landmark study *The Destruction of the European Jews*, containing the now famous charts demonstrating that all the anti-Semitic policies set in place by the Nazis—with the sole exception of extermination—had already been instituted by the church in previous centuries.[12]

THE ANTI-SEMITIC LEGACY OF THE CHURCH

It was church leaders who were first responsible for passing discriminatory laws against the Jews, forcing them to wear a yellow star, herding them together in ghettos, and even expelling them from their countries (to mention just a few of the indignities). The Nazis merely renewed previously instituted anti-Semitic measures, but with an unprecedented vengeance, cruelty, and coldly calculated murderous hatred.

As Dennis Prager and Joseph Telushkin pointed out:

> Christianity did not create the Holocaust—indeed, Nazism was anti-Christian—but it made it possible. Without Christian antisemitism, the Holocaust would have been inconceivable....
>
> Hitler and the Nazis found in medieval Catholic anti-Jewish legislation a model for their own, and they read and reprinted Martin Luther's virulently antisemitic writings. It is instructive that the Holocaust was unleashed by the only major country in Europe having approximately equal numbers of Catholics and Protestants. [Both traditions were saturated with Jew-hatred.] ...
>
> While it is true that many Nazis were anti-Christian (and that Nazism itself was anti-Christian), they were all, as the Jewish philosopher Eliezer Berkovits has pointed out, the children of Christians.[13]

This was the terrible end result of fifteen hundred years of church-sponsored or church-approved or church-tolerated anti-Semitism. And, in perhaps the greatest perversion in the history of religion, hatred of the Jews was carried out in the name of Jesus—himself a Jew to his dying breath. How did a faith that was founded by a Jewish rabbi (and whose first adherents were all Jews) become so hostile to the Jewish people?

Raul Hilberg charts the progression:

Since the fourth century after Christ there have been three anti-Jewish policies: [forced] conversion, expulsion, annihilation. The second appeared as an alternative to the first, and the third emerged as an alternative to the second.... The missionaries of Christianity had said in effect: You have no right to live among as Jews. The secular rulers who followed proclaimed: You have no right to live among us. The Nazis at last decreed: You have no right to live....

The German Nazis, then, did not discard the past; they built upon it. They did not begin a development; they completed it.[14]

How can this possibly be?

When my family lived in Maryland, I often visited a Jewish bookstore located a few miles from our home, developing a very good relationship with the owner, Mr. E., and his son Menachem, both of them Orthodox Jews. I stopped in one day to look at some books, and Menachem came up to me with excitement: "I spotted this new book on false messiahs in Jewish history, and I picked up two copies, one for you and one for my dad."

I immediately began to look through the table of contents (the book was written in Hebrew), thanking Menachem for getting it for me and assuring him it was right up my alley. With a smile, though, I pointed to the first chapter and said, "Obviously, I don't agree with that chapter!" Yes, the first chapter was about Jesus, viewed by the author as the ultimate false messiah and not even mentioned by name in the chapter title. He was simply "That man" ('oto ha'ish in Hebrew).

Writing from Israel, the Orthodox Jewish author of the book expressed his views with passion:

> Instead of bringing redemption to the Jews, the false Christian messiah has brought down on us base libels and expulsions, oppressive restrictions and burning of [our] holy books, devastations and destructions. Christianity, which professes to infuse the sick world with love and compassion, has fixed a course directly opposed to this lofty rhetoric. The voice of the blood of millions of our brothers cries out to us from the ground: "No! Christianity is not a religion of love but a religion of unfathomable hate! All

history, from ancient times to our own day, is one continuous proof of the total bankruptcy of this religion in all its segments."[15]

There is some obvious hyperbole in these words, but the author can surely be forgiven. Everything he knows about "Christianity" tells him that it *is* a totally corrupt, anti-Jewish faith. And he is not the only Jew to share these sentiments: when religious Jews say the name Jesus, they pronounce it Yeshu, which is also a Hebrew acronym for, "May his name and memory be obliterated!" (Hebrew, *yimach sh'mo v'zikro*).[16] For many religious Jews, when they speak that name, they are uttering a curse against him as well. Cursing the name of Jesus?

But wait. Jesus wasn't only a Jew himself, but he is the first man in recorded history to be called "Rabbi." The only possible exception would be his cousin, Rabbi Yochanan the Immerser, better known as St. John the Baptist.[17] Think of it: Yeshua, the rabbi from Nazareth, and his cousin, Rabbi Yochanan, who called his fellow Jews to do *teshuvah* (repentance) and be ritually immersed (as religious Jews do in the *mikveh* today). This is the beginning of "Christianity"?

The Jewishness of Jesus

As for Yeshua, he taught in the synagogues, read from the Torah scrolls, and initially sent his first followers—all of them Jews—to reach out to fellow Jews alone: "Do not go among the Gentiles or enter any town of the Samaritans," he said. "Go rather to the lost sheep of Israel" (Matt. 10:5–6; the prophets often pictured the children of Israel as lost or scattered sheep).[18]

On another occasion he told a Gentile woman, "I was sent only to the lost sheep of the house of Israel" (Matt. 15:24, esv; he did, however, have mercy on her and heal her daughter). On yet another occasion he explained to a Samaritan woman,[19] "You people don't know what you are worshipping; we worship what we do know, because salvation comes from the Jews" (John 4:22, cjb).[20] Yes, these are the words of Jesus, found directly in the New Testament: "salvation comes from the Jews." And some Jews won't even say his name? Some Jews still curse his name? What happened?

Followers of Jesus believe that after he was crucified, he rose from the dead and then gave his disciples (*talmidim*, students, followers, in Hebrew) a commission to make *talmidim* in all the nations, but the priority remained the same: start in Jerusalem, then go to Judea, then Samaria, then the ends of the earth. (See Acts 1:8.) As expressed in Luke 24:47, "Repentance and forgiveness of sins will be preached in his name to all nations, beginning at Jerusalem."

And that's exactly what his followers did, declaring the good news that the Messiah had come and died and risen from the dead, in accordance with the ancient Hebrew prophecies, and in his name the forgiveness of sins was being offered. Preaching at the Temple in Jerusalem during the festival of *Shavu'ot* (Weeks; Pentecost), Peter (in Hebrew, *Shimon Kefa*) said to his fellow Jews, "And you are heirs of the prophets and of the covenant God made with your fathers. He said to Abraham, 'Through your offspring all peoples on earth will be blessed.' When God raised up his servant, he sent him first to you to bless you by turning each of you from your wicked ways" (Acts 3:25–26). Yes, God sent the Messiah first to the Jewish people!

Interestingly, after a number of years, when the first Gentiles became followers of Yeshua, a controversy arose among his faithful disciples: Do these Gentiles first have to become Jewish to follow him? Do the men have to be circumcised, and do both men and women have to become Torah observant? (See Acts 15.) *That* was the big controversy they had to address, rather than, Can you be Jewish and follow Jesus? To the contrary, Jews were the only followers Yeshua had until the Gentiles began to join their ranks.

Almost thirty years after Yeshua's death and resurrection, his Jewish followers in Jerusalem were still zealous for the Torah and totally devoted to their people. As their leaders stated, "You see, brother, how many thousands of Jews have believed, and all of them are zealous for the law" (Act 21:20).

In complete contrast, by the Middle Ages, Jews converting to Catholicism often had to promise on oath that they would break all association with their people, that they would no longer observe the Sabbath or any festivals or holy days, that they would not circumcise their sons, and that they would even force themselves to take a liking to pork![21] To ask once again: What in the world happened?

THE JEWISHNESS OF PAUL

Perhaps Paul changed everything? Absolutely not. (I'll take this up in more detail in chapter 7.) He wrote to Gentile believers in Rome that the message of the good news about the Messiah (called the gospel) was "God's powerful means of bringing salvation to everyone who keeps on trusting, to the Jew especially, but equally to the Gentile" (Rom. 1:16, CJB; or, "first for the Jew, then for the Gentile"). And lest the Roman believers thought that being Jewish no longer had any spiritual significance, he wrote, "What advantage, then, is there in being a Jew, or what value is there in circumcision? Much in every way! First of all, they have been entrusted with the very words of God" (Rom. 3:1–2).

As for Paul's love for his people Israel—for whom he grieved, since he was convinced they had missed the Messiah when he came—he spoke these words of anguish:

> I am speaking the truth—as one who belongs to the Messiah, I do not lie; and also bearing witness is my conscience, governed by the *Ruach HaKodesh* [Holy Spirit]: my grief is so great, the pain in my heart so constant, that I could wish myself actually under God's curse and separated from the Messiah, if it would help my brothers, my own flesh and blood, the people of Isra'el! They were made God's children, the *Sh'khinah* [divine presence] has been with them, the covenants are theirs, likewise the giving of the Torah, the Temple service and the promises; the Patriarchs are theirs; and from them, as far as his physical descent is concerned, came the Messiah, who is over all. Praised be ADONAI [the Lord] for ever! Amen.
>
> —ROMANS 9:1–5, CJB

Later he explained to the Roman believers that, despite many Jewish people being hostile to the message of Jesus the Messiah, nonetheless, "with respect to being chosen they are loved for the Patriarchs' sake, for

God's free gifts and his calling are irrevocable" (Rom. 11:28–29, CJB). And just as Jeremiah had prophesied that the day would come when God would be the God of all the families of Israel, so too Paul declared that the day would come when "all Israel will be saved, as it is written: 'The deliverer will come from Zion; he will turn godlessness away from Jacob. And this is my covenant with them when I take away their sins'" (Rom. 11:26–27).[22]

So who changed things then, if it wasn't Paul? Actually, the change was gradual, over the course of several centuries, and it began when Gentile followers of Yeshua failed to heed Paul's exhortations. "Do not be arrogant, but be afraid," he wrote to the Romans (Rom. 11:20), with specific reference to their attitude toward Israel. "I don't want you to become conceited" (paraphrasing his words in verse 25).

He didn't want these Gentile believers to forget that God had made room for them to share at the table with their older Jewish brothers and sisters (the Messiah's own people!). Otherwise they might begin to think that *they* were now the new Israel and that God was finished with the old Israel. Paul rebuked this notion strongly: "Again I ask: Did they [meaning the people of Israel] stumble so as to fall beyond recovery? Not at all!" (v. 11). He was emphatic that God's promises to his chosen nation would ultimately come to pass (vv. 11–16).

FROM JEWISH JESUS MOVEMENT TO GENTILE CHURCH

What happened, then, was this. At first the Jesus movement was entirely Jewish, recognized as another Jewish sect (like the Pharisees or Sadducees or Essenes), but over a period of centuries, a period longer than America has existed as the United States, more and more Gentiles joined the movement, and the Jewish believers found themselves between a rock and a hard place.

The Gentile church no longer understood them, having lost sight of their Jewish roots (just as Paul had warned!) and basically saying to them: "If you want to be part of us, you have to give up your Jewishness." (Yes, there were Jewish followers of Yeshua who were Torah observant several centuries after his death.) The rest of the Jewish community basically told them, "If you want to be part of us, you have to give up Jesus." And so, after three hundred to four hundred years (although some claim it took up to six hundred or seven hundred years), these Jewish believers were completely swallowed up into the church.[23]

But that's only part of the story. By this time (meaning the fourth century), the church had become so detached from its Jewish roots that it had turned Peter (Shimon Kefa, the Jewish *talmid* of Yeshua!) into the first pope, banned Christians from observing the seventh-day Sabbath (changing it to Sunday), and celebrated Easter in place of Passover (rather than celebrating the Messiah's death and resurrection during the Passover season, as the first believers did).

Thankfully, a major change has been taking place, and if you visited Israel today, you would find as many as ten thousand Jews who are following Yeshua as Messiah, with scores of Messianic Jewish congregations all over the land, meeting together to worship and pray on *Shabbat* (Sabbath).

And following in the footsteps of the "Righteous Gentiles" who risked their lives to save Jews during the Holocaust,[24] there have been meetings in America where thousands of Christians have symbolically put on the Yellow Star that marked Jews during the Holocaust (and before), making a public pledge to give their own lives to save Jewish lives should another terrible calamity arise. And it is well-known that evangelical Christians have become Israel's very best friends, as even the Knesset (Israel's house of representatives) acknowledges. In fact, when I tell these precious people about the horrors of "Christian anti-Semitism," they are absolutely shocked, having never been exposed to it before.[25]

Now, in 2012, the man known as "America's most famous rabbi," my friend Shmuley Boteach, has written a book encouraging Jews to reclaim Jesus for themselves, saying that now is the opportune time. I wholeheartedly concur!

What is interesting, though, is that Jews have been reclaiming Jesus-Yeshua as one of their own for the last one hundred years—and even longer. Let's continue on our journey, then, with the excitement of children on a treasure hunt. There are some real treasures to be found.

2

WHAT'S SO NEW ABOUT JEWS
RECLAIMING JESUS?

ALTHOUGH THE PUBLICATION of Rabbi Shmuley Boteach's *Kosher Jesus* was attended with a flurry of media attention (rightly so), and although it stirred up a considerable amount of controversy in the religious Jewish world (understandably), there's really nothing new about a rabbi or Jewish scholar reclaiming Jesus as one of their own. In fact, as I sit in my office and scan the wall-to-wall bookshelves, my eyes immediately fall on quite a few similar books written by Jewish scholars of the past and present, not to mention scores of books by Christian scholars seeking to place Jesus in a Jewish context.[1]

These Jewish rabbis, professors, and philosophers run the full gamut of strong criticism of Jesus to great appreciation for him. But the general pattern is that they were more interested in reclaiming him than rejecting him. This is highly significant, since the earliest rabbinic sources that appear to refer to Jesus-Yeshua, written within the first five hundred years of his life, speak of him as a reprobate sinner, a deceiver who was damned to hell.[2] Consequently, this was how many religious Jews viewed him through the centuries.

But within the last two hundred years a major shift began to take place. As Matthew Hoffman noted in his book *From Rebel to Rabbi: Reclaiming Jesus and the Making of Modern Jewish Culture*:

> From the end of the eighteenth century, Jewish proponents of modernization, enlightenment (Haskalah), and reform began to reject the traditionally negative Jewish views of Jesus in favor of increasingly sympathetic appraisals of him. This complex

and intriguing trend in modern Jewish history has come to be known by scholars as the Jewish reclamation of Jesus.[3]

Although that trend was stalled because of the horrors of the Holocaust—in the Jewish mind, often associated with Christianity—the Jewish reclaiming of Jesus has continued in more recent decades.

In 1984 Donald Hagner, a professor at Fuller Theological Seminary and a top New Testament scholar, wrote a volume summarizing Jewish research on Jesus through the early 1980s entitled *The Jewish Reclamation of Jesus.*[4] Since then the floodgates of Jewish scholarship on Jesus have opened wide, and a major cultural and religious shift is taking place before our eyes. As noted in 2008 by Prof. John T. Pawlikowski, a Catholic leader heavily involved in interfaith dialogue:

> The "Jesus question" is definitely making a comeback on the agenda in certain Jewish circles, much more than it was even a decade ago. The new Jewish quest for Jesus, however, is now being done much more in collaboration with Christian scholarship than was the case in the late nineteenth and early twentieth centuries. Where it will lead remains an open question.[5]

The changes have been so dramatic that in 2011 Zev Garber, professor emeritus and chair of Jewish studies and philosophy at Los Angeles Valley College, edited a major collection of essays entitled *The Jewish Jesus: Revelation, Reflection, Reclamation.*[6] The last essay in the volume, by Shaul Magid, addressed the subject, "The New Jewish Reclamation of Jesus in Late Twentieth-Century American: Realigning and Rethinking Jesus the Jew."[7]

Let's go back through the years and see what these different Jewish authors had to say. Jesus is clearly being reclaimed by his Jewish people.

The first book I see on my shelves is the classic 1922 volume by Joseph Klausner, *Jesus of Nazareth: His Life, Times, and Teaching,* a book hailed by some as, "The best biography and history of Jesus ever written."[8] Klausner, while taking issue with key aspects of Jesus' teaching and philosophy, wrote that, "Jesus was a Jew and a Jew he remained till his last breath. His one idea was to implant within his nation the idea of the coming of the Messiah and, by repentance and good works, hasten the 'end.'...From the standpoint of general humanity, he is, indeed, 'a light to the Gentiles.'"9

Klausner, who was a pioneer professor at Hebrew University, beginning his tenure there in 1920, wrote his Jesus book in an early form of Modern Hebrew, meaning that he wrote the book mainly for his fellow Jews. The edition I have was printed by Bloch Publishing, and it contains a foreword by Sydney B. Hoenig, professor emeritus of Jewish History at Yeshiva University. (Hint: Bloch Publishing is not a Christian publishing house, and Yeshiva University is not a Christian seminary.)10

FROM HEBREW UNIVERSITY TO OXFORD UNIVERSITY

One generation later another brilliant professor at Hebrew University, David Flusser, spent decades studying Jesus the Jew along with the Jewish background to the New Testament. A seven-hundred-page volume of his combined essays entitled *Judaism and the Origins of Christianity* was published by Hebrew University's very own Magnes Press.11 Flusser also authored the book *Jesus* (translated into multiple languages), now published in an updated edition with the title *The Sage from Galilee: Rediscovering Jesus' Genius*.12 So, two of the most prominent professors at the most famous Jewish institution in the world spent considerable time writing about Jesus the Jew.

Also writing in Modern Hebrew for Jewish readers, Yehezkel Kaufmann, another pioneer professor at Hebrew University and one of the greatest biblical scholars of his generation, noted in 1929–30 that:

> It is the opinion of [Abraham] Geiger, [Solomon] Graetz, and other Jewish scholars—and also many more liberal Christian scholars—that Jesus was wholly Jewish in outlook. Jesus did not intend to break with tradition, or to found a new religion; and certainly he did not imagine that he was founding a religion of the Gentiles.13

His own opinion was that, "There was, then, no contradiction between the views of Jesus and of contemporary Jewish orthodoxy with respect to the written Torah and the ceremonial law as a whole. Jesus accepted the oral law as taught by the Pharisees."[14]

As expressed by Rabbi Ben Zion Bokser in 1967:

> The Jesus of history was a son of his people, who shared their dreams, who was loyal to their way of life, who died a martyr's death because of a commitment to his vision of their highest destiny. The image of Jesus as depicted in Christian writings was not founded on historical reality.[15]

This is hardly an isolated opinion among Jewish scholars.

Moving now to Oxford University, Prof. Geza Vermes, one of the world's leading authorities on the Dead Sea Scrolls, authored a series of books on Jesus, beginning with *Jesus the Jew: A Historian's Reading of the Gospels* (1973), followed by *Jesus and the World of Judaism* (1983), then *The Religion of Jesus the Jew* (1993), then *The Changing Faces of Jesus* (2000), then *The Authentic Gospel of Jesus* (2003).[16] As if this was not enough, in 2010 he released *The Real Jesus: Then and Now*.[17]

Vermes begins the preface to *The Authentic Gospel of Jesus* speaking of "The historical Jesus, a religious genius" and explains his approach to the study of this Jesus:

> Acting as a sympathetic historian and discarding denominational biases, both the deification of Jesus by Christians and his traditional Jewish caricature as an apostate, a magician and an enemy of the people of Israel, I have simply tried to put the record straight and to reconstruct a genuine likeness of Yeshua, son of Joseph of the Galilean townlet of Nazareth.[18]

JESUS THE PHARISEE

In 2003 Hyam Maccoby, professor of Jewish studies at the University of Leeds, wrote *Jesus the Pharisee*, a book that deeply influenced Shmuley's thinking in *Kosher Jesus*, as he freely acknowledges.[19] Apparently unknown to Maccoby, almost twenty years earlier a Brooklyn rabbi named Harvey Falk wrote a book with the identical title, *Jesus the Pharisee: A New Look at the Jewishness of Jesus*.[20] And Falk cited at length a letter from the respected eighteenth-century rabbi and Talmudic scholar Jacob Emden, a letter that is not widely known today, despite Emden's stature.

Writing in 1757, Rabbi Emden explained:

> Therefore you must realize—and accept the truth from him who speaks it—that we see clearly here that the Nazarene and his Apostles did not wish to destroy the Torah from Israel, God forbid; for it is written so in Matthew (Mt. 5), the Nazarene having said, "Do not suppose that I have come to abolish the Torah. I did not come to abolish, but to fulfill. I tell you this: So long as heaven and earth endure, not a letter, not a stroke, will disappear from the Torah until it is achieved. If any man therefore sets aside even the least of the Torah's demands, and teaches others to do the same, he will have the lowest place in the Kingdom of Heaven, whereas anyone who keeps the Torah, and teaches others so, will stand high in the Kingdom of Heaven." This is also recorded in Luke (Lk. 16). It is therefore exceedingly clear that the Nazarene never dreamed of destroying the Torah.[21]

Rabbi Emden also wrote that, "The Nazarene brought about a double kindness in the world. On the one hand, he strengthened the Torah of Moses majestically....And on the other hand, he did much good for the Gentiles...."[22]

In 1875 a respected Orthodox rabbi named Elias Soloweyczk (Soloveitchik) produced a rabbinic commentary in Hebrew on the Gospel of Matthew, entitled *Kol Koreh* ("a voice cries out"), which was then followed by a commentary on the Gospel of Mark, in which he sought to demonstrate that the Gospels did not contradict either the Hebrew Scriptures or the Talmud. At the beginning of his commentary on Mark he wrote: "In the preface to my first volume of Kol Koreh I promised to show that the New Testament, contrary to popular belief, is neither in disagreement with the Old or even with the Talmud. I fulfilled my commitment regarding the first Gospel, and now I work on the second."[23] Rabbi Soloweyczk made reference to Rabbi Jacob Emden's writings as well.

Just a few years later the German Reform rabbi Abraham Geiger ignited a firestorm of controversy when he argued that Jesus was a teacher of Judaism rather than the founder of Christianity, but in many ways that has become a common Jewish point of view.[24] More sympathetic was the 1939 novel of Sholem Asch, *The Nazarene*, written as if by first-century eyewitnesses.[25] (Asch, of course, was a famed Yiddish author.)

In 1911 Gerald Friedlander published *The Jewish Sources of the Sermon on the Mount*,[26] but a more substantial work was released by Claude G. Montefiore in two volumes, *The Synoptic Gospels, Edited With an Introduction and a Commentary* (second edition, 1927).[27]

MORE JEWISH VIEWS OF JESUS

Then, in 1931, Hyman Gerson Enelow's *A Jewish View of Jesus* was published,[28] and by that same year, enough books and articles had been written about Jesus by Jewish authors that Thomas T. Walker released his study, *Jewish Views of Jesus; An Introduction and an Appreciation* (1931).[29] After the devastation of World War II, Jewish publications on Jesus and the New Testament began once more, and in 1956 two important studies came out: *A Jewish Understanding of the New Testament* by Reform Rabbi Samuel Sandmel and Prof. David Daube's volume *The New Testament and Rabbinic Judaism*.[30] As for the 1967 study by the German Jewish scholar Schalom Ben-Chorin, the title says it all: *Brother Jesus: The Nazarene Through Jewish Eyes*.[31] Jumping ahead to 1983, Israeli scholar and Orthodox Jew Pinchas Lapide published *The Resurrection of Jesus* in which he also affirmed that "Jesus was utterly true to the Torah, as I myself hope to be. I even suspect that Jesus was even more true to the Torah than I, an Orthodox Jew."[32] But Lapide went one step further, and it was quite a big step at that: he affirmed that Yeshua rose from the dead!

> I accept the resurrection of Easter Sunday not as an invention of the community of disciples, but as a historical event.... I believe that the Christ event leads to a way of salvation which God has

opened up in order to bring the Gentile world into the community of God's Israel.[33]

The fact is that more and more Jews are recognizing Jesus-Yeshua as one of their own, often claiming that he has been wrongly represented by the church (or the New Testament itself).

As I look around my personal library, I see books such as *Jesus and the Judaism of His Time* by Irving M. Zeitlin (1991),[34] *Jesus of Nazareth, King of the Jews: A Jewish Life and the Emergence of Christianity* by Paula Fredriksen (1999),[35] and with strikingly similar names (both, coincidentally, published in 2007), *Jesus the Misunderstood Jew: What the New Testament Really Says About the Man From Nazareth* by Robert Kupor[36] and *The Misunderstood Jew: The Church and the Scandal of the Jewish Jesus*, by Amy-Jill Levine.[37] Who is this "misunderstood Jew"?

JEWISH-CHRISTIAN COLLABORATIONS AND JEWISH NEW TESTAMENT COMMENTARIES

There are now collaborative works by Jewish and Christian scholars, such as *Christianity and Rabbinic Judaism: A Parallel History of Their Origins and Early Development* (1992),[38] *Jews and Christians Speak of Jesus* (1994),[39] or *Jesus Through Jewish Eyes: Rabbis and Scholars Engage an Ancient Brother in a New Conversation* (2001),[40] just to mention a few. There are even whole series of books written jointly by Jewish and Christian scholars, all focused on Jesus-related issues, such as those produced by Jacob Neusner and Bruce Chilton.[41]

As I noted in my 2000 article in the Israeli journal *Mishkan*:[42]

> The very fact that collaborative Jewish-Christian volumes such as *Hillel and Jesus*[43] can be written is a huge step forward, especially since such scholarship is not just the occasional research of a Jewish professor (like Joseph Klausner's work of a previous generation) but rather is reflective of mainstream trends. How can it be negative when Lawrence H. Schiffman, a traditional Jew and a leading authority on the Dead Sea Scrolls, writes on "The Jewishness of Jesus: Commandments Concerning Interpersonal

Relations";[44] when Prof. Irving Zeitlin authors a volume entitled, *Jesus and the Judaism of His Time*;[45] when Rabbi Philip Sigal discusses the halakhah [approach to Jewish law] of Jesus according to Matthew's Gospel;[46] when Israeli scholars such as David Flusser and Shmuel Safrai lead the Jerusalem School for the Study of the Synoptic Gospels in its efforts to recover (and thereby rediscover) the Jewish background to the Gospels?[47] All this presupposes the Jewishness of Jesus and the fact that he can only be rightly understood as a Jew among Jews—in terms of his message, his mission, and his mindset.

And there are more and more Jewish studies of the New Testament being published, such as *A Rabbinic Commentary on the New Testament: The Gospels of Matthew, Mark and Luke*, by Samuel Tobias Lachs (1987),[48] *Rabbinic Perspectives on the New Testament*, by Dan Cohn-Sherbok (1990),[49] and *Modern Jews Engage the New Testament: Enhancing Jewish Well-Being in a Christian Environment*, by Michael Cook (2008).[50] And in a landmark publication in 2011, Oxford University Press released *The Jewish Annotated New Testament*, the exclusive work of Jewish scholars, making this virtually a Jewish version of a Christian study Bible.[51] I should also mention a controversial new volume by Talmud scholar Daniel Boyarin, *The Jewish Gospels: The Story of the Jewish Christ* (2012).[52] Talk about Jews reclaiming Jesus!

And remember: I am only citing books written *by* Jews *about* Jesus and the New Testament (with the exception of the collaborative works I mentioned). Otherwise, I would have to list an almost endless stream of books written by Christian scholars about the Jewishness of Jesus with titles such as *Jesus Within Judaism* (1989),[53] *Rabbi Jesus: An Intimate Biography* (2002),[54] *Sitting at the Feet of Rabbi Jesus: How the Jewishness of Jesus Can Transform Your Faith* (2009),[55] or the multi-volume study by John P. Meier, *A Marginal Jew: Rethinking the Historical Jesus*.[56]

Is There More to This Rabbi From Nazareth?

By now, though, the message should be clear: Jesus was Jewish, and many Jewish scholars want to reclaim him as one of their own, which leads to an important observation. In these different Jewish studies Jesus has been depicted as a great rabbi, a Pharisee par excellence, a charismatic healer and exorcist, a holy man, an enlightened religious teacher, an exceptional sage, or the leader of a rebellion against Rome. But even if all of these depictions of Jesus were true, there's a nagging question that remains. Why are we still talking about *this particular Jew* almost two thousand years after his death?

There were other great rabbis and preeminent Pharisees, others who claimed to be healers and exorcists or who were hailed as enlightened religious teachers, and still others who fought to overthrow the tyranny of Rome, but most of the world has never heard of them. In fact, some of them are virtually unknown even in much of the contemporary *Jewish* world. Why does Jesus-Yeshua stand out from all the others like a brilliant flare piercing the darkness of the night?

Why, indeed, has the Western world divided time by BC (Before Christ) and AD (Anno Domini, the year of our Lord)? Why is the name of Jesus revered today by more than two billion Christians (roughly one-third of the world's population)? And why is Jesus revered by many Hindu teachers (who consider him another important divine incarnation), Buddhist teachers (who consider him an especially enlightened person), and Muslim teachers (who recognize him as one of the great prophets and who even believe that he will return!)?[57]

Could it be that, while there is truth to some of these Jewish descriptions of Jesus, he was actually more than the sum of all of them combined? Could it be that the very thing these Jewish scholars reject—namely, that Yeshua was the Messiah, who, in a unique and unprecedented way, brought the presence of God to earth—is the key to unlocking the mystery of the Jewish rabbi from Nazareth? Could it be that while the church of history has, at times, turned Jesus into a wonderfully exalted but almost unrecognizable "unkosher Christ," and while contemporary Jewish scholars have recognized him merely as a faithful Jew of his times, both sides have missed the forest for the trees?

The Jewish scholars we have cited discovered many wonderful things about Jesus (although, to be clear, he was certainly not a freedom fighter who called for an armed uprising against Rome, as we shall see). But even as a beautiful diamond can be turned to reveal new facets of its brightness and splendor, the same is true about Jesus.

Who *was* this Jewish man who dared to say, "Heaven and earth will pass away, but my words will never pass away" (Matt. 24:35)? Two thousand years later his words ring truer than ever, being quoted and memorized and passed on in more than twenty-five hundred languages and dialects. Even as you read this book, Jewish and Gentile followers of Yeshua in every corner of the world are studying his words, from a candle-lit hut in an isolated jungle village in India to an army outpost in the heart of Israel. Who was this man?

Jewish scholars and rabbis have recognized aspects of what made Yeshua so extraordinary, but they have lost sight of the amazing whole. Just think of someone so transcendent that calling him a "great rabbi"[58] *and* a "charismatic virtuoso"[59] *and* a "master *darshan* (orator)"[60] *and* a "religious genius"[61] *and* a "luminous figure"[62] *and* a "Galilean Hasid"[63] *and* a "great, world-changing patriot for Judaism"[64] *and* a "prophetic Pharisee"[65] *and* an "astute socioeconomic commentator"[66] *and* a "religious reformer"[67] *and* a "Jew of Jews"[68] *and* the "conscience of Israel"[69] doesn't begin to do him justice, any more than describing the Grand Canyon as a "really, really big, beautiful hole in the earth" conveys a fraction of the canyon's majestic grandeur.

So the burning question remains: Who is this Jesus-Yeshua? How do we describe him? Rabbi? Rebel? Reformer? Religious teacher? Reprobate sinner? Righteous one? Revolutionary? Redeemer?

Addressing Congress in 1893, Prof. Kaufman Kohler, the second president of Hebrew Union College, said:

> No ethical system or religious catechism, however broad and pure, could equal the efficiency of this great personality, standing, unlike any other, midway between heaven and earth, equally near to God and to man....
>
> Jesus, the helper of the poor, the friend of the sinner, the brother of every fellow-sufferer, the comforter of every sorrow-laden, the healer of the sick, the up-lifter of the fallen, the lover of man, the redeemer of woman, won the heart of mankind

by storm. Jesus, the meekest of men, the most despised of the despised race of the Jews, mounted the world's throne to be earth's Great King.[70]

Is Kohler on the right track? And is it possible that there is more to Jesus-Yeshua than even Kohler was able to grasp?

Albert Einstein was also enthralled with the figure of Jesus. In a 1929 interview in *The Saturday Evening Post* he explained that, "As a child I received instruction both in the Bible and in the Talmud. I am a Jew, but I am enthralled by the luminous figure of the Nazarene....Jesus is too colossal for the pen of phrase-mongers, however artful."[71]

When asked if he believed in the historical existence of Jesus, Einstein replied, "No one can read the Gospels without feeling the actual presence of Jesus. His personality pulsates in every word. No myth is filled with such life."[72]

And the famed Jewish philosopher Martin Buber once wrote:

From my youth onwards I have found in Jesus my great brother. That Christianity has regarded and does regard him as God and Savior has always appeared to me a fact of the highest importance which, for his sake and my own, I must endeavor to understand....I am more than ever certain that a great place belongs to him in Israel's history of faith and that this place cannot be described by any of the usual categories.[73]

In light of this, Buber stated, "We must overcome the superstitious fear which we harbor about the Messianic movement of Jesus, and we must place the movement where it belongs, namely, in the spiritual history of Judaism."[74]

It is to that spiritual history that we return. Are you ready to continue on the journey?

3

A RABBI LIKE NO OTHER

Julius Wellhausen (1844–1918) was a German Bible critic with little sympathy for ancient Judaism. Yet his insights about Jesus have been quoted by many Jewish leaders through the years: "Jesus was not a Christian; he was a Jew. He did not preach a new faith, but taught men to do the will of God; and in his opinion, as also in that of the Jews, the will of God was to be found in the Law of Moses and in other books of Scripture."[1]

Jesus not a Christian, but a Jew? Prof. Shaye I. D. Cohen, a Jewish historian who has taught at the Jewish Theological Seminary, Harvard University, and Brown University, reminds us of just how Jewish Jesus was:

> Was Jesus a Jew? Of course Jesus was a Jew. He was born of a Jewish mother in Galilee, a Jewish part of the world. All of his friends, associates, colleagues, disciples—all of them were Jews. He regularly worshipped in Jewish communal worship, what we call synagogue. He preached from Jewish texts from the Bible. He celebrated the Jewish festivals. He was born, lived, died, taught as a Jew.[2]

According to Prof. Joseph Klausner, Jesus:

> ...keeps the ceremonial laws like an observing Jew: he wears "fringes";[3] he goes up to Jerusalem to keep the feast of Unleavened Bread, he celebrates the "Seder" [the traditional Passover meal], blesses the bread and the unleavened cakes and breaks them and says the blessing over the wine; he dips the various herbs into

the *haroseth*,[4] drinks the "four cups" of wine [again, referring to the Passover meal] and concludes with the *Hallel* [a prayer based on the Psalms].[5]

As for Jesus not being a "Christian," the word was not coined until more than a decade after his death, it occurs just three times in the New Testament (Acts 11:26; 26:28; 1 Pet. 4:16), and it was not widely used as a designation for Jesus' followers until the second century. And from what we can tell, the term "Christian" was coined by outsiders, possibly as a term of derision,[6] the equivalent of calling followers of Muhammad something like "Muhammadites."

Obviously, Jesus was not a Christian but a Jew. Yet he was more than that. He was also a rabbi (although, to be clear, not in the sense of a modern congregational rabbi).

This, of course, is common knowledge to many, but for others it is startling news. After all, the traditional thinking goes like this: A *Jewish* religious leader is called a rabbi, but a *Christian* religious leader is called a pastor. And since Jesus was the founder of Christianity, his disciples would have called him a pastor, as in Pastor Christ.

Well, that certainly would have been news to his first disciples, all of them Jews. They never heard of "Christianity" in their lifetimes. And Yeshua's first followers went to synagogue on Saturday not church on Sunday, celebrated Hanukkah not Christmas (come to think of it, they never heard of Christmas either), and referred to any popular teacher as rabbi, using it as a title of honor and respect.[7]

Does this sound confusing to you? Does it appear that I'm mixing two religions together or that I'm claiming that Christianity doesn't exist—or that it's actually Jewish? Then let's take a look at the New Testament documents and see what they have to say.

A First-Century Rabbi

One night a respected Jewish leader who came to talk to Yeshua, not wanting to be seen inquiring of him. "Now there was a man of the Pharisees named Nicodemus [Hebrew, *Nakdimon*], a ruler of the Jews. This man came to Jesus by night and said to him, 'Rabbi, we know that you are a teacher come from God, for no one can do these signs that you do unless God is with him'" (John 3:1–2, ESV).[8]

So, a Jewish leader—a Pharisee at that—recognizes Jesus as a gifted teacher, a man sent by God, and he calls him rabbi, a title by which he is addressed a total of thirteen times in the New Testament (along with being called a teacher many more times),[9] and this leads us to a very important observation: *we cannot understand who Jesus-Yeshua is unless we recognize him as a first-century Jewish rabbi.* I could cite a small mountain of books and articles penned by Jewish and Christian scholars that agree with this assessment, and it is a foundational premise of Rabbi Shmuley Boteach's *Kosher Jesus* as well.[10]

So, if Jesus was a rabbi, what would that look like in the first century?

A first-century rabbi would gather together a group of disciples (or students; *talmidim* in Hebrew).

One of the most famous sayings in the *Mishnah* (a collection of Jewish legal traditions that form the basic component of the *Talmud*, the central text of Judaism) is the exhortation to "make many disciples" (m. Pirke Avot, 1:1), and this was something Jesus did with distinct purpose, saying to his potential disciples, "Follow me!"[11] As noted by David Stern:

> Teachers, both itinerant like Yeshua and settled ones, attracted followers who wholeheartedly gave themselves over to their teachers (though not in a mindless way, as happens today in some cults). The essence of the relationship was one of trust in every area of living, and its goal was to make the *talmid* like his rabbi in knowledge, wisdom and ethical behavior.[12]

As Jesus taught, "A disciple is not above his teacher, nor a servant above his master. It is enough for the disciple to be like his teacher, and the servant like his master" (Matt. 10:24–25, ESV). It is striking that there are more than two hundred references to Yeshua's disciples (*talmidim*) in the Gospels, and his final commission to his eleven core disciples was to "go and make people from all nations into *talmidim*" (Matt. 28:19, CJB).

A first-century rabbi would instruct his disciples in God's Word and offer his interpretations.

Matthew sums up Yeshua's pattern of ministry in three words, in this order: teaching, preaching, and healing. "Jesus went through all the towns and villages, teaching in their synagogues, preaching the good news of the kingdom and healing every disease and sickness" (Matt. 9:35; see also 4:23; I'll discuss more about his healing ministry later in this chapter).

In a clear parallel to the Torah being given on Mount Sinai, when Jesus was about to deliver one of his most famous teachings, "he went up on a mountainside and sat down. His disciples came to him, and he began to teach them" (Matt. 5:1–2). As for the teaching he delivered that day on the mountainside (called the "Sermon on the Mount," found in Matthew 5–7), whole books have been written to show its connection to Jewish thought of the day.[13]

Prof. Geza Vermes pointed out that, "The Bible played a fundamental part in the religious and literary creativity of the Jews in the intertestamental era"—by which he means the period between roughly 200 BCE to 200 CE—"with the career of Jesus falling almost exactly in the middle." And so, Vermes notes, "In their teaching and interpretative activity Jewish masters made use of the Bible, their Holy Scripture, in simple and complex ways."

Vermes then explains five main types of Scripture interpretation found in the entire gamut of Jewish literature of that day, noting that, with only one exception, "all these exegetical methods are attested in the Synoptic Gospels," with Jesus himself quoting from the Hebrew Scripture more than forty times.[14] This is exactly what would be expected of a rabbi/teacher of the day, and many of Yeshua's teaching methods are in keeping with the main categories of Jewish biblical interpretation.

He also made great use of parables, a literary form highly prized by the later rabbis as well, as stated in the Midrash: "Our rabbis say: Let not the parable be lightly esteemed in your eyes, since by means of the parable a man can master the words of the Torah" (Song of Songs Rabbah 1:1, 8–9). Prof. Brad Young, a student of David Flusser at Hebrew University, wrote an entire volume on *Jesus and His Jewish Parables*,[15] comparing them to the parables found extensively in later rabbinic literature. And Klausner spoke of the "shrewdness and sharpness of his proverbs," noting that "his forceful epigrams serve, in an exceptional degree, to make ethical ideas a popular possession."[16]

To this day little children delight in Jesus' parables while brilliant scholars try to unfold the depths of their meaning. He once taught that, "The kingdom of heaven is like yeast that a woman took and mixed into a large amount of flour until it worked all through the dough" (Matt. 13:33). Do you understand what Rabbi Yeshua meant?[17]

A first-century rabbi would encourage his disciples to acts of piety and devotion.

This Jesus did constantly, showing them how to pray, encouraging them to do their charitable acts in secret, and continually calling them to care for the poor and the outcast.[18] It was in this context that the famous parable of the good Samaritan was delivered.

An expert in the law had asked Jesus what he needed to do to inherit eternal life, and Jesus told him he must love the Lord God with all his heart, soul, and strength as well as love his neighbor as himself. (In saying this, of course, Jesus was reaffirming mainstream Jewish thought, emphasizing the two greatest commandments.) "But he [the legal expert] wanted to justify himself, so he asked Jesus, 'And who is my neighbor?'" (Luke 10:29). Perhaps he was thinking to himself, "Only Jews are my neighbors!"[19]

Jesus then tells a parable about a Jewish man who was robbed, beaten, stripped naked, and left for dead on the side of the road, only to be passed by and ignored by two Jewish men who should have been the most spiritual in their community (a priest and a Levite). It was only a Samaritan—a despised half-breed in the eyes of many Jews—who stopped and cared for the man, even at his own personal sacrifice. (This was a shocking, pride-killing story, one that attacked the very notion of ethnic superiority.)

Yeshua then asked him, "'Which of these three do you think was a neighbor to the man who fell into the hands of robbers?' The expert in the law replied, 'The one who had mercy on him.' Jesus told him, 'Go and do likewise'" (Luke 10:36–37).

What a surprise ending! "You go and be the neighbor. Your selfish, legally narrow, self-justifying perspective is the exact opposite of what the Torah intended."

That is how Jesus often taught, coming from unexpected angles, using vivid illustrations, pricking the conscience, and always calling for practical action that would help the hurting and oppressed. He was the ultimate rabbi/teacher!

A first-century rabbi would make legal pronouncements or settle legal disputes.

Although not every rabbi was expected to do this, because of Yeshua's popularity, different Jewish groups would often come to him, asking for his legal opinion, sometimes even wanting to trap him in his words. On one occasion, "Some Pharisees came to him to test him. They asked, 'Is it lawful for a man to divorce his wife for any and every reason?'" (Matt. 19:3).

Does this seem like an odd question? Who would want to know if it was lawful for a man "to divorce his wife for any and every reason"?

Actually, it is well known that there was a dispute between the two main Pharisaical camps of the day, the school of Hillel and the school of Shammai. As recorded in the Mishnah:[20]

> The House of Shammai say, "A man should divorce his wife only because he has found grounds for it in unchastity, since it is said, *Because he has found in her indecency in anything* (Dt. 24:1)." And the House of Hillel say, "Even if she spoiled his dish, since it is said, *Because he has found in her indecency in anything.*" R. Aqiba says, "Even if he found someone else prettier than she, since it is said, *And it shall be if she find no favor in his eyes* (Dt. 24:1)."[21]

These Pharisees wanted to know where Jesus stood. His answer, while mostly in line with the House of Shammai ("A man should divorce his wife only because he has found grounds for it in unchastity"), went even further, explaining God's intention from "the beginning":

> "Haven't you read," he replied, "that at the beginning the Creator 'made them male and female,' and said, 'For this reason a man

will leave his father and mother and be united to his wife, and the two will become one flesh'? So they are no longer two, but one. Therefore what God has joined together, let man not separate."

—MATTHEW 19:4–6

When asked why Moses in the Torah gave specific instructions regarding divorce, Yeshua explained, "Moses permitted you to divorce your wives because your hearts were hard. But it was not this way from the beginning. I tell you that anyone who divorces his wife, except for marital unfaithfulness, and marries another woman commits adultery" (vv. 8–9).

How did Jesus know that Moses only gave this law because of human sinfulness, recognizing that not everyone would be faithful to their marital commitment? What was his source of information? And what kind of rabbi was he?

It is at this point that we make the most important discovery so far: It is absolutely true that Jesus was a rabbi, but he was *far more than just an ordinary first-century rabbi*. In fact, it can safely be said that Jesus stands out from every rabbi who ever lived.

Of course, I could spend hundreds of pages citing examples of how his teaching paralleled that of other ancient Jewish sages, or how his sayings can best be understood by re-creating them in Hebrew or Aramaic,[22] or how the Jewish background to a given passage helps illuminate its meaning, but others have done that, and there is no point proving what we already know.

There's not even much point in trying to classify Jesus into one of the Jewish groups of the day (the primary ones being the Pharisees, Sadducees, and Essenes),[23] other than giving a context for some of the religious disputes that took place. For example, in Matthew's Gospel—written with a Jewish audience clearly in mind—the Pharisees are acknowledged as the teaching leaders of the day (Matt. 23:1–3), yet they are almost always depicted as being in conflict with Yeshua, and he rebukes them in the strongest terms (especially in Matthew 23:4–39).

Some scholars reject this as a later projection back into the text, assuring us that no such conflict took place. This is reflected in Rabbi Shmuley's comments: "If Jesus was such a devout Pharisee and rabbi, then, why would the Jews want him dead? The truth is: they didn't. *The rabbis had no problem whatsoever with Jesus.*"[24]

Others, however, have suggested that the reason for such intense conflicts was precisely *because* Jesus was a Pharisee! In other words, these were internal squabbles, family differences, and those tend to be especially animated. This, of course, would be the exact opposite of the traditional Christian reading of the Gospels, one that saw the Pharisees as the outsiders, the enemies, the hypocrites par excellence, with Jesus being anything but a Pharisee. (Klausner would be one of a number of Jewish scholars who believed that Jesus was not a Pharisee.[25])

Other scholars have pointed to alleged connections between Jesus and the Essenes (best known today in connection with the Dead Sea Scrolls), while still others have made Jesus into a proto-Karaite, meaning a Jew who only accepted the authority of the written Scriptures and rejected the authority of the oral traditions. These theories would also explain some of the conflicts between Yeshua and the religious leaders. And from still another angle, Prof. David Flusser stated that, "In those days there was an understandable tension between the charismatic holy man and the Pharisaic establishment."[26]

Clearly, Jesus accepted many of the Pharisaical traditions (such as attending synagogue),[27] while at other times he took issue with those traditions (e.g., Matt. 15:1–20; Mark 7:1–19, discussed further, below). At the same time he definitely rejected key doctrines of the Sadducees (they denied the future resurrection of the dead; obviously, Jesus did not).[28]

Yet I repeat: if we put all our emphasis here, seeking to understand Jesus simply as a first-century rabbi, we will badly miss the mark, and we will not be able to answer the big questions we have been asking.

Why *is* he the most influential Jew who ever lived? Why *do* more than two billion people today see him as more than a mere man? Why are they reading the words of *this particular rabbi* rather than the words of Hillel or Akiva?

Why do more than three and a half billion people (Muslims and Christians combined) believe him to be a prophet? And why do more than two hundred thousand Jews around the world today believe him to be the Messiah of Israel?

A Rabbi and Much More

We have established that we cannot rightly understand who Jesus is until we understand him first as Jew and second as a Jewish rabbi, but now we must now go one step further. *We cannot rightly understand who Jesus is unless we understand him to be a rabbi like no other, a rabbi and much more.*

Here are just four things that set Yeshua apart as a rabbi like no other. They will give you a further glimpse into just who he was.

Rabbi Jesus reached out to the marginalized and disenfranchised.

He was often criticized by the other religious leaders for hanging out in public with "sinners"—including the notoriously corrupt tax collectors, not to mention prostitutes. How scandalous! But this was an integral part of his mission:

> While Jesus was having dinner at Matthew's house, many tax collectors and "sinners" came and ate with him and his disciples. When the Pharisees saw this, they asked his disciples, "Why does your teacher eat with tax collectors and 'sinners'?" On hearing this, Jesus said, "It is not the healthy who need a doctor, but the sick. But go and learn what this means: 'I desire mercy, not sacrifice.' For I have not come to call the righteous, but sinners."
>
> —Matthew 9:10–13

What an unusual rabbi!

Today we often hear about the importance of being "inclusive," but what people often mean by inclusion is, "Accept me as I am and affirm me as I am." (I call this "affirmational inclusion.") Yeshua did something much better. He practiced what I call "transformational inclusion": he met people where they were and changed them.

Here's a typical—and amazing—picture of Rabbi Jesus in action. Please take a moment to read the entire account:

Jesus entered Jericho and was passing through. A man was there by the name of Zacchaeus; he was a chief tax collector and was wealthy. He wanted to see who Jesus was, but being a short man he could not, because of the crowd. So he ran ahead and climbed a sycamore-fig tree to see him, since Jesus was coming that way.

When Jesus reached the spot, he looked up and said to him, "Zacchaeus, come down immediately. I must stay at your house today." So he came down at once and welcomed him gladly. All the people saw this and began to mutter, "He has gone to be the guest of a 'sinner.'"

But Zacchaeus stood up and said to the Lord, "Look, Lord! Here and now I give half of my possessions to the poor, and if I have cheated anybody out of anything, I will pay back four times the amount."

Jesus said to him, "Today salvation has come to this house, because this man, too, is a son of Abraham. For the Son of Man came to seek and to save what was lost."

—LUKE 19:1–10

How remarkable! First Jesus calls this stranger by name (how did he know his name?) and then invites himself for a meal at the home of this well-known sinner. Holy men don't do that! Then, before Jesus even says a word, Zacchaeus is so overcome by the consciousness of his sin that he repents on the spot and pledges to make dramatic amends. Jesus then says, "That's exactly why I came! My mission is to reach people just like you."

And Jesus did something else that was very different. He involved women in his ministry.[29] The Gospels even tell us that it was some of these women who were the first to see him after he rose from the dead.[30] It's not surprising, then, that as the message of Jesus spread through the ancient world, in particular among the Gentiles, many women embraced his words. It liberated them from a spiritually inferior position, and—in contrast with pagan culture—the Jesus movement required men to be chaste and not just women. This too brought about powerful social changes.[31]

In keeping with this, Yeshua spoke of himself as a shepherd of the sheep, and an exceptional one at that. No one could take his precious sheep away from him, no matter what:

> I am the good shepherd. The good shepherd lays down his life for the sheep. The hired hand is not the shepherd who owns the sheep. So when he sees the wolf coming, he abandons the sheep and runs away. Then the wolf attacks the flock and scatters it. The man runs away because he is a hired hand and cares nothing for the sheep. I am the good shepherd; I know my sheep and my sheep know me....
>
> My sheep listen to my voice; I know them, and they follow me. I give them eternal life, and they shall never perish; no one can snatch them out of my hand.
>
> —John 10:11–14, 27–28

Do you see why I say that Jesus cannot simply be categorized as a first-century Jewish rabbi?

Rabbi Jesus was a miracle worker like no other.

Some of the miracles of Jesus paralleled that of earlier miracle workers in Israel's history (such as Elisha),[32] placing him firmly in that tradition of Spirit-empowered holy men. And it is well known that a few early rabbis were also renowned as miracle workers (in particular Honi the Circle Drawer and Hanina ben Dosa).[33] But the scope and nature of Yeshua's miracles far exceeded them all—and it is in many of those miracle accounts that he is called "Rabbi."

- A blind beggar named Bartimaeus was crying out to Jesus as he passed by, recognizing him as Messiah, and asking for mercy. Jesus had the man brought to him and asked him, "'What do you want me to do for you?' The blind man said, *'Rabbi, I want to see.'* 'Go,' said Jesus, 'your faith has healed you.' Immediately he received his sight and followed Jesus along the road" (Mark 10:46–52).[34]

- Before raising his friend Lazarus from the dead—Lazarus had been dead for *four days*—Jesus was addressed by one of his disciples as "Rabbi." (See John 11, specifically verse 8.) And to Martha, the sister of Lazarus, he said, "I am the resurrection and the life. He who believes in me will live, even though he dies; and whoever lives and believes in me will never die [meaning, spiritually]. Do you believe this?" (vv. 25–26). Then he demonstrated this by raising Lazarus from the dead. Not your typical rabbi!

- When he demonstrated his power over nature by cursing a fig tree, his disciples called him "Rabbi," marveling at who he was and what he did. (See Mark 11:21.)

- One night, after feeding thousands of people, Jesus' disciples took a boat and crossed over the lake, but Jesus stayed behind. Then he walked several miles across the water, meeting his shocked disciples in their boat in the midst of a storm. The next morning, the crowd was stunned to find him on the other side of the lake, since they knew he didn't have a boat. So they asked him, "Rabbi, when did you get here?" (John 6:25). A rabbi who walks on water!

Scenes like this were the norm when Yeshua and his disciples showed up in a town or village:

> And when they got out of the boat, the people immediately recognized him and ran about the whole region and began to bring the sick people on their beds to wherever they heard he was. And wherever he came, in villages, cities, or countryside, they laid the sick in the marketplaces and implored him that they might touch even the fringe of his garment. And as many as touched it were made well.
> —MARK 6:54–56, ESV[35]

No disease was too hard for him:

> And great crowds came to him, bringing with them the lame, the blind, the crippled, the mute, and many others, and they put them at his feet, and he healed them, so that the crowd wondered, when they saw the mute speaking, the crippled healthy, the lame walking, and the blind seeing. And they glorified the God of Israel.
>
> —MATTHEW 15:30–31, ESV

If you have never read these accounts before, you might be saying, "That's crazy! Those are just made-up stories. There's no way things like that ever happened"—and I certainly understand your skepticism. But ask yourself this question: Is it possible that this is one of the reasons Jesus stood out from his contemporaries?

Even critical historians generally agree that Jesus was known as a great miracle worker, and we know that as the Jesus movement began to spread among Jews and Gentiles, his followers also had a reputation for healing power (just as he promised; see John 14:12).[36] There are even some accounts in the Talmudic literature that attribute healing power to one of Yeshua's early Jewish disciples.[37] Some even claim that he is still healing today. Could it be true?[38]

Rabbi Jesus pointed to a new and better approach to the Torah.

On a number of occasions in the Gospels Jesus healed a sick person on the Sabbath, causing a good deal of controversy.[39] "Why couldn't he heal on another day? Isn't he violating the Sabbath? After all, this was not a life-threatening situation." He even claimed that some of the Jewish teachers were making the Word of God void through their traditions (Mark 7:8–9).

Now, we know that the Sabbath is of central importance to observant Jews, and it has often been said that, throughout history, Jews didn't keep the Sabbath as much as the Sabbath kept the Jews. And yet the rabbis developed a massively complex system of Sabbath laws (they are still being refined every year); in contrast, Jesus pointed to a more organic, relational approach.

Since the *Torah* (the "five books of Moses," which are the first five books of the Bible) forbids work on the Sabbath (Exod. 20:8–11), the rabbis needed to determine what exactly constituted work—a noble, God-honoring goal for sure, but one that became incredibly complex, as they broke "work" down into thirty-nine subdivisions, and that was just the start.[40] Is this what God intended?

Here is the beginning of the Talmudic tractate (book) called Shabbat (in the Talmud—this tractate is 157 very difficult, dense pages, and these, again, are just the opening lines, and the focus is on bringing an item from one domain into another):

> The carryings out of the Sabbath are two which are four within, and two which are four without. How so? The poor man stands without and the master of the house within: [i] if the poor man stretches his hand within and places [an article] into the hand of the master of the house, or [ii] if he takes [an article] from it and carries it out, the poor man is liable, and the master of the house is exempt. [Again] [i] if the master of the house stretches his hand without and places [an object] in the poor man's hand, or [ii] takes [an object] therefrom and carries it in, the master is liable, while the poor man is exempt. [iii] If the poor man stretches his hand within and the master takes [an object] from it, or places [an object] therein and he carries it out, both are exempt; [iv] if the master stretches his hand without and the poor man takes [an object] from it, or places [an article] therein and he carries it inside, both are exempt. (m. Shabbat 1:1)[41]

Does this sound confusing? Here it is an outline format for easier reading:

1:1   A   [Acts of] transporting objects from one domain to another [which violate] the Sabbath

            (1) are two, which [indeed] are four [for one who is] inside,

            (2) and two which are four [for one who is] outside.

B How so?

I C [If on the Sabbath] the beggar stands outside and the householder inside,

D [and] the beggar stuck his hand inside and put [a beggar's bowl] into the hand of the householder,

E or if he took [something] from inside it and brought it out,

F the beggar is liable, the householder is exempt.

II G [If] the householder stuck his hand outside and put [something] into the hand of the beggar,

H or if he took [something] from it and brought it inside,

I the householder is liable, and the beggar is exempt.

III J [If] the beggar stuck his hand inside, and the householder took [something] from it,

K or if [the householder] put something in it and he [the beggar] removed it,

L both of them are exempt.

IV M [If] the householder put his hand outside and the beggar took [something] from it,

N or if [the beggar] put something into it and [the householder] brought it back inside,

O both of them are exempt.[42]

I repeat: These are just the opening lines. The discussion gets infinitely more complex as it goes on, and then there are commentaries added to this, and then law codes, and then legal responses, and on and on it goes. Traditional Jews will tell you that, for them, the holiness is in the details, but that still begs the question: Is this really what God intended? Is this truly what he means by "rest"?

Asher Intrater, a Messianic Jewish leader who has lived with his family in Israel since 1992, explained the contrast in the two approaches well:

Yeshua also spoke of the Sabbath. In Judaism we have developed mountains of "halachic" rules about what to do and not do. Yeshua believed that such a compendium of added ritual laws diminished the ability to observe the Sabbath in the way it had originally been intended. He summarized His approach to dealing with Sabbath laws in three simple statements:

1. The Sabbath was made for mankind, not mankind for the Sabbath—Mark 2:27

2. The Son of Man is lord of the Sabbath—Mark 2:28

3. It is lawful to do good on the Sabbath—Mark 3:4

His teaching on this subject was miraculous and revolutionary in its simplicity and purity. In addition, His teaching was more than just a commentary about the Sabbath. In the Jewish world there is a position called "Posek Ha Dor"—the top rabbi who passes judgment and determines what becomes law in his generation. Yeshua was speaking as "Posek Ha Dor." He was not suggesting law, He was setting the law. He was not making commentary about the law, He was determining it.[43]

And even here Yeshua went beyond the other rabbis, both of his generation and throughout history. He actually spoke with divine authority: "When Yeshua had finished saying these things [referring to the Sermon on the Mount, Matt. 5–7], the crowds were amazed at the way he taught, for he was not instructing them like their Torah-teachers but as one who had authority himself" (Matt. 7:28–29, cjb). In fact, he spoke as the prophets spoke, not just giving an opinion or an interpretation or an insight. He spoke with the authority of the Lord, which leads us to our last point.

Rabbi Jesus was a prophet.

The Jewish Gospel scholar Claude G. Montefiore understood that Jesus spoke as a prophet, contrasting him with the other rabbis of his era. He wrote that, "We do, I think, know enough about the great Rabbis of the first century A.D. to say that, however fine and noble their teaching may have been or was, it cannot properly be called prophetic. They were not called prophets, and they could not properly have been called so."[44] What exactly did he mean?

> However much they may have recognized that, at bottom, the Pentateuchal laws of morality were greater than its laws about sacrifice or "clean and unclean," they could not, they did not, deal with the subject in the same way and spirit as Jesus. Hillel was ever the servant of the Law and never its judge. In a sense he was more consistent than Jesus, but for that very reason he was less prophetic. Sabbath conflicts, such as happened to Jesus, could not have happened to him. That is why—or that is *one* reason why—the production of parallels from the teaching of Hillel with the teaching of Jesus is mostly futile. *The spirit is different. The prophetic touch is present in the one case and absent in the other, and it is the prophetic touch that makes the difference.*[45]

For rabbi and professor Dan Cohn-Sherbok, it is the prophetic element in the life of Jesus that helps to explain the very real conflicts he *did* have with other religious leaders: "His attack on the scribes and Pharisees can be seen, not as a rejection of the Torah, but as a prophetic renunciation of a corrupt religious establishment."[46] Exactly!

Cohn-Sherbok also observed:

> Placing himself in the line of the prophetic tradition, Jesus was anxious to call the people back to the true worship of God, and his words and actions testify to his dedication to compassion and loving-kindness. For this reason he healed the sick on the Sabbath in violation of Pharisaic law; he conspicuously turned his attention to the lowly, to sinners, to children, and to foreigners. In the case of those who were most sorely in need, Jesus illustrated the love and concern that all human beings are to exhibit. Jesus established fellowship with all those who were at the margin of society; he continually took the side of

the weak who were ostracized and condemned by the general public.[47]

Yes, a rabbi like no other!

Montefiore summed things up well: "The combination at least was new: Jesus was teacher, pastor, and prophet in one, and in this combination too lies something of his originality."[48]

The picture is becoming clearer, and our vision of Jesus-Yeshua is getting more wonderful by the minute. The journey continues.

4

A THREAT TO THE ESTABLISHMENT

IT'S NOT EASY being a prophet. Prophets are called to go against the grain, upset the applecart, expose hypocrisy, challenge the status quo, and get deeply under our skin. That's why Israel's prophets were often hated, rejected, and even killed—only to be praised and celebrated after their deaths.

As expressed in the pithy prose of Christian author Leonard Ravenhill:

> The prophet is violated during his ministry, but he is vindicated by history. He is the villain of today and the hero of tomorrow. He is excommunicated while alive and exalted when dead! He is dishonored with epithets when breathing and honored with epitaphs when dead. He is friendless while living and famous when dead. He is against the establishment in ministry; then he is established as a saint by posterity.[1]

How true! And note well Ravenhill's observation that the prophets stand "against the establishment in ministry"—be it the religious or the secular or the political establishment. Prophets are a threat to our monopoly and our control.

And prophets make us uncomfortable since, if they are right, we are wrong—and nobody likes to be wrong. How dare that self-righteous, self-anointed, self-appointed prophet confront good people like us!

Abraham Joshua Heschel, one of the greatest Jewish thinkers of the last century, cut to the heart of the matter: "The prophet is an iconoclast, challenging the apparently holy, revered, and awesome. Beliefs cherished as certainties, institutions endowed with supreme sanctity, he exposes as scandalous pretensions."[2]

How dare that prophet smash our sacred idols? How dare he claim to speak for God? We can hear the Lord's voice too.[3] What gives *him* the right to say that our worship is in vain, that our religious practices are an abomination, that our acts of piety are a sham?[4] Who does he think he is?

The great Hebrew prophet Isaiah had the audacity to address the esteemed Jerusalem leaders as the "rulers of Sodom," also calling his very own people the "people of Gomorrah." And he claimed that God was speaking through him. Who can listen to words like these?

> "The multitude of your sacrifices—what are they to me?" says the LORD. "I have more than enough of burnt offerings, of rams and the fat of fattened animals; I have no pleasure in the blood of bulls and lambs and goats. When you come to appear before me, who has asked this of you, this trampling of my courts? Stop bringing meaningless offerings! Your incense is detestable to me. New Moons, Sabbaths and convocations—I cannot bear your evil assemblies. Your New Moon festivals and your appointed feasts my soul hates. They have become a burden to me; I am weary of bearing them. When you spread out your hands in prayer, I will hide my eyes from you; even if you offer many prayers, I will not listen. Your hands are full of blood.
>
> —ISAIAH 1:11–15

What? God won't listen to our prayers? God won't accept our Sabbath observance? God won't receive our offerings? God doesn't want us frequenting his Temple? *Our hands* are full of blood? Isaiah should be put to death! (Jewish tradition confirms that he was.[5])

One century later the prophet Jeremiah brought a searing rebuke to our people as they gathered for worship in the holy Temple. He too claimed to be speaking directly for God:

> Will you steal and murder, commit adultery and perjury, burn incense to Baal and follow other gods you have not known, and then come and stand before me in this house, which bears my Name, and say, "We are safe"—safe to do all these detestable

things? Has this house, which bears my Name, become a den
of robbers to you? But I have been watching! declares the LORD.

—JEREMIAH 7:9–11

He actually prophesied that the Temple, the Lord's sacred sanctuary,
would be destroyed by invading armies.

And what was the response to Jeremiah's message? "As soon as
Jeremiah finished telling all the people everything the LORD had commanded him to say, the priests, the prophets and all the people seized
him and said, 'You must die!'" (Jer. 26:8).[6] Jeremiah barely escaped with
his life, as the text makes clear that opposition against him was virtually universal, speaking of "the priests, the prophets and all the people."

Tragically, his words proved true, and less than twenty-five years after
his prophetic sermon, Jerusalem lay in ruins, the Temple was destroyed,
and thousands were killed or exiled, just as Jeremiah predicted.

Six centuries later history repeated itself when another bold prophet
stood in the Temple of Jerusalem—the Second Temple, which had
been rebuilt after the Jewish exiles returned home. He too exposed religious hypocrisy, rebuked the corrupt establishment, and prophesied the
destruction of the Temple. He too was viciously opposed, and his words,
like Jeremiah's, also came to pass. I will have more to say about this
prophet shortly.

But these accounts should not surprise us in the least. Rather, as
British journalist A. G. Gardiner explained, such reactions are to be
expected: "When a prophet is accepted and deified, his message is lost.
The prophet is only useful so long as he is stoned as a public nuisance,
calling us to repentance, disturbing our comfortable routines, breaking
our respectable idols, shattering our sacred conventions."[7] We will always
have a love-hate relationship with the prophets.

"The prophet is human," Heschel explains, "yet he employs notes one
octave too high for our ears.... Often his words begin to burn where
conscience ends."[8]

It is not easy to listen to the voice of the prophet! He is too shrill, too
intense, too strict, an unbearable extremist to whom everything seems
black and white. As expressed again by Ravenhill, the prophet:

...is ordained of God but disdained by men. The degree of his effectiveness is determined by his measure of unpopularity. Compromise is not known to him. He marches to another drummer! He is a "seer" who comes to lead the blind. He is a scourge to the nation before he is scourged by the nation.[9]

The prophet lives in holy tension, and his words make others tense. Let Heschel instruct us once more:

> To a person endowed with prophetic sight, everyone else appears blind; to a person whose ear perceives God's voice, everyone else appears deaf....The prophet hates the approximate, he shuns the middle of the road. Man must live on the summit to avoid the abyss....The prophet's word is a scream in the night. While the world is at ease and asleep, the prophet feels the blast from heaven.[10]

That's why prophets are often rejected before they are accepted and murdered before they are memorialized. Jesus-Yeshua suffered that very same fate.

Jesus the Prophet

Yes, it was Jesus who was that bold prophet who stood in the Temple courts, just as Jeremiah did six centuries earlier, calling for repentance and warning of imminent judgment. And as it happened with his predecessor Jeremiah (or *Yirmiyahu* in Hebrew), Yeshua's message was also rejected, but while Jeremiah the prophet escaped with his life, Yeshua the prophet did not.

Yet his words came to pass with striking accuracy, and barely forty years after his death, Jerusalem again was in ruins, the Temple again destroyed, and thousands again killed or exiled—except this time the death toll was massively higher and the devastation massively greater.

It is only when we see Jesus as a prophet that we can rightly understand the conflict and controversy that surrounded him. In fact, if the New Testament painted a picture of him being in an easy-going, cozy relationship with his fellow Jewish leaders, embraced by the religious hierarchy and praised by the religious aristocracy, then we would have known that something was wrong with the picture. That's not how prophets are treated by the establishment they confront.

"But," you say, "it's one thing to say that Jesus was in conflict with some of the religious leadership. It's another thing to say that any of them would want him killed."

To the contrary, the Talmud and rabbinic writings claim that the Jewish people—my own people—have often been guilty of killing the prophets, going all the way back to Mount Sinai itself. (Surely no one can accuse Jewish texts of being anti-Semitic![11])

- The Talmud and Midrash teach that the Israelites killed the prophet Hur shortly after receiving the Ten Commandments, with some of the texts claiming that the children of Israel killed all the elders as well.[12]

- The Talmud records that Manasseh, king of Judah, killed Isaiah, one of the greatest prophets of the Hebrew Scriptures.[13]

- The Scriptures also speak of the people of Israel murdering other prophets, like Uriah son of Shemaiah and Zechariah son of Jehoiada, with Talmudic expansions on these biblical accounts as well.[14] Jewish tradition even states that Isaiah's words in Isaiah 1:21 (calling the people "murderers") refer to the murder of Uriah.[15]

- First Kings 18:4 tells us that Jezebel, the queen of Israel, was killing off the Lord's prophets to the point that a righteous man trying to save their lives hid one hundred of them in two caves. Things got so bad that Elijah the prophet said to the Lord, "The Israelites have rejected your covenant, broken down your altars, and put your prophets to death with the sword. I am the only one left, and now they are trying to kill me too" (1 Kings 19:14).

- The Midrash states that Jeremiah the prophet protested to the Lord, "I cannot prophesy about them [meaning the people of Israel]; what prophet went out to them whom they did not seek to kill?"[16]

There was certainly no hyperbole in Yeshua's words when he addressed Jerusalem, the seat of Jewish leadership and the national capital, as "the city that kills the prophets and stones those who are sent to it" (Matt. 23:37, esv). In fact, when he uttered these words of rebuke to hypocritical religious leaders in his day, he was standing right in the middle of the Bible's prophetic tradition:

> You build tombs for the prophets and decorate the graves of the righteous. And you say, "If we had lived in the days of our forefathers, we would not have taken part with them in shedding the blood of the prophets." So you testify against yourselves that you are the descendants of those who murdered the prophets.
> —Matthew 23:29–31

Almost any great prophet in Israel's history could have stood in the city of Jerusalem and spoken these very same words to many of the leaders of his generation. This is prophetic truth, completely faithful to the Hebrew Bible and Jewish traditions.

Jesus Lines Up With Other Prophets

As expressed by Prof. Dan Cohn-Sherbok:

> Like the prophets of the Hebrew Bible, Jesus can be seen as the conscience of Israel....In his confrontation with the leaders of the nation, Jesus echoed the words of the prophets by denouncing hypocrisy and injustice....As a prophetic figure, this image of Jesus should be recognizable to all Jews.[17]

In the words of Claude G. Montefiore, "Jesus does not preface his speeches with 'Thus saith the Lord,' but in the conviction of inspiration, in the assurance that he too was called and chosen by God to do a certain work, he entirely resembles Amos, Isaiah, and Ezekiel."[18]

I can illustrate this in the form of a ten-question, multiple choice test. Let's see how you score. I'll list a series of quotes from the Hebrew Scriptures and the New Testament, and you have to identify the speaker. Is it: (a) Moses, (b) Jesus, (c) Jeremiah, (d) Isaiah, or (e) Ezekiel?

Take a minute and go through all the quotes, jotting down your answers as you go, and then you can score yourself at the end. And remember: all of these words were spoken to or about the Jewish people by Moses, Jesus, Jeremiah, Isaiah, or Ezekiel, and each of these prophets claimed to be speaking for the Lord himself:

1. The LORD saw this and rejected them because he was angered by his sons and daughters. "I will hide my face from them," he said, "and see what their end will be; for they are a perverse generation, children who are unfaithful."

2. Tell the Israelites, "You are a stiff-necked people. If I were to go with you even for one moment, I might destroy you."

3. Go now, write it on a tablet for them, inscribe it on a scroll, that for the days to come it may be an everlasting witness. These are rebellious people, deceitful children, children unwilling to listen to the LORD's instruction.

4. For you are like whitewashed tombs, which outwardly appear beautiful, but within are full of dead people's bones and all uncleanness. So you also outwardly appear righteous to others, but within you are full of hypocrisy and lawlessness.

5. For I know how rebellious and stiff-necked you are. If you have been rebellious against the LORD while I am

still alive and with you, how much more will you rebel after I die!

6. [God said to the prophet]: Son of man, I am sending you to the Israelites, to a rebellious nation that has rebelled against me; they and their fathers have been in revolt against me to this very day. The people to whom I am sending you are obstinate and stubborn.... But the house of Israel is not willing to listen to you because they are not willing to listen to me, for the whole house of Israel is hardened and obstinate.

7. Ah, sinful nation, a people loaded with guilt, a brood of evildoers, children given to corruption! They have forsaken the LORD; they have spurned the Holy One of Israel and turned their backs on him.

8. "Your wickedness will punish you; your backsliding will rebuke you. Consider then and realize how evil and bitter it is for you when you forsake the LORD your God and have no awe of me," declares the Lord, the LORD Almighty.

9. You have let go of the commands of God and are holding on to the traditions of men.... You have a fine way of setting aside the commands of God in order to observe your own traditions!

10. And so the Lord says, "These people say they are mine. They honor me with their lips, but their hearts are far from me. And their worship of me is nothing but man-made rules learned by rote."

Let's see how you scored.

1. Spoken by Moses at the end of Israel's wandering in the wilderness (Deut. 32:19–20).

2. Also spoken by Moses—claiming to be speaking God's very words—after the children of Israel made the golden calf idol at Mount Sinai (meaning, just days after receiving the Ten Commandments; Exod. 33:5).

3. Spoken by Isaiah (yes, God told him to write down these words about our people; Isa. 30:8–9).

4. Spoken by Jesus, rebuking the religious hypocrites (Matt. 23:27–28, esv).

5. Spoken by Moses, shortly before his death (Deut. 31:27).

6. Spoken by Ezekiel, when God sent him on his prophetic mission (Ezek. 2:3–4; 3:7; God even told him that if he sent him to the Gentiles, they would listen to him, but the Jews would not, because they were too rebellious; Ezek. 3:5–6).

7. Spoken by Isaiah (Isa. 1:4).

8. Spoken by Jeremiah (Jer. 2:19)

9. Spoken by Jesus, rebuking the superficial worship of our people (Mark 7:8–9).

10. Spoken by Isaiah, also rebuking the superficial worship of our people (Isa. 29:16, nlt). In fact, before Jesus gave the word of rebuke in #9, he quoted these very words from Isaiah. (See Mark 7:6–8; Jesus began by saying, "Isaiah was right when he prophesied about you hypocrites.")

The purpose of this little exercise should be clear by now: *Jesus spoke as a prophet to his Jewish people.* And if you are going to reject his words as anti-Semitic or un-Jewish, then you have to do the same with the words of Isaiah, Jeremiah, Ezekiel, Moses, and even God himself! It is only when we wrongly see Jesus as a hostile outsider rather than a loyal insider that we can so badly misread his words. It is imperative that we reclaim him as the last, great national prophet in the history of Israel.

It is true that he called some hypocritical Jewish leaders "snakes" and a "brood of vipers" (Matt. 23:33).[19] But earlier Isaiah had said of his people, "They hatch the eggs of vipers and spin a spider's web" (Isa. 59:5), labeling them "sons of a sorceress...offspring of adulterers and prostitutes...a brood of rebels, the offspring of liars" (Isa. 57:3–4). He even said, "But your iniquities have separated you from your God; your sins have hidden his face from you, so that he will not hear. For your hands are stained with blood, your fingers with guilt. Your lips have spoken lies, and your tongue mutters wicked things" (Isa. 59:2–3).

Isaiah's message was far harsher than the message of Jesus, yet Jews still revere the words of Isaiah but often revile the words of Jesus. Why? They both addressed their people as faithful prophets of the Lord, and they both suffered the penalty of death for their obedience. Shouldn't we honor them both?

Some of Jeremiah's contemporaries wanted him dead or silenced (e.g., Jer. 11:18–19; 20:10), and some of Jesus' contemporaries wanted him dead or silenced (e.g., Mark 3:6; John 5:18). Why do many traditional Jews find the accounts about Jeremiah to be believable but then claim the accounts about Jesus must have been fabricated by later editors trying to make the Jews look bad?[20]

Most of Jeremiah's opposition came from the religious leaders,[21] to which Jewish readers would respond, "The leaders in his day must have been very sinful. That's why he took them to task." Jesus experienced the same kind of opposition as he rebuked corruption and hypocrisy and man-made tradition. Yet the same people who believe Jeremiah was right when he confronted the priests and the prophets read Yeshua's words and say, "How unfair of him! Those were saintly men he was rebuking."

Why the Double Standard?

Could it be that Yeshua's words hit too close to home? Could it be that he really was sent here to warn his generation about impending judgment from God, just as his predecessors had done? Could it be that the conflicts recorded in the Gospels make perfect sense against this backdrop?

Prof. Craig Evans, a specialist in New Testament and Aramaic studies, noted that when other scholars explain away most of the conflict in Jesus' life, they thereby omit "a convincing explanation of what led to Jesus' death."[22] But those conflicts make perfect sense, especially when we realize that shortly before his death Jesus told a series of parables at the Temple in Jerusalem,[23] a number of which were directed against the leadership—and the leaders were stung by his words: "When the chief priests and the Pharisees heard Jesus' parables, they knew he was talking about them. They looked for a way to arrest him, but they were afraid of the crowd because the people held that he was a prophet" (Matt. 21:45–46).[24]

It was against this backdrop that Jesus "entered the temple area and drove out all who were buying and selling there. He overturned the tables of the money changers and the benches of those selling doves" (Matt. 21:12). This was the ultimate prophetic confrontation—the prophet, burning with zeal for the house of God and the honor of God and the purity of God, now, literally, "cleaning house"—his Father's house! And by this prophetic action he was certainly sealing his fate.

As Prof. Craig Keener observes:

> Most likely, Jesus' act in the Temple challenged the Jerusalem aristocracy that controlled the Temple system, hence related in some way to Jesus' prophecy of the Temple's impending destruction....
>
> Before Jesus could become the chief cornerstone, however, he had to be rejected by the builders—the establishment who controlled Herod's temple (Mk. 12:10–12). Opposition to the Temple would generate hostility from most of mainstream Judaism, and perhaps even martyrdom at the hands of the authorities. For Jesus to offer this provocation, then refuse to flee Jerusalem or arm his followers [see chapters 5–6], suggests that he intended to face the authorities' hostility.[25]

His prophetic words and acts would certainly provoke a hostile reaction from the religious establishment whose monopoly and whose authority he threatened, and for them it was easier to eliminate the prophet than to admit their guilt. As Jesus once remarked, "Surely no prophet can die outside Jerusalem!" (Luke 13:33).

Following in the footsteps of our nation's greatest prophets, Yeshua wept over Jerusalem, as Isaiah and Jeremiah had done before:

> As [Jesus] approached Jerusalem and saw the city, he wept over it and said, "If you, even you, had only known on this day what would bring you peace—but now it is hidden from your eyes. The days will come upon you when your enemies will build an embankment against you and encircle you and hem you in on every side. They will dash you to the ground, you and the children within your walls. They will not leave one stone on another, because you did not recognize the time of God's coming to you."
>
> —LUKE 19:41–44[26]

And it was immediately after speaking these words of agony that he entered the Temple and "began driving out those who were selling," delivering this prophetic rebuke on behalf of his heavenly Father: "It is written," he said to them, "'*My house will be a house of prayer*'; but you have made it '*a den of robbers*'" (vv. 45–46). Note carefully those italicized words: The first is a direct quote from the book of Isaiah (Isa. 56:7); the second is a direct quote from the book of Jeremiah (Jer. 7:11). Through Jesus-Yeshua, the prophet from Nazareth, these two ancient prophets continued to speak.

Now, we know that Jeremiah was a true prophet of the Lord because he predicted the destruction of the First Temple and the exiling of the Jewish people and it happened, just as he said it would.[27] And we know that Jesus was a true prophet of the Lord because he predicted the destruction of the Second Temple and the exiling of the Jews, and it happened, just as he said it would.[28]

And this forces us to ask some difficult questions. Although the Jewish people were guilty of all kinds of atrocities in Jeremiah's day—idolatry, immorality, and the shedding of innocent blood (including burning children alive as a sacrifice to the false god Molech)—the Temple was rebuilt roughly seventy years after it was destroyed. But after it was destroyed for the second time in 70 CE, it has not been rebuilt since. Why?

By the time the Talmud was completed, the Second Temple had been destroyed for more than five hundred years.[29] Why was it still in ruins? It seemed that Israel's guilt during the time of the First Temple was far greater than Israel's guilt while the Second Temple stood. Why then such a severe punishment?

The Talmud addresses these questions:

> Why was the first Sanctuary destroyed? Because of three [evil] things which prevailed there: idolatry, immorality, bloodshed....
>
> But why was the second Sanctuary destroyed, seeing that in its time they were occupying themselves with Torah, [observance of] precepts, and the practice of charity? Because therein prevailed hatred without cause. That teaches you that groundless hatred is considered as of even gravity with the three sins of idolatry, immorality, and bloodshed together (b Yoma 9b).

So, the Talmud states that at the time of the First Temple (including the time of Jeremiah), the people were guilty of idolatry, immorality, and bloodshed, yet at the time of the Second Temple (including the time of Jesus), the people "were occupying themselves with Torah, [observance of] precepts, and the practice of charity." Yet the destruction of the Second Temple has now lasted more than twenty-five times as long. How can that be?

The Talmud's answer was that in those days, there "prevailed hatred without cause." Could that be the clue we have been looking for? Could it be that the Jewish people were guilty of rejecting the words of a prophet greater than Jeremiah, still not recognizing him as a prophet to this day? And could it be that Yeshua's own people committed the sin of "baseless hatred" against him? Jesus said that some of the leaders were guilty of this very thing—hating him without a cause (John 15:18–25). Could there be a connection?

And what if Jesus was not just *a* prophet but *the* prophet, the one the Jewish people were expecting in those days? And what if, rather than this great prophet accompanying the Messiah (in accordance with some of the ancient Jewish expectations), this prophet *was* the Messiah—and yet Israel's leaders scorned his words and were guilty of hating him without a cause? Could that explain why the judgment was so severe?[30]

Six hundred years earlier, in the days of Jeremiah, a biblical historian recorded these words:

> The LORD, the God of their fathers, sent word to them through his messengers again and again, because he had pity on his people and on his dwelling place. But they mocked God's messengers, despised his words and scoffed at his prophets until the wrath of the LORD was aroused against his people and there was no remedy.
>
> —2 CHRONICLES 36:15–16

Did history repeat itself, except this time with a greater prophet and greater consequences? And if, as Jews, we can believe that God judged us for rejecting his prophets in 600 BCE, why can't we believe that he judged us for rejecting his Prophet—King Messiah—in 30 CE? And if Jeremiah and his fellow prophets were a threat to the political and religious establishment, why wouldn't it follow that Yeshua too was a threat to the political and religious establishment? By recovering him as Israel's greatest prophet, Israel's history now makes much more sense.

And so the journey of discovery continues. Israel's long-hidden Messiah is being revealed.

5

HOW JESUS GOT HIJACKED BY
A WELL-MEANING RABBI

I T READS LIKE a thriller, and as the story unfolds, you are on the edge of your seat.

"On the night before the final confrontation, the rabbi gathers his disciples together."

What happens next?

"He orders them to collect swords. They must prepare to seize the Temple by force."

The suspense builds.

"They will demonstrate to the people of Jerusalem their teacher's courage and fearlessness in the face of Rome."

And then?

"When the people see, they will follow him, sparking a massive rebellion. The Romans will have no choice but to retreat."

This is positively breathtaking.

But wait. There's something wrong with the picture. The rabbi has only eleven men in his army, and between them they have only two swords. Two! Yet they are about to take on the armies of Rome and "seize the Temple by force"?

Not to fear. There's more to the story.

The rabbi "relies not on the sword alone. If he but makes the effort to begin the fight, God will take over and rescue His people. Just as the Israelites in their flight from Egypt needed to demonstrate faith by plunging into the churning waters, after which God parted the Red Sea, likewise the teacher and his disciples need only demonstrate sincere willingness to take on the enemy. Then, God will do the rest."[1]

Could it be true?

Not a chance. And despite the passionate story-telling, it is nothing more than that: a made-up story, a fictional account, a re-creation of history without any historical support—and in saying this I mean no insult to my esteemed colleague Rabbi Shmuley Boteach, the teller of the story.

REINVENTING JESUS

For Shmuley, Jesus was a hero, a man of boundless courage, a rabbi who hated oppression and injustice, a Jewish leader who could not tolerate a pagan kingdom ruling over the people of God, a potential Messiah who believed that the moment of liberation had come and who decided that he would inaugurate the Messianic era by force. But the Jesus of Shmuley's book exists only in Shmuley's mind.

Put another way, you can boil down the essence of these six words, "*Kosher Jesus* by Rabbi Shmuley Boteach," to just three words: *Jesus by Shmuley.* Yes, my dear friend Shmuley has manufactured a Jesus-Yeshua that never was, a fictional character no closer to reality than the European, blue-eyed, blond-haired version sometimes seen in media and art. As Augustine once commented, "If you believe what you like in the gospels, and reject what you don't like, it is not the gospel you believe, but yourself."[2]

But that's not the worst of it. Shmuley's depiction of Jesus as an armed freedom fighter is not only untrue, but it is also downright pathetic: Shmuley's Jesus was totally deceived. Such a leader should be pitied, not praised.

It would be like Moses *really believing* that God called him to challenge Pharaoh to "Let my people go," only to find out he was wrong—dead wrong—with disastrous consequences for his people, not to mention certain execution for him. (And would we be honoring the memory of Moses if he led our nation into the Red Sea *really believing* that God would part the waters for them, only to watch them drown?)

It would be like Noah spending decades of his life building a massive boat, *really believing* that the Lord told him to make it, warning his neighbors that a terrible flood was coming and that all the animals would come marching to his boat before the flood came, only to see that the torrential downpour never came, let alone the elephants and the giraffes or the lions and tigers and bears (oh my).

It would be like the prophet Elijah *really believing* that he was supposed to call for a confrontation with 850 false prophets on Mount Carmel, *convinced* that God wound send down fire from heaven to confirm his words, only to discover that he had concocted the whole thing in his own head and that he, not the false prophets, was about to be hacked to pieces.

Shmuley's Jesus is no better—really, he is worse—since he not only imagined that he was about to lead a successful revolt against Rome, but he also imagined himself to be the Messiah, the Hope of Israel, the Redeemer, only to fail miserably. To repeat: leaders like this are to be pitied, not praised, and to the extent they cause harm to others and bring dishonor to the name of God, they are to be repudiated rather than respected.

In Shmuley's version, Jesus and his eleven disciples, brandishing those two swords, make their dramatic move (it really is quite a picture), but there is no uprising of the people to support them, no divine intervention, no massive rebellion. Instead, Jesus is arrested, flogged, and nailed to a cross, while his disciples flee for their lives.

This is something glorious? This is a noble story? This is why Jews today should reclaim this Jesus for themselves?

If this was the true and real story of Rabbi Yeshua, I assure you he would not be the best known and most influential Jew in history. And if Shmuley's version of the story was true—although this is something he seems not to have countenanced—there would have been massive reprisals by Rome leading to an ocean of Jewish blood being spilled for an attempted revolt by a deluded Messianic pretender. And this is supposed to enhance our appreciation of Jesus as Jews?

The fictional Jesus is a deceived religious teacher, a man with a Messiah complex who was willing to lead his closest friends on a suicide mission on the hunch that God was about to work a miracle on his behalf. He was a failed leader who not only died an ignominious death as a seditious rebel—a death against his will as opposed to a self-sacrificing act of love—but whose story ends right there, since the fictional Jesus never rose from the dead.

In Shmuley's own words, "The legacy of the rabbi has little future. Persecuted by Rome, devastated after the loss of their beloved leader, the teacher's followers become fewer and fewer."[3] Thus ends the fictional account of the manufactured, unhistorical Jesus, whose legacy "has little future."

The reality is that there would be little reason to be talking about Shmuley's Jesus two millennia after his death, and Shmuley is quite right in saying that the legacy of *that* rabbi would have little future. The very fact that, two thousand years later, there is passionate discussion about him in our Jewish community (let alone that his name is on the lips of hundreds of millions people around the world) means that there is far more to the story. As noted by David Flusser, "it would be absolutely absurd to suppose that Christianity adopted an unambitious, unknown Jewish martyr and catapulted him against his will into the role of chief actor in a cosmic drama."[4] Exactly.

THE JERUSALEM SYNDROME

Have you ever heard of something called "the Jerusalem syndrome"? It is a recognized psychiatric condition often contracted by visitors to the ancient city. While there, they become convinced that they are one of the figures from Bible times, like Elijah the prophet or even Jesus himself. Those who develop this temporary form of insanity include "the would-be messiahs, the misfits, the misguided, the spiritually involved,"[5] and most of them are drawn especially to the Western ("Wailing") Wall, the last remnant of the outer structures of the Temple destroyed by the Romans forty years after Yeshua's death.

The online Jewish Virtual Library reports that "Jerusalem psychiatrist, Dr. Jordan Scher, claims that many disturbed people flock to the Holy City seeking the special spiritual atmosphere that imbues the capital, especially the Old City. 'Jerusalem is flooded by messiahs; those who come to meet him, to wait for him or to settle the turmoil in their own souls.'"[6]

Yet Rabbi Shmuley's fictional Jesus is no better than these poor deluded souls, since he too wrongly thought of himself as the Messiah and he too had a special attraction to the Holy City and the holy Temple, with one glaring addition: Shmuley's Jesus actually tried to start an armed revolt.

Who is more to be pitied? A harmless, modern day tourist who contracts the Jerusalem syndrome, spends a few days in a hospital, comes to his senses, apologizes profusely, and then returns home, or a failed leader who falsely raises the hopes of his nation, who dies still believing he is the Messiah (when he is not), who is crazy enough to attack tens of thousands of heavily armed troops with a handful of men carrying two swords, and who risks a bloodbath in order to live out his delusions?

Which one of these two is more dangerous? More deceived? More to be pitied?

Putting this in contemporary terms, would we praise a religious leader who was convinced that the time had come to overthrow the American government, showing up at the White House with a few loyal followers and a pistol, believing that he was God's anointed deliverer? And as the police dragged him away in handcuffs, would we celebrate his noble intentions and commend his courage?

To be sure, in his book Shmuley gets many things right about Jesus, embracing him as a faithful Jew, appreciating him as a great rabbi, esteeming him as a gifted teacher, recognizing him as a passionate prophet.[7] And Shmuley is to be commended for having the courage to speak of Jesus in such glowing terms. But the things that made Yeshua transcendent and that demonstrated that he was, in fact, our Messiah are the very things Shmuley missed or, I should say, struck from the historical record.

Now Shmuley would be the first to admit that he is neither a professional historian nor a biblical scholar—although he is widely read, well informed, and a brilliant speaker. And so, in his radical reconstruction of the New Testament, he largely follows the scholarship of others, most particularly Hyam Maccoby (as he acknowledges) in order to create his fantasy Jesus.[8]

Dismissing the New Testament

On what basis, then, do these other scholars—few in number, to be sure—concoct a similar version of Jesus, also making him into the leader of an armed revolt?[9] Well, the first thing they have to do is dismiss completely the New Testament as we have it (a very shaky way to start, as I'll explain shortly), since the Jesus of the New Testament is *not* a freedom fighter against Rome. Second, they have to comb through the New Testament looking for clues that support their theory (obviously, this runs the risk of finding what you're looking for, even if it's not there). Third, they have to build a mountain out of a molehill, or, more exactly, a national revolt out of two swords. Fourth, they have to finish where they started and explain away the overwhelming evidence that still stands against their position.

That's why only the tiniest minority of academic experts hold to this position, even though biblical scholars who take liberties with the sacred text are famous for coming up with all kinds of unusual—and sometimes even crazy—theories about what the biblical authors "really" said or how biblical history "really" unfolded. And that's why a few years after the latest theory has come out, it's quickly replaced by a new one, just as unlikely or preposterous.

To be perfectly clear, it's wonderful when new archeological finds come to light, shedding new light on the Scriptures, or when linguistic insights open up the meaning of a passage. Those of us involved in biblical scholarship live for moments like that, since our goal is to rightly understand what is written. It's another thing entirely, though, when scholars try to rewrite the Bible based on their own particular theory, often trying to make a giant square peg fit into a tiny round hole.

The story is told about a famous German philosopher who was giving his theory of history to his students. When he was done, one of the students said to him, "But professor, the facts of history are in direct contradiction to your theory!" The professor replied, "So much for history!" In the case before us here, the scholars who try to make Jesus into the leader of an armed revolt must say, "So much for the New Testament!"

Let me give you a very simple analogy, but one that will certainly drive home the point. A fire inspector finds two scorched lollipops lying in the corner of a burned-down shoe store and concludes that it was actually a clandestine candy factory. True, there are thousands of shoes scattered everywhere, and yes, there are hundreds of charred shoe boxes along with lots of pairs of socks, not to mention jars of shoe polish—in other words, everything you would expect to find in a shoe store. But those two lollipops—how can they be explained?

Well, it turns out there was a woman in the store when the fire started, and when she was interviewed, she said she was buying shoes for her daughter when she smelled smoke. So she grabbed her little girl by the arm and ran out the door, and she thinks her daughter dropped those lollipops in the process.

But the fire inspector, who prides himself on thinking outside of the box, postulates that there must be a cover-up and that this store, which had a permit to sell shoes but not to manufacture candy, must have been doing something illegal. And so he dismisses the clear, consistent, and comprehensive evidence, imagining it instead to be some kind of ruse, and then puts forth his candy factory theory as the most plausible explanation.

In the same way, the clear, consistent, and comprehensive testimony of the authors of the New Testament, most of whom were eyewitnesses to the events they describe, must be completely dismissed. (For more on this, see the next chapter, "The Lamb Who Was Slain.") The biggest difference is that we're dealing with two swords rather than two lollipops.

The Two Swords Theory

Yes, much of this elaborate reconstruction that turns the Prince of Peace into Rabbi Rambo finds its strongest alleged support in *one short passage* in the Gospel of Luke where Jesus, knowing that he is about to be betrayed by a duplicitous disciple, has this discussion with his remaining *talmidim*, eleven in number:

> Then Jesus asked them, "When I sent you without purse, bag or sandals, did you lack anything?"
> "Nothing," they answered.

> He said to them, "But now if you have a purse, take it, and also a bag; and if you don't have a sword, sell your cloak and buy one. It is written: 'And he was numbered with the transgressors'; and I tell you that this must be fulfilled in me. Yes, what is written about me is reaching its fulfillment."
>
> The disciples said, "See, Lord, here are two swords."
>
> "That is enough," he replied.
>
> —LUKE 22:35–38

What was going on here? First, let's use some logic and ask ourselves a question. Was this passage left in Luke's account by accident? Certainly not, since Luke put his account together with meticulous care, as many historians and archeologists will confirm, and the idea of a passage "accidentally" finding its way into the text is ridiculous.

In fact, this is how Luke begins the book, which was written for someone named Theophilus:

> Many have undertaken to draw up an account of the things that have been fulfilled among us, just as they were handed down to us by those who from the first were eyewitnesses and servants of the word. Therefore, since I myself have carefully investigated everything from the beginning, it seemed good also to me to write an orderly account for you, most excellent Theophilus, so that you may know the certainty of the things you have been taught.
>
> —LUKE 1:1–4

This means that Luke did his homework well and compiled his account with the greatest of care, so it's patently absurd to think that he "accidentally" left this incriminating piece of evidence in the text. In fact, it's patently absurd to think that he would ever have put such an account in his book unless he wanted it there.

As the author of more than twenty books, some as long as seven hundred pages with more than fifteen hundred detailed endnotes, I can tell you that I don't "accidentally" include passages in my books that I don't want to be there. And if I spot a typo in the text of one of my books, even if it's just weeks before publishing, I try to get it corrected. If I can't, that single typo will be on my mind until we can correct it in the next printing. That's the way careful authors think. But in Luke's case he had years to change the text if he wanted to—he didn't have to worry about rushing it to the printer to meet a publishing deadline—and yet he never changed these words. Obviously he didn't find them incriminating.

I know this should be self-evident, but sometimes when people start to believe in conspiracy theories, they check their rational thinking at the door, and frankly, that's what has happened with the "two sword, armed revolt" theory. For the sake, however, of the "armed revolt" theorists, let me take things one step further before looking back at the text in Luke.

Luke's Gospel was not only carefully written, but it was also copied countless times by those who wanted to spread the message. Yet all the manuscript copies we have contain these verses, which means that no one tried to remove them. This is very significant, since someone writing out a copy of a text might think that a particular passage didn't seem to fit, or they might fear that the words could be potentially dangerous or misleading, or they might remember another manuscript they saw that didn't contain these words, making them wonder if the text was completely accurate. In such cases, if they were not careful, professional scribes, they might just expunge the troublesome passage (or, in a professional way, put special marks around it to highlight it). That's why textual scholars look at the ancient manuscripts so carefully, comparing all the evidence to arrive at the most accurate reading.[10] Yet the verses in question were neither removed nor highlighted in the hundreds of relevant manuscripts we have.

So, not only is it ridiculous to think that Luke accidentally left the verses in this Gospel, but also there's no manuscript evidence that would suggest it either, nor is there a hint that someone added it in "secretly" later (another absurd argument). In fact, the context requires that the verses were there all along.

Getting back, then, to the context, we read that soon after Yeshua finished talking with his disciples, an armed crowd came to take him by force. (He was very popular with the people, so the strategy was to capture him at night.)

> When Jesus' followers saw what was going to happen, they said, "Lord, should we strike with our swords?" [These are the two swords that were mentioned just a few verses earlier.] And one of them struck the servant of the high priest, cutting off his right ear. But Jesus answered, "No more of this!" And he touched the man's ear and healed him.
>
> —Luke 22:49–51

Commenting on this passage, Prof. Craig Keener, a highly respected New Testament scholar and an expert in the Jewish background to the world of Jesus, made an interesting observation: "Many people associated Messiahs with popular revolt and the overthrow of the Gentile kingdoms that oppressed Israel; *a Messiah who would heal his attackers was not part of anyone's messianic picture.*"[11] Jesus was a healer, not an armed rebel, a message that Luke—along with the rest of the New Testament authors—makes emphatically clear.[12]

As if this wasn't clear enough, after Jesus rebuked Peter for his violent act and then healed the victim's ear (his name was Malchus), Jesus rebuked the armed crowd that came to arrest him:

> Then Jesus spoke to the leading priests, the captains of the Temple guard, and the elders who had come for him. "Am I some dangerous revolutionary," he asked, "that you come with swords and clubs to arrest me? Why didn't you arrest me in the Temple? I was there every day. But this is your moment, the time when the power of darkness reigns."
>
> —Luke 22:52–53, nlt

Or, as paraphrased in *The Message*, "Jesus spoke to those who had come—high priests, Temple police, religion leaders: 'What is this, jumping me with swords and clubs as if I were a dangerous criminal? Day after day I've been with you in the Temple and you've not so much as lifted a hand against me. But do it your way—it's a dark night, a dark hour.'"

This, then, is what we know about what Luke wrote:

1. The passage about the two swords was an integral part of the story Luke was relating. In fact, out of the four Gospel accounts, only Luke shares this information, meaning that he wanted readers to be specially aware of it.

2. It occurs in a context that completely repudiates any possible notion that Jesus was planning an armed revolt.

So, we're back to where we started. What is the passage actually saying? The best interpretation is quite simple. As explained by Lucan scholar I. Howard Marshall:

> The section begins with an appeal by Jesus to the experiences of their earlier mission when they went out in faith and yet experienced no lack. But now conditions are different: the growth of opposition to Jesus and to his followers means that they must be well prepared, even going to the length of regarding a sword as an indispensable accompaniment. The saying can be regarded only as grimly ironical, expressing the intensity of the opposition which Jesus and the disciples will experience, endangering their very lives. They are summoned to a faith and courage which is prepared to the limit.... This situation arises for there is an OT prophecy which must be fulfilled in Jesus, the saying that associates the Servant of Yahweh with evil-doers; Jesus sees it as a prophecy of his death, for his life is now drawing to an end. But the disciples fail to understand; taking Jesus literally, they produce two swords, and Jesus has to rebuke them for their lack of comprehension—a lack that will become more evident when Jesus is arrested....
>
> A reference to preparation for an anticipated eschatological [end-time] or messianic conflict is highly improbable, since this idea plays no part in the thinking of Jesus or the early church

(except in a non-literal sense). Nor is it likely that Jesus is contemplating armed resistance in the manner of the Zealots.[13]

Joseph Fitzmyer, one of the world's premier scholars of the Gospel of Luke, also noted that, "This verse [speaking of Luke 22:36] has no zealot tendency...Jesus' words about equipping oneself with purse, knapsack, and sword have to be taken in a symbolic sense....The symbolic sense of his counsel is derived from the reaction that he gives to the literal interpretation of his words in v. 38."[14]

And what did Jesus say in Luke 22:38? When his disciples said, "See, Lord, here are two swords," he replied with, "No more of this!" or, "Enough of that!" As Fitzmyer explains, "I.e., the apostles have so misunderstood the import of my words."[15]

Returning to Marshall's comments, he was making reference to Isaiah 53, a passage from the Hebrew Bible that speaks of a righteous individual who suffers and dies, not for his own sins, but rather for the sins of his people, going as a lamb to the slaughter. Yet those for whom he died thought he was a guilty sinner, dying for his own guilt. In retrospect they confessed, "Yet it was our weaknesses he carried; it was our sorrows that weighed him down. And we thought his troubles were a punishment from God, a punishment for his own sins!" (Isa. 53:4, NLT).

Yeshua reminded his followers that this text, composed as much as seven hundred years before he was born, was actually a prophecy about him, and he drew attention to the closing line of the prophecy (with the specific text he quoted italicized here): "For he exposed himself to death *and was numbered among the sinners*, whereas he bore the guilt of the many and made intercession for sinners" (Isa. 53:12, NJV).

Do you see it? Jesus was saying, "My brothers, the prophecy declares that I will be misunderstood and wrongly judged and that people will count me among the rebellious sinners" (in other words, guilt by association; as rendered in the NLT, Jesus would be "counted among the rebels"). "So," he says to them ironically, "now is the time to get a few swords, so my critics can have some fodder for their false accusations. After all, that's what is written in the text!"

The disciples, however, took him literally and said, "Look, we have two swords," at which point he said, "Enough!" In harmony with the comments of Fitzmyer, cited above, Marshall also explains: "It is most probable that this simply means, 'That's enough (sc. of this conversation)' and is meant as a rebuke."[16] As noted by Keener, "By mentioning the 'sword' here Jesus is not inviting revolution like the Zealots did.... Instead, Jesus calls for a temporary and symbolic act—two are sufficient (v. 38)—so he may be charged as a revolutionary and hence 'reckoned among transgressors' in accordance with Isaiah 53:12."[17]

How ironic it is that the "Rabbi Rambo" theorists have unknowingly played right into the false accusation against Jesus, based on the disciples having two swords at that, just as Jesus said. "Look," these theorists say, "he was hanging out with armed zealots!" As to the fact that they had swords at all, Marshall again notes, "Since the wearing of swords was not uncommon (Shab. 6:4), there is nothing surprising about this detail."[18] (The text he cites is from the Mishnah, Shabbat 6:4, which discusses the legality of carrying a sword out of one's house on the Sabbath.)

A further word of wisdom is added by another top Lucan scholar, John Nolland:

> The directive to buy a sword deserves a measure of separate consideration. Lined up as it is with purse, bag, and sandals, we can eliminate at once any idea that zealot sympathies are coming to expression with the commendation of the sword. [In other words, if Yeshua's point was to get an army ready for battle, he wouldn't tell them they needed a purse or sandals!] The sword is thought of as part of the equipment required for the self-sufficiency of any traveller in the Roman world. Nothing more than protection of one's person is in view. Similarly there can be no thought that the swords might be used to make a defense of Jesus...or might be for use in an anticipated eschatological armed struggle.[19]

Some have pointed to Yeshua's words in Matthew 10:34 to support the violent revolutionary theory. There he said, "Do not suppose that I have come to bring peace to the earth. I did not come to bring peace, but a sword." Once again, however, the context is perfectly clear. He is talking about the sword of conflict and division within families: "For I have come to turn 'a man against his father, a daughter against her mother, a daughter-in-law against her mother-in-law—a man's enemies will be the members of his own household'" (vv. 35–36).

In fact, when he spoke of turning "a man against his father... a man's enemies will be the members of his own household," he was quoting directly from the Hebrew prophet Micah, and it is this very verse (Micah 7:6) that is cited in the Mishnah to describe the difficult days that will exist immediately before the Messiah arrives (see m. Sotah 9:15).

As I noted in a study of this passage:

> In other words, there was a Jewish interpretation current in the days of Jesus (and continuing for some time after that) associating family upheaval with the coming of the Messiah (m. Sotah 9:15). This was part of a scenario predicted by the rabbis in which the moral fabric of society would disintegrate in the days immediately preceding the advent of the Messiah.[20]

Consider also the words of Doron Mendels, professor of ancient history at the Hebrew University, in his book *The Rise and Fall of Jewish Nationalism*:

> Although Jesus and his disciples knew what an army at that time was like (Luke 14:31–32), it was not of any major importance for their thought. Even the wars of the days according to the Gospels were to come from heaven, with the elect on earth remaining passive.... Jesus is depicted in the narrative parts of the New Testament as a pacifist who has nothing to do with the politics of his own time. Nevertheless, at a certain juncture he does become somewhat aggressive, and says, "Do not think that I have come to bring peace on earth; I have not come to bring peace but a sword" (Matt. 10:34, and see also Luke 12:51 and 22:36–38); but this passage can be seen as being in keeping with Jewish prophecy, which metaphorically and symbolically used phrases of that kind.... This statement does not fit the way he

was portrayed and is not repeated anywhere else. Jesus as well as his disciples never mention an earthly army when they had the Kingdom of God in mind (John 18:36).[21]

So, we can now summarize our findings: (1) As we learned in chapter 4, Jesus' cleansing of the Temple was a prophetic act of public rebuke and not an attempt to foment violence. (2) The reference to the "two swords" in Luke is found in a context that totally repudiates violence, which is in keeping with the rest of the New Testament evidence. (3) Jesus referred to Isaiah's prophecy that he would be falsely accused of being part of a sinful crowd of rebels, telling his disciples that they might as well play the part, but when they took him literally, he said, "Enough!"[22] (4) When he said in Matthew that he didn't come to bring a peace but a sword, he was talking about the sword of division within families, as they would divide over following him or rejecting him.

Now, there is other "evidence" that the "armed revolt" advocates have put forth, but for the most part, it is even more tenuous than what we have already reviewed.[23] That's why scholars such as Martin Hengel, one of the world's most respected authorities on ancient Jewish revolutionary movements,[24] have been so dismissive of the arguments used. As Hengel observed, "The sources have been selectively treated, in a one-sided way, supplemented in part with *pure fantasy*."[25] For a sober scholar of Hengel's stature, those are very strong words.

As to the question of whether the evidence pointed to Jesus being "a messianic pretender" with violent revolutionary intentions, Hengel replied, "Certainly not! Neither his behavior during the last dramatic days in Jerusalem nor his total activity and proclamation support such assumptions. *They rest upon details which are torn out of context and are arbitrarily interpreted.*"[26]

JESUS THE REVOLUTIONARY?

Was there in any sense, then, in which Jesus was a revolutionary? Hengel, in fact, was especially sensitive to the danger of re-creating Jesus as a violent rebel, having lived through the horrors of Nazism. (He was born in 1926 and conscripted into the German army at the age of seventeen, but he threw away his weapons and uniform while in France toward the end of the war.) And Hengel witnessed Nazi theologians who not only denied that Jesus was Jewish but who also described him as "Fighter, Hero, and Leader (*Führer*)....No good service was rendered his message by doing so....Consequently, there is no common ground between the charismatic physician Jesus of Nazareth and the erstwhile Che Guevara."[27]

But Hengel realized that, in a far more radical way, Jesus really was a revolutionary. On the one hand, he made totally clear that:

> [Jesus] cannot be party to those who—then as now—seek to improve the world by violence which begins with a hate-filled defamation and escalates to bloody terror, to torture and mass murder, where each party shifts all the blame on the opponent. The Jewish War (A.D. 66–70) is a striking paradigm for that. The errors of church history, crusades, inquisition, and religious wars, should put us on guard...against a romantic justification of revolutionary violence.[28]

Truly we make a tragic mistake when we try to change the Yeshua of the Bible into a mythological freedom fighter. Surely he knew there was a better way, a more revolutionary way.

Hengel explains:

> Jesus pointed a quite different way with *agape* [love]: the way of nonviolent protest and willingness to suffer, a way which deserves more fully the designation "revolutionary" than does the old, primitive way of violence. During his activity of one or two years he was a greater force in the world and intellectual history than all agents of revolutionary violence from Spartacus [leader of the slave uprising against Rome] to Judas the Galilean [a Jewish freedom fighter] till today.[29]

As noted by Gerhard Lohfink, a German theologian:

> It is true that Jesus never called for a political, revolutionary transformation of Jewish society. Yet the repentance which he demanded as a consequence of his preaching of the reign of God sought to ignite within the people of God a movement in comparison to which the normal type of revolution is insignificant.[30]

To the extent Christians have focused on the real Jesus—the authentically kosher Jesus—they have brought blessing to multitudes. To the extent they have made him into someone else, including a leader who advocated changing the world by force, they have brought pain and suffering. And since Jesus calls us to follow his example,[31] the stakes are very high when we change him from a preacher of nonviolence who overcame evil with good into a rebel who died in an attempted bloody overthrow of Rome.

Thank God the Mother Teresas of this world are changing the world by caring for the poor and the dying rather than by recruiting violent revolutionaries to go on suicide missions to blow up the rich oppressors. That is not the Jesus way.

Christian educator Vernon C. Grounds expressed it so well:

> A Christian who...becomes a revolutionary will serve as a revolutionary catalyst in the Church; and by the multiplication of revolutionized Christians, the Church will become a revolutionary catalyst in society; and if society is sufficiently revolutionized, a revolution of violence will no more be needed than a windmill in a world of atomic energy.[32]

Precisely. Our journey continues.

6

THE LAMB WHO WAS SLAIN

THE LAMB. IT is the picture of nonresistance, the image of non-protest. And so it was only fitting that Isaiah the prophet spoke of one who did not resist his own death in terms of a lamb: "He was oppressed, and he was afflicted, yet he opened not his mouth; like a lamb that is led to the slaughter, and like a sheep that before its shearers is silent, so he opened not his mouth" (Isa. 53:7, ESV).[1] And it is this title and figure—"the Lamb"—that is applied to Jesus throughout the New Testament.

John, one of Yeshua's closest disciples, wrote, "The next day [John the Baptist] saw Jesus coming toward him, and said, 'Behold, the Lamb of God, who takes away the sin of the world!'" (John 1:29, ESV; see also verse 36.)

Writing to Gentile believers in the city of Corinth, Paul explained, "For our Pesach [Passover] lamb, the Messiah, has been sacrificed" (1 Cor. 5:7, CJB).

In the words of Peter, "You should be aware that the ransom paid to free you from the worthless way of life which your fathers passed on to you did not consist of anything perishable like silver or gold; on the contrary, it was the costly bloody sacrificial death of the Messiah, as of a lamb without defect or spot" (1 Pet. 1:18–19, CJB).

Then, in the Book of Revelation, the last book of the New Testament, the image of Jesus as the Lamb becomes more prominent, occurring a striking twenty-eighty times in the course of twenty-two chapters.[2] In this unique book filled with mystical visions—called "apocalyptic" by scholars—John describes what he saw: "And between the throne [of God] and the four living creatures and among the elders I saw a Lamb standing, as though it had been slain, with seven horns and with seven eyes, which are the seven spirits of God sent out into all the earth" (Rev. 5:6, ESV).

Now what is fascinating is that Jesus is also described in Revelation as "the Lion of the tribe of Judah, the Root of David" (Rev. 5:5), but this description only occurs once. Why? It is because the Jesus of history was a Lamb—not resisting his death by crucifixion, advocating servant-hood rather than domination (Matt. 20:25–28), teaching his followers to bless those who cursed them and to pray for those who persecuted them (Matt. 5:43–48)—whereas the Jesus who will return one day in the future, leading the armies of heaven, will be a Lion, hailed as "the King of kings and the Lord of lords" (Rev. 19:11–16).

Consider the evidence:

- John the Baptist, the forerunner of Jesus, called him a lamb.

- The apostle Paul, writing less than thirty years after Jesus' death, called him a lamb.

- Peter, his passionate and loyal disciple, a man who tried to stop Yeshua's arrest with a sword (John 18:10–11), called him a lamb.

- Twenty-eight times in the Book of Revelation, written roughly sixty years after the death of Jesus, he is called a lamb.

Now ask yourself a question. Have other freedom fighters who called for the violent overthrow of their oppressors been consistently and comprehensively described as lambs?

One hundred sixty-five years before the time of Jesus, Judah Maccabee took on the armies of Greece, in the process becoming one of the greatest warriors in Jewish history. Did anyone ever describe him as a lamb? Three hundred years later, Simeon Bar Kochba, a fearless general, led the ill-fated second Jewish revolt against Rome. Did his followers commonly depict him as a lamb? Yet Jesus is consistently depicted as a lamb rather than as a warring king or violent general. What does this tell us?

Ancient sources inform us that when the Jewish people revolted against Rome in 66–70 CE (with tragic results, which you see later in this chapter), Yeshua's Jerusalem-based, Jewish followers did not participate in the revolt. Instead they fled to Pella (in what is now Jordan), preferring to be falsely branded as traitors by their countrymen rather than participate in an armed revolt.[3] Why?

In *Kosher Jesus*, Shmuley argues that Yeshua's exhortation to "turn the other cheek" in the Sermon on the Mount (Matt. 5:39) relies on Lamentations 3:30, a verse found in the Hebrew Scriptures, and therefore this is not a new, innovative teaching from Jesus.[4] Yet at the same time, Shmuley wants us to believe that Jesus advocated the violent overthrow of Rome. This is hardly "turning the other cheek"![5]

In fact, in this very same Sermon on the Mount—actually, in this very same section of verses—Yeshua said to his disciples:

> You have heard that our fathers were told, 'Eye for eye and tooth for tooth.' But I tell you not to stand up against someone who does you wrong. On the contrary, if someone hits you on the right cheek, let him hit you on the left cheek too! If someone wants to sue you for your shirt, let him have your coat as well! And if a soldier forces you to carry his pack for one mile, carry it for two!
>
> —Matthew 5:38–41, cjb

Do these sound like the words of a freedom fighter gathering violent revolutionaries to overthrow Rome? "Listen, boys! Here's the plan: Whatever happens to you, don't retaliate. Around here, we overcome evil by good! And if you meet up with one of those oppressive Roman soldiers and he forces you to carry his equipment for a mile, carry it for two miles. We'll show them!"

Yeshua continued:

> You have heard that our fathers were told, 'Love your neighbors—and hate your enemy.' But I tell you, love your enemies! Pray

for those who persecute you! Then you will become children
of your Father in heaven. For he makes his sun shine on good
and bad people alike, and he sends rain to the righteous and the
unrighteous alike.

—MATTHEW 5:43–45, CJB

Love your enemies? Pray for those who persecute you? That's what
you tell a band of freedom fighters poised to take down their vicious and
well-armed Roman foes?

Someone might argue that the New Testament was *rewritten* to make
Jesus into a teacher of love and an advocate of nonviolence. Is this plausible or even possible?

Aside from the fact it is quite an interesting argument—in other
words, the more witnesses and the more solid testimony, the more we
should question the evidence!—serious, critical, meticulous scholarship
also dismisses completely this argument. In short, it is the picture of
Jesus as the Lamb that emerges from every strand of authorship in the
writings of the New Testament. It is consistent, it is without contradiction, and it is how Jesus was remembered by his first disciples and, in
turn, their disciples: he was the one who laid down his life for us, the
one who came to serve rather than to be served.

In complete contrast one must literally make a mountain out of a
molehill—and a very small one at that, consisting of just two swords, as
we learned in the previous chapter—in order to turn Jesus into a violent
revolutionary. You might as well say that that Mahatma Gandhi was
actually a bloody Islamic terrorist who was subsequently reinvented as a
Hindu pacifist, and all this within a generation of his death.

The night that Jesus was betrayed after praying with his closest followers in a garden called Gethsemane (meaning "olive press," pro-
nounced *Gat Sh'manim* in Hebrew), "a crowd with swords and clubs"
burst on the scene, ready to take him by force. (See Matthew 26:47;
Mark 14:43. The Gospel authors tell us the crowd was sent by the Jewish
Temple leadership; see Appendix A.)

Jesus pointed out the absurdity of the situation, addressing them with
these words: "So you came out to take me with swords and clubs, the

way you would the leader of a rebellion? Every day I sat in the Temple court, teaching; and you didn't seize me then" (Matt. 26:55, CJB). Jesus was a holy rabbi, not "the leader of a rebellion."

To be sure, his teachings were radical and revolutionary, and, without a doubt, he did call for world transformation. But his methods were not the methods of the world. As noted by H. S. Vigeveno in his book *Jesus the Revolutionary*:

> Our world has witnessed many a revolution, but none as effective as the one that divided history into B.C. and A.D. Every revolution involves the shedding of blood. So did this one. Not as much blood, perhaps, but the quality of the One far outweighs the quantity of others. Revolutionary, indeed, this mission, to begin with a cross and sway the whole world through suffering love. Revolutionary to build a Church on the sacrifice that offers man forgiveness and atonement with God.[6]

It is revolutionary indeed to "sway the whole world through suffering love."

A LEGACY OF NONVIOLENCE

That is what Jesus taught, that is what Jesus emulated, and that is what he passed on. And that is why, for more than three hundred years after Yeshua's death, there is not a single recorded act of religious violence carried out by Jesus' followers against their opponents. In contrast, Paul could say this about the early disciples: "As it is written, 'For your sake we are being killed all the day long; we are regarded as sheep to be slaughtered'" (Rom. 8:36, ESV, quoting from Ps. 44:22). Yes, Christians really were fed to the lions in the Coliseum in Rome and butchered by the gladiators for the entertainment of the crowd. In contrast, there was no such thing as a Christian gladiator! In fact, as the Jesus movement gained traction among the Romans, gladiatorial combat came to an end.[7]

Paul also wrote, "For although we do live in the world, we do not wage war in a worldly way; because the weapons we use to wage war are not worldly" (2 Cor. 10:3–4, CJB). In other words, followers of Jesus *are* in a war and they *are* participating in a revolution, but it is a spiritual war and a revolution of the heart.

And so Paul gave these instructions to the Christians living in Rome:

> Never pay back evil with more evil. Do things in such a way that everyone can see you are honorable. Do all that you can to live in peace with everyone. Dear friends, never take revenge.... Instead, "If your enemies are hungry, feed them. If they are thirsty, give them something to drink. In doing this, you will heap burning coals of shame on their heads." Don't let evil conquer you, but conquer evil by doing good.
> —ROMANS 12:17–21, NLT (QUOTING FROM PROV. 25:22)

Paul learned all this from the example and teachings of Jesus, and for his efforts to spread the Good News, he was beheaded under Nero around 64 CE.

Without a doubt Yeshua's disciples were perceived to be a threat, since their ultimate allegiance was to King Jesus (in Hebrew, *Yeshua HaMelekh*) rather than to Caesar, and they spoke of another kingdom and prayed for its full manifestation on the earth. In fact, the famous words of what is called the Lord's Prayer, "May your Kingdom come...may your will be done on earth as it is in heaven" (Matt. 6:10), have exact parallels in Jewish prayers of the day.[8] But these were prayers for God to bring about his kingdom and his will, not calls for armed resistance, and thus, when the followers of Jesus were called subversive, it was because of their message and their morals.

We see this in Acts 16:20–21, where Paul and Silas, both Jews, are accused of throwing the city of Philippi into an uproar, by "advocating customs that are not lawful for us to accept or practice, since we are Romans" (NET). And in the very next chapter of Acts, some Jewish troublemakers who were opposed to Paul and his team tried to incite the city officials against them, knowing exactly what charges to bring: "These people who have stirred up trouble throughout the world have come here too.... They are all acting against Caesar's decrees, saying there is another king named Jesus!" (Acts 17:6–7, NET).[9] This will certainly stir up the opposition!

But note carefully: Paul and the other disciples were not involved in an armed conflict, nor were they violent revolutionaries, and when a Roman soldier got Paul confused with a dangerous terrorist, it made for an amusing account (Acts 21:37–38):

> Roman soldier: "Aren't you the Egyptian who started a revolt and led four thousand terrorists out into the desert some time ago?"
>
> Paul: "I am a Jew, from Tarsus in Cilicia, a citizen of no ordinary city. Please let me speak to the people [meaning, his fellow Jews who were creating an uproar at the Temple because of Paul's presence]."

To paraphrase, "No, I'm not your guy! I'm a well-bred Roman citizen from the city of Tarsus, and I'd like to share my story with my Jewish brothers here in the city."

It was this same Paul who once explained to believers in Ephesus that their battle was not with people but with spiritual forces, and the "sword" they were to fight with was God's Word—the Bible!—while the greatest weapon they had was prayer (Eph. 6:10–18).

These believers *were* engaged in a conflict, but it was an ideological conflict, a conflict of ultimate loyalty. And if violence ever came into play, it was *by* the ruling authorities (or angry mobs) *against* the followers of Jesus. In fact, during the early decades of the Jesus movement, the Greek word for "witness" came also to mean "martyr," since if you held your ground as a "witness" of your faith in Jesus, you might well pay the ultimate price. (Our English word *martyr* comes from this very Greek word for witness, namely, *martys* or *martyros*.) The spirit of transformation by nonviolence that was taught and emulated by their Master was now alive and well in them.

In the previous chapter we saw that it was utterly ludicrous to argue that Jesus was planning to lead a bloody, armed revolt against Rome (indeed, according to the theory, this was part of what made him so great), especially when we remember that just a few years after his death, he was universally depicted as a gentle lamb, advocating love for one's enemies. Such a reconstruction strains credulity, to put it mildly. It would be the equivalent of convincing the world that General George MacArthur was actually an outspoken pacifist who never picked up a gun in his life, pulling off this ruse with complete success within a few years of World War II.

But there's more. According to the "violent rebellion" theory (which, as we noted, is espoused by the smallest minority of Jewish and Christian scholars),[10] it was the very hope of armed revolt that drew Yeshua's closest followers to him, meaning that these men were being groomed to become the trusted leaders of his ragtag army. And yet, if this theory were true, after Yeshua's death these warriors in training were the very ones who reinvented him as a preacher of non-retaliation, a rabbi who advocated submission to the Roman authorities. What's more, they loyally followed their newly reinvented Jesus the rest of their lives, even to the point of martyrdom. Who can take this seriously?

It would require a scenario like this: A band of Jewish men become captivated by a charismatic leader named Yeshua, with dreams of driving out the Romans in a bloody revolt, and it is the hope of an armed rebellion that inspires them and draws them to Jesus. But when he is killed for sedition against Rome, they rewrite history to make him into a lamb who called for submission to the authorities, and they themselves become lambs, making this lamblike attitude one of the hallmarks of the Jesus movement. Who can believe such a theory?

I, along with a host of other biblical scholars and historians, find it much more reasonable to believe the words of Peter, the acknowledged leader of those very first disciples, who wrote:

> Indeed, this is what you were called to; because the Messiah too suffered, on your behalf, leaving an example so that you should follow in his steps. "He committed no sin, nor was any deceit found on his lips." When he was insulted, he didn't retaliate with insults; when he suffered, he didn't threaten, but handed them over to him who judges justly.
> —1 Peter 2:21–23, CJB (QUOTING ISAIAH 53:9)

Interestingly, the Gospels inform us that Peter didn't always have this perspective, and they share some very embarrassing moments in the life of this passionate and impulsive Jewish fisherman who would have been known in Hebrew as Shimon Kefa. (This, by the way, is one of the best pieces of evidence that the accounts about Peter are trustworthy, since it is counterproductive to memorialize the embarrassing words and deeds of one of the main leaders of your movement, let alone to create them out of thin air.[11])

Matthew, Mark, and Luke all record that, after Peter declared that Yeshua was the Messiah, the Son of the living God, "Jesus began to show his disciples that he must go to Jerusalem and suffer many things from the elders and chief priests and scribes, and be killed, and on the third day be raised" (Matt. 16:21, ESV; see also v. 16).[12] This, however, came as a shock to Peter, who moments ago had made a clear profession that Yeshua was indeed the Messiah—meaning, he thought, the one who presumably would overthrow Rome and set up the kingdom of God on earth.[13]

So Peter took Jesus aside and began to rebuke him—yes, Peter rebuked his leader, the one whom he had just called the Son of God—saying, "Far be it from you, Lord! This shall never happen to you." In response, Jesus said to Peter, "Get behind me, Satan! You are a hindrance to me. For you are not setting your mind on the things of God, but on the things of man" (Matt. 16:22–23, ESV). In other words, "Peter, you've got it all wrong, and it's really the devil who is speaking through you. Your perspective is completely carnal and earthly. I'm going to change the world by laying down my life, not by taking the lives of others."

Roughly two years later, when the armed crowd came to arrest Jesus as he prayed in the Garden of Gethsemane, Peter did something even more embarrassing: he drew his sword and chopped off the ear of the servant of the high priest.

Once again Jesus rebuked Peter: "Put your sword back into its place. For all who take the sword will perish by the sword" (Matt. 26:52, ESV). These are not the words of a violent revolutionary! The Gospel authors make it perfectly clear that Jesus planned to go willingly to his death, as

John records: "Jesus commanded Peter, 'Put your sword away! Shall I not drink the cup the Father has given me?'" (John 18:11).

Wanting to drill home the point after Peter's violent act, Yeshua asked him, "Do you think that I cannot appeal to my Father, and he will at once send me more than twelve legions of angels? But how then should the Scriptures be fulfilled, that it must be so?" (Matt. 26:53–54). "Yes, Peter, I am the Son of the living God, and if it was a fight we wanted, my Father could send more than twelve thousand angels to rescue me and to crush our foes. But that's not my purpose. I came to give my life as a ransom for my people and for the world. Let it be."

In the same way, when Jesus stood before Pontius Pilate, the ruthless Roman procurator who had the power to spare his life,[14] he told him, "My kingship does not derive its authority from this world's order of things. If it did, my men would have fought to keep me from being arrested by the Judeans. But my kingship does not come from here" (John 18:36, CJB).

And when Jesus had been nailed to the cross by Roman soldiers, rather than cursing them and calling down judgment on their heads, he prayed for them: "Father, forgive them, for they do not know what they are doing" (Luke 23:34). From beginning to end this is the exact opposite of a violent leader planning an armed uprising.

Peter followed his Master's example, dying by crucifixion around 64 CE, just as Yeshua did, but with one notable exception: ancient sources tell us that he was crucified upside down, since he didn't feel worthy to die the same way his Savior did.[15]

It is striking and sobering to note that of those first eleven disciples, only two died natural deaths (John and probably Matthew), while the rest, according to tradition, were martyred:

- Peter was crucified upside down.

- Andrew, his brother, was crucified on an x-shaped cross.

- Jacob (James), son of Zebedee, was beheaded.

- Philip was crucified upside down.

- Bartholomew was drowned in a sack.

- Thomas was speared to death (or shot with arrows).

- Jacob (James), son of Alphaeus, was stoned to death (or crucified).

- Thaddaeus was shot with arrows.

- Judah (Judas, not Iscariot) was crucified and shot with arrows.

- Simon the Zealot was crucified.[16]

And why were they put to death? Was it because they were engaged in violent acts against Rome or other tyrannical powers? No, they were killed because their message and lifestyle were perceived to be a threat to the religious and secular powers.[17] These men followed the example of the Lamb who was slain, themselves becoming lambs, and by giving their lives for the movement, they helped to spark a revolution that has continued until this day.

THE LEGACY CONTINUES

Speaking to an overflowing church crowd in Selma, Alabama, on March 8, 1965, Dr. Martin Luther King Jr., who learned the principles of nonviolent resistance from Jesus and Gandhi,[18] proclaimed, "Deep down in our nonviolent creed is the conviction that there are some things so dear, some things so precious, and some things so eternally true that they are worth dying for."[19] And that's why King renounced the philosophy of violent confrontation espoused by Malcom X and others, preferring to confront injustice and inequality through the powerful principles of nonviolent resistance.

Jesus is the ultimate inspiration behind that nonviolent creed! How it cheapens him when we make him into a violent rebel, as if his ideals could only be accomplished by slicing the throats of Roman soldiers, thereby leaving a trail of thousands of widows and orphans, both Jewish and Roman alike. And let it be declared clearly and without equivocation:

during those tragic, dark times in history when professing followers of Jesus have taken up the sword to conquer and convert, they have denied his name, made a mockery of his teachings, and defiled his legacy.

The Jesus-Yeshua we revere is the one whose truly revolutionary message and example have transformed and inspired hundreds of millions of lives for two thousand years. And while there is a necessary place for armies and weapons—thank God for the troops who defeated Hitler and the Nazis—this was not the method of the Messiah. He knew that violence begets violence and that hatred begets hatred, and the only way to break the cycle of violence and hatred is by self-sacrificing love.

While speaking at a church service in the early 2000s, pointing back to the turbulent nature of the 1960s, I asked the attendees if any of them had been involved in any radical religious or political movements. (Amusingly, a man in his fifties said that he was the first one to grow his hair long in high school, but now he was quite bald.) A few raised their hands and said they had been involved in Buddhism or TM (Transcendental Meditation) in the sixties, while others had been into radical campus movements.

Then a white man raised his hand and said that, in those days, he had been involved in the Ku Klux Klan. Immediately after that, a black man sitting next to him—but a stranger to him—raised his hand and said that he had been a member of the Black Panthers! The two of them laughed and hugged while the audience cheered. That is how Jesus deals with racial hatred and prejudice, by changing the heart and bringing reconciliation, not by violent confrontation.

Mahatma Gandhi, one of the most revered leaders of the twentieth century and a man who defeated the British Empire by practicing these nonviolent principles, spoke of Jesus as "a man who was completely innocent, [who] offered himself as a sacrifice for the good of others, including his enemies, and became the ransom of the world. It was a perfect act."[20]

As I've mentioned in previous chapters, less than forty years after that perfect act, Jewish freedom fighters completely unrelated to the Jesus movement tried to break the grip of Rome, leading to monumental Jewish suffering.[21] The Jewish historian Josephus actually claims that *one million Jews* perished in the uprising, including thousands of Jewish men who were crucified. And the Temple of the Lord in Jerusalem, one of the wonders of the ancient world and the holy sanctuary of the God of Israel, was burned to the ground.[22] It has not been rebuilt to this day.

Barely sixty years after this catastrophe, another Jewish rebellion was launched under the leadership of Simeon bar Kochba, hailed as the Messiah by none other than Rabbi Akiva, the greatest rabbi of his day. Again, the results were catastrophic, with Roman claims of 985 Judean villages destroyed. Although this figure might be exaggerated, it is in harmony with the fact that:

> ...without exception, all Judean villages excavated appear to have been razed following the Bar Kochba Revolt. This supports the distinct impression of almost total regional destruction following the war. Historical sources note the vast number of captives sold into slavery in Palestine and shipped abroad.
>
> The Judean Jewish community never recovered from the Bar Kochba War. In its wake Jews no longer formed the majority in Palestine.[23]

As if this was not enough, there was one more indignity that was to be experienced, and if you ever wondered how the Jewish homeland came to be known as Palestine, this is your answer: "An additional, more lasting punitive measure taken by the Romans involved expunging Judea from the provincial name, changing it from *Provincia Judea* to *Provincia Syria Palestina*."[24] As for Rabbi Akiva, looking for a warring Messiah and swayed by Bar Kochba's military prowess, he died a terrible, martyr's death, being skinned alive at the age of ninety.[25]

Yeshua knew there was a better way, weeping over Jerusalem as he foresaw the coming destruction (Luke 19:41–44). A few days later, as he was being led to his crucifixion with his body ripped apart by Roman whips, he was thinking about his people, not himself. "Daughters of Yerushalayim," he exclaimed, "don't cry for me; cry for yourselves and your children! For the time is coming when people will say, 'The childless women are the lucky ones—those whose wombs have never borne a child, whose breasts have never nursed a baby!'" (Luke 23:28–29, CJB).

That's how intense the suffering was going to be, and this would be the inevitable fruit of violent revolution.

Jesus called for a different revolution, a more radical revolution, a revolution of the spirit and the heart. We degrade him when we make him into a mere patriot and freedom fighter. His patriotism was of a higher order, and the freedom for which he fought was an eternal freedom, one that liberates the very soul. And that's why Yeshua and not Bar Kochba, the fierce warrior and false Messiah, is praised worldwide today.

What a revolutionary! What a Lamb! Our journey continues.

Section II

FROM KOSHER JESUS TO UNKOSHER CHRISTIANITY?

7

WAS PAUL THE ONE WHO
CHANGED IT ALL?

Aᴄᴄᴏʀᴅɪɴɢ ᴛᴏ Mɪᴄʜᴀᴇʟ Shapiro, author of the book *The Jewish
100: A Ranking of the Most Influential Jews of All Time*, Saul of
Tarsus, better known as the apostle Paul, was the sixth most
influential Jew of all time—ahead of Karl Marx (#7), Theodor Herzl
(#8), Baruch de Spinoza (#10), King David (#11), Anne Frank (#12), The
Prophets (of biblical times; #13), Maimonides (#16), Moses Mendelssohn
(#18), Rashi (#20), Benjamin Disraeli (#21), David Ben-Gurion (#23),
Hillel (#24), and King Solomon (#29), just to round out the top thirty.[1]
Shapiro listed only Moses, Jesus, Einstein, Freud, and Abraham ahead of
Paul (in that order).

Yet there are some who question whether Paul was really Jewish (or at
least, whether he was born Jewish), while others grant that he was born
Jewish but then accuse him of lying about his pedigree. (He claimed to
have been brought up in Jerusalem, where he studied under Gamaliel,
one of the greatest Pharisaic teachers of the day; see Acts 22:3.)

Many Jews (along with many Gentile critics of Christianity) believe
that, "Jesus was really all right. He was a good Jew and a fine rabbi.
It was Paul who messed everything up and founded Christianity."[2]
As expressed by Prof. Eugene Fischer, a Catholic leader who has been

involved in Jewish dialogue for years, "Jesus was a good guy. Paul was a bad goy."[3] (*Goy* is a Hebrew term for Gentile, used non-colloquially by non-Hebrew speakers.) Yes, Paul was the real troublemaker (or, in the words of Prof. Hyam Maccoby, "the mythmaker"[4]), the one who transformed the Jewish-Jesus movement into an unrecognizable Gentile religion. Is there any truth to this?

If you recall, in Rabbi Shmuley Boteach's narrative, Jesus had died as a failed Messiah, thwarted in his attempt to overthrow Rome: "The legacy of the rabbi has little future," Rabbi Shmuley wrote. "Persecuted by Rome, devastated after the loss of their beloved leader, the teacher's followers become fewer and fewer."[5]

But in Shmuley's version (influenced primarily by Hyam Maccoby's controversial theories), this was not the end of the story. Rather, it was the beginning—and not because Shmuley accepts the resurrection of Yeshua. Instead it was because of a stranger who entered the scene, and this stranger changed everything.

So important is this stranger to Shmuley's thesis that the opening chapter of his book *Kosher Jesus* is entitled "The Rabbi and the Stranger," the rabbi being Jesus and the stranger being Paul.

> Without warning, a mysterious stranger arrives. He presents himself to the teacher's remaining followers. They fear he has been sent only to harass them further; perhaps he is in the employ of the high priest, an agent of Rome, his job to undermine any and all sedition against the emperor. Yet he claims to be on the side of the rabbi's followers.[6]

Paul then tells these "remaining followers" that their "fallen rabbi appeared to him in a vision. The experience changed him. He now hopes to follow the rabbi's teachings—though as the disciples will soon learn, his agenda is very different."[7]

To their shock, Paul explains to them that: (1) "The rabbi was more than a man, more even than the messiah. He suggests the rabbi was outright divine—literally, the son of God." (2) "The stranger ascribes a meaning to the rabbi's death that the original followers never could. The rabbi did not die in vain, the stranger argues. His demise constituted part of his mission from God, the fulfillment of an ancient, divine plan. The rabbi had been sent to die for the sins of mankind." (3) "Furthermore, the rabbi came to this earth on a spiritual mission rather than a political one. His purpose involved not freedom from Rome but rebellion against a corrupt Jewish establishment and Torah observance that had calcified into an obstacle to salvation." (4) "[T]he stranger tells the stunned disciples that their rabbi's death brought all the laws of the Torah to completion. His execution abrogated all obligations specified in the Law."

How do Yeshua's followers respond to this new message? "The disciples are dumbfounded. No teaching could have given greater shock to a Jewish system. The Torah is not eternal? The rabbi was God Himself? Impossible. The small collection of disciples—devout Jews all—banishes the stranger."

But that doesn't stop Paul. "Undaunted, he disseminates his theory of the rabbi's identity among the gentile Romans, launching his campaign at a most opportune time." The results are dramatic: "The new message suits their predisposition. It spreads quickly with unprecedented enthusiasm."[8]

How should we assess this narrative?

Simply stated, it is not just fiction; it is fantasy—and I say that as a serious student of the Scriptures for more than forty years, much of that time spent in intensive study of both the biblical texts and the best scholarly literature available. In short, this narrative does not just strain credulity; it insults it.

WHERE RABBI SHMULEY GOT HIS IDEAS

I am fully aware of the fact that the intentions of my esteemed colleague Rabbi Shmuley are quite noble, and for that I am deeply appreciative. He has taken a courageous stand at great professional risk in his desire to remove any barrier between our Jewish people and Jesus (meaning, of course, what Shmuley understands to be the Jesus of history). He wants to eliminate the accusation that it was Jesus who founded a non-Jewish faith called "Christianity," placing the blame for that squarely on Paul.

But good intentions do not equal good scholarship, nor are they a valid excuse to rewrite the sacred texts of another religion.

Shmuley did not, however, create his thesis out of whole cloth. As stated above, he relied on Hyam Maccoby's work,[9] specifically his 1986 book, *The Mythmaker: Paul and the Invention of Christianity*.[10] Ironically, although Maccoby intended the title of his book to refer to Paul, the alleged "mythmaker," it actually serves as an unintentionally ironic description of the book itself: the late Prof. Maccoby, not Paul, was the mythmaker.

Yet Shmuley is not the only one to follow this thesis. It has also been embraced by another popular Jewish author, journalist David Klinghoffer in his 2005 book, *Why the Jews Rejected Jesus: The Turning Point of Western History*.[11]

Among recognized New Testament scholars, however, Maccoby's *Mythmaker* is either ignored or else dismissed in the strongest of terms. What makes this all the more significant is that these scholars frequently quote Maccoby's other writings on early Judaism and the Jewish background to legal disputes in the Gospels,[12] and Maccoby was a contributor to the prestigious volume *Dictionary of Paul and His Letters*.[13]

But when it comes to *The Mythmaker*, experts in the field have barely given it the time of day, so far-fetched are Maccoby's proposals—and I'm not talking here about supposedly close-minded "fundamentalist Christian scholars," but about critical scholars who are open to all kinds of new ideas. I have actually spoken with some of the top New Testament scholars about *The Mythmaker*, and although they are intimately familiar with the important literature in their field, they had never even heard of the book.

Reviewing *The Mythmaker* in *The Jewish Quarterly Review*, John E. Gager, until 2006 the William H. Danforth Professor of Religion at Princeton University, stated bluntly that it was, in part, a "perverse misreading" of the relevant texts. Gager's conclusion was that Maccoby's book "is not good history, not even history at all." This is not typical of scholarly reviews, which tend not to use such forceful language, but that's how unsubstantiated the theories put forth in *The Mythmaker* are.

Prof. Gager noted in his review that, "There is a grave, if largely unrecognized, danger in all new departures, for they can take us in either of two directions—forward or backward. This book, I fear, moves us backward in virtually every area." Strong words once again!

Gager, however, did feel there was one way the book could have been redeemed: "Still, the book might have been redeemed with an ever so slight shift in its self-description. If, instead of representing it as a work of historical scholarship, the author had described it as a piece of historical romance...*we might have been able to enjoy it as fiction.*"[14]

Fiction! Yet this book is the primary basis for Shmuley's rewriting of much of the New Testament and the early history of the Jesus movement. And Gager is not alone among scholars in dismissing Maccoby's *Mythmaker* in such strong terms.

James D. G. Dunn, for many years the Lightfoot Professor of Divinity in the Department of Theology at the University of Durham, England, is one of the leading authorities on Paul. His 2006 volume *The Theology of Paul the Apostle*—just one of his many books on Paul—is more than eight hundred pages long.[15] And Dunn, like Gager, cannot possibly be described as some kind of narrow-minded, fundamentalist Christian. To the contrary, he is one of the leaders in what is called the "new perspectives on Paul,"[16] which is constantly challenging traditional Christian understandings and always looking for fresh new approaches to Paul.

What does Dunn say about Maccoby's thesis, which includes the idea that Paul was a convert to Judaism and did not have a Pharisaical background? Dunn wrote:

> Paul shows that he is as firmly located within Judaism as anyone can be; he is no first- or even tenth-generation proselyte. Maccoby's counter suggestion (*Mythmaker*, 95–96), that Paul was a Gentile whose claim here is totally invented and fictitious, is *wildly fanciful* and shows *no sensitivity* to Paul's whole argument in Romans. [Dunn is speaking of Paul's statement in Rom. 11:1, "I am an Israelite myself, a descendant of Abraham, from the tribe of Benjamin."][17]

Yes, it is Maccoby, not Paul, who is the mythmaker, and when Maccoby argues that Paul's claim to be a true Israelite from the tribe of Benjamin is invented and fictitious, Dunn rightly counters that what is invented and fictitious is Maccoby's thesis. To repeat Dunn's words, it "is wildly fanciful and shows no sensitivity to Paul's whole argument in Romans."[18]

Similar sentiments were expressed by a reviewer in the *Library Journal*, who much preferred Jewish scholar Alan Segal's book, *Paul the Convert: The Apostolate and Apostasy of Saul the Pharisee*,[19] "to the *polemical speculation* of Hyam Maccoby's *The Mythmaker*"—and Segal's study was hardly traditional in its own approach.[20] Even a Jewish scholar like Prof. Adam Gregerman, reviewing *Kosher Jesus* in the *Forward*, the oldest Jewish daily newspaper, noted that "Boteach seems not to know that this strange, conspiratorial reading [of Maccoby] has been almost universally rejected by scholars since it appeared."[21]

Now, I want to say once more that scholars of Paul are constantly looking for new approaches to his writings and his life, and over the years, some *very* odd theories have been entertained, to put it mildly.[22] And there is no question that Paul is a complex Jewish thinker, to the point that one of the New Testament books, attributed to Peter, states that, "[Paul's] letters contain some things that are hard to understand, which ignorant and unstable people distort, as they do the other Scriptures, to their own destruction" (2 Pet. 3:16). So, if Peter acknowledged that Paul could easily be misunderstood, you can only imagine that scholars from all backgrounds could have a field day with his writings.

Yet even in this environment of scholarly speculation and exploration, Maccoby's *Mythmaker* has been consistently dismissed or ignored. In fact, even in volumes that have been written simply to summarize and discuss the latest developments in Pauline scholarship, citing scores (if not hundreds) of relevant studies, *The Mythmaker* is not considered worthy of discussion.[23]

John Gager, whose scathing review of *The Mythmaker* was cited previously, actually wrote a book in 2000 entitled *Reinventing Paul*,[24] evaluating the most recent, new approaches to Paul and putting forth his own theory, yet in that book too Maccoby's study wasn't cited a single time.

Nonetheless, a theory that undermines the fundamental doctrines of the New Testament is built on this intellectual castle of sand. Words fail to express how presumptuous it is to tell more than two billion people that their religious beliefs are completely wrong—really, nothing more than myths—based primarily on one book that almost all serious scholars have either dismissed or ignored.

THE NEW TESTAMENT ACCORDING TO RABBI SHMULEY

It is one thing to challenge common historical or religious assumptions and beliefs based on solid evidence and serious scholarship. In fact, if our beliefs and assumptions can't withstand scrutiny, then there is something wrong with them. It is another thing entirely, though, to offer a radical reconstruction and rereading of the entire New Testament based on a book promoting an indefensible, unsupportable, extremely fringe theory.

At this point you might be saying to yourself, "Well, if the book is so bad, why spend so much time dismissing it? And could it be that other scholars have ignored it because they simply don't want to face the truth? Maybe Maccoby was rejected because he wasn't part of the 'club' or because the implications of his thesis were too dangerous."

Those are certainly fair questions, and they deserve a response. First, I spent this much time on the subject because popular books by Orthodox Jewish authors (such as David Klinghoffer's *Why the Jews Rejected Jesus* and Rabbi Shmuley's *Kosher Jesus*) put a lot of stock in Maccoby's thesis, and most Jews reading those books will not have the ability to evaluate Maccoby's radical claims, since they are not professional scholars in that field or even serious students of the New Testament. (The same is true for all of us in many different areas that lie outside of our expertise.)

Second, scholars studying Paul come from all kinds of backgrounds—from atheists to evangelical Christians and from liberal critics who don't believe the Bible is inspired to Jewish professors who put no religious stock in Paul—and even in this wide-open "Let's hear your latest theory" environment, Maccoby's book has not been a serious factor. And having studied the relevant literature for years, I can tell you that some of the wildest theories have been put forth, with "dangerous" implications for

Christian beliefs if true. One author even suggested that Paul's alleged bouts with malarial fever caused him to be self-contradictory and confused![25]

Third, there are plenty of Jewish scholars who recognize Paul as a Pharisaical Jew with a solid Jewish background and clear patterns of Jewish thought. As stated by Rabbi Jacob Emden in 1757, "Paul was a scholar, an attendant of Rabban Gamaliel the Elder, well-versed in the laws of the Torah."[26] (As I mentioned in chapter 2, Emden was one of the most respected rabbinic authorities of the eighteenth century, and I can assure you that he holds infinitely more weight in the traditional Jewish community than does Maccoby.)

Rabbi Emden, however, was hardly alone. Hebrew University professor Joseph Klausner (also mentioned in chapter 2), followed up his book on Jesus with *From Jesus to Paul* also written originally in Hebrew.[27] While he, like others before and since him, felt that Paul was more responsible for "Christianity" than was Jesus, he had no doubt about Paul's Jewishness and rabbinic heritage, writing:

> Truly, Paul was a Jew not only in his physical appearance, but he was also a typical Jew in his thinking and in his entire inner-life. For Saul-Paul was not only "a Pharisee, a son of Pharisees," but also one of those disciples of the Tannaim who were brought up on the exegesis of the Torah, and did not cease to cherish it to the end of their days. It would be difficult to find more typically Talmudic expositions of Scripture than those in the Epistles of Paul.[28]

Klausner was also of the opinion that:

> Paul lived by Jewish law like a proper Jew; also, he knew the Old Testament in its Hebrew original and meditated much upon it....If Paul was a "Hebrew of the Hebrews" and "a Pharisee, a son of Pharisees," educated in Jerusalem and able to make speeches in Hebrew (or Aramaic), obviously he was not a "Septuagint Jew" [meaning, a Jew dependent on the

Greek translation of the Bible]...only, as various Christian scholars have been accustomed to picture him.[29]

More recently, Alan Segal wrote that, "Paul is a trained Pharisee who became the apostle to the Gentiles,"[30] while Aramaic scholar Daniel Boyarin noted that, "Paul has left us an extremely precious document for Jewish studies, the spiritual autobiography of a first-century Jew....Moreover, if we take Paul at his word—and I see no a priori reason not to—he was a member of the Pharisaic wing of first-century Judaism."[31] And Rabbi Dr. Burton Visotzky, a distinguished professor at Jewish Theological Seminary, wrote that, "The Pharisee Saul of Tarsus is arguably one of the most influential religious figures in the history of Western culture."[32] Yet Maccoby's myth-made Paul couldn't even read Hebrew!

According to Dr. Julie Galambush, a former Baptist minister who converted to Judaism:

> For much of the twentieth century, Paul of Tarsus was considered the founder of a new religion, Christianity. Jesus had been a Galilean teacher, but Paul, a hellenized Jew of Asia Minor, brought Jesus' message, both physically and philosophically, to the Gentiles. In recent years the image of the "Christian Paul" has fallen out of favor. Just as in the nineteenth and twentieth centuries scholars rediscovered the Jewishness of Jesus, so now they have begun to reclaim the Jewishness of Paul. The reality of a Jewish Paul—a Paul who never dreamed that his missionary endeavors would spread anything but a new stage in Jewish belief—carries a particular poignancy in light of later Christian history.[33]

Fascinating!

Let's consider what the New Testament would look like if the Maccoby-Klinghoffer-Boteach reconstruction was correct. First, we would have to strike out quite a few verses in the New Testament where Paul speaks about himself, simply because they would all be lies:

• I ask then: Did God reject his people? By no means! ~~I am an Israelite myself, a descendant of Abraham, from the tribe of Benjamin.~~ (Rom. 11:1)

• ~~Are they Hebrews? So am I. Are they Israelites? So am I. Are they Abraham's descendants? So am I.~~ (2 Cor. 11:22)

• ~~For you have heard of my previous way of life in Judaism,~~ how intensely I persecuted the church of God and tried to destroy it. ~~I was advancing in Judaism beyond many Jews of my own age and was extremely zealous for the traditions of my fathers.~~ (Gal. 1:13–14)

• If anyone else thinks he has reasons to put confidence in the flesh, I have more: ~~circumcised on the eighth day, of the people of Israel, of the tribe of Benjamin, a Hebrew of Hebrews; in regard to the law, a Pharisee; as for zeal, persecuting the church; as for legalistic righteousness, faultless.~~ (Phil. 3:4–6)

• ~~I am a Jew, born in Tarsus of Cilicia, but brought up in this city. Under Gamaliel I was thoroughly trained in the law of our fathers and was just as zealous for God as any of you are today.~~ (Acts 22:3; Paul said this to a large crowd of Jews at the Temple in Jerusalem.)

• ~~My brothers, I am a Pharisee, the son of a Pharisee.~~ I stand on trial because of my hope in the resurrection of the dead. (Acts 23:6; Paul spoke these words in Jerusalem, but this time to the Sanhedrin, the Jewish ruling council.)

• ~~The Jews all know the way I have lived ever since I was a child, from the beginning of my life in my own country, and also in Jerusalem. They have known me for a long time and can testify, if they are willing, that according to~~

~~the strictest sect of our religion, I lived as a Pharisee.~~ And now it is because of my hope in what God has promised our fathers that I am on trial today. (Acts 26:4–6; Paul in his defense before King Agrippa)

- I have done nothing wrong ~~against the law of the Jews or against the temple or~~ against Caesar. (Acts 25:8; Paul in his defense before the governor Festus)

- ~~My brothers, although I have done nothing against our people or against the customs of our ancestors,~~ I was arrested in Jerusalem and handed over to the Romans. (Acts 28:17; speaking to the Jewish leaders in Rome)

Do you feel comfortable striking out verses in the Christian Bible— from autobiographic accounts, at that? Are you happy with the fact that medieval Catholic censors edited out texts from the Talmud and rabbinic writings that they deemed offensive but now Jewish leaders are effectively striking out verses in the New Testament by calling them outright lies?[34] Well, we're just getting started.

According to the fictional narrative put forth in *Kosher Jesus*, it was Paul who introduced the idea that Yeshua was "outright divine—literally, the son of God." This means that all the verses in the New Testament that refer to Jesus as the Son of God would also have to be expunged, let alone all the verses that describe him as in any sense divine.[35] It also raises the question of how these verses got there in the first place, since many of them are found in the writings of the original Jewish followers of Yeshua who allegedly rejected Paul and his theology.

To give you an idea of what we're talking about, if Paul introduced the idea that Jesus was the Son of God, that would mean that every time Jesus was referred to as such in the Gospels, those verses would reflect later additions or changes—meaning that later editors or authors somehow changed the "original" New Testament books to comport with the new theology of "the stranger."[36]

In order, then, to get back to the alleged "original" Gospel sources of which Shmuley speaks,[37] we would have to delete these verses from the Gospels as later additions or changes. Yet these verses are deeply imbedded in their immediate contexts, meaning that, if you pull them out, you pull out most of the verses surrounding them. This would be similar to being left with a restaurant that has no menus and that doesn't serve food, or a bank that has no money and that doesn't offer loans, checking accounts, or saving accounts.

How often, then, is Jesus referred to as "Son of God" in the Gospels alone? The verses in question are: Matthew 4:3, 6; 8:29; 14:33; 16:16; 26:63; 27:40, 43, 54; Mark 1:1; 3:11; 5:7; 15:39; Luke 1:32, 35; 4:3, 9, 41; 8:28; 22:70; John 1:34, 49; 5:25; 11:27; 19:7; 20:31. Those are a lot of texts! And quite a few of them occur in parallel accounts where the Gospel authors repeat the same stories from different angles, yet these accounts are in harmony in terms of calling Jesus the Son of God.

And who is it that refers to Yeshua as "Son of God" in these texts? It is a host of different witnesses, both friendly and hostile, including:

- The Gospel authors themselves

- All his disciples

- Specific disciples (Peter, Nathaniel, Martha)

- John the Baptist

- The high priest and other chief priests

- Jewish teachers and elders

- A Roman soldier

- Demons

- Satan

- The angel Gabriel

- Yeshua himself

What a list!
If we include the verses in the Gospels where God testifies from

heaven that Jesus is "my Son," then we have to add Matthew 3:17; 17:5; Mark 1:11; 9:7; Luke 3:22; 9:35. (We also have to add God himself to the host of witnesses.) And then there are all the verses where Jesus refers to God as "Father" (in a clearly unique and individual sense) or to himself as "the Son," which adds a lot more verses in the four Gospels alone.[38]

And we would have to completely trash some of the most famous passages in the Bible, including John 3:16–18, which would now read like this:

> For God so loved the world that he gave ~~his one and only Son~~, that whoever believes ~~in him~~ shall not perish but have eternal life. For God did not send ~~his Son~~ into the world to condemn the world, but to save the world ~~through him~~. Whoever believes ~~in him~~ is not condemned, but whoever does not believe stands condemned already because he has not believed in the name of ~~God's one and only Son~~.

In reality, we would have to trash the entire Gospel of John (attributed, again, to John-Yochanan, one of Yeshua's first followers and, again, one of those who allegedly rejected Paul's so-called new theology). We would have to trash the letters of John as well, since 1 John alone, consisting of just five short chapters, refers to Jesus as God's Son twenty-one times.

And we haven't mentioned the Letter to Hebrews—written exclusively to Jewish believers in Yeshua—where Jesus as the Son of God is a prominent theme. This is true right from the opening verses, which explain that:

> ...in these last days [God] has spoken to us by his Son, whom he appointed heir of all things, and through whom he made the universe. The Son is the radiance of God's glory and the exact representation of his being, sustaining all things by his powerful word. After he had provided purification for sins, he sat down at the right hand of the Majesty in heaven.
>
> —HEBREWS 1:2–3 (SEE ALSO 1:5, 8; 3:6; 4:14; 5:5, 8; 6:6; 7:3, 28; 10:29)

You would literally have to cut out of the heart and soul of Hebrews to remove the concept of Jesus as the Son of God—and this concept is thoroughly embedded in a totally Jewish book.

Yet somehow, we are told, all this got written back into these texts (the alleged work of the "redactors") and was magically weaved—seamlessly!—into the very core of book after book and narrative after narrative and teaching after teaching. That would be like weaving the Communist Manifesto into the American Constitution without leaving an editorial trace (to the point that some of the original signers lent their names to the newly created document) or like merging the face of Princess Diana into Da Vinci's *Mona Lisa* without art critics being able to spot the changes. This is just one of the reasons I said that the theory espoused by Maccoby and Rabbi Boteach not only strains credulity but also insults it.

And remember: I have only considered the first alleged innovation made by "the stranger," and even so, I haven't even covered all of the New Testament (excluding, of course, Paul's own writings).

The second allegation is that Paul introduced the concept that, "The rabbi had been sent to die for the sins of mankind." This too is a core, foundational New Testament truth. (For a small sampling of non-Pauline texts that say this same thing, see Matthew 1:21; 20:28; Mark 10:45; Luke 22:20; Hebrews 9:15.) As for the third allegation, namely, that Paul introduced the concept that "the rabbi came to this earth on a spiritual mission rather than a political one," we have already seen how the whole of the New Testament makes plain that Yeshua's mission was *not* a political one.[39] (See chapters 5 and 6.) And let us not forget that Paul explicitly states that he received "from the Lord" the fact that Jesus, on the night he was betrayed, called his disciples to commemorate his sacrificial death in what we call "the Last Supper," memorialized in the church as "Holy Communion" or "the Eucharist." (See 1 Corinthians 11:23–26.) This last Passover meal with the disciples is described in all four Gospels and became a sacrament universally recognized by the early church. It was surely not an innovation by Paul. He too knew that the mission of Jesus was *not* a political one.

In short, these alleged innovations supposedly introduced by the so-called "stranger" are really the very foundations of the Jesus movement, as integral to the whole New Testament message as the concepts of the Torah, the chosenness of Israel, and the importance of tradition are to rabbinic Judaism, the root and trunk of the tree as opposed to the tips of the branches.

So then, if Paul didn't change everything, who did? How *did* we get from a kosher Jesus to an allegedly unkosher Christianity? The journey now takes an interesting turn.

8

THE JEWISH GENIUS WHO BROUGHT
THE GOD OF ISRAEL TO THE NATIONS

W HY DID GOD choose the Jewish people? Was he guilty of favoritism? Did he care about only one group of people on the earth? Quite the contrary: he chose the people of Israel, beginning with Abraham, because he wanted to bless the entire world. The Jewish people were called to be a light to the nations.

As a boy I heard that as Jews, we were the "chosen people," but I never heard exactly what we were chosen for. And I was certainly not alone. Many Jews cannot answer the question, "Chosen for what?"

Before the Torah is read in the synagogue every Sabbath, a prayer is recited, praising God for choosing Israel out of all the nations and for giving the Jewish nation the Torah. But is that the extent of Israel's chosenness, namely, that the Jewish people were chosen to receive the wonderful gift of God's Torah?[1] And to what purpose? Is there more to being chosen by Almighty God?

This is what is written in the *Tanakh*, the Hebrew Scriptures or Old Testament, about God's purpose in choosing the Jewish people:

1. God said to Abraham (then called Abram), "I will make you into a great nation and I will bless you; I will make your name great, and you will be a blessing. I will bless those who bless you, and whoever curses you I will curse; and *all peoples on earth will be blessed through you*" (Gen. 12:2–3, emphasis added).[2] The Lord was looking for one man who would listen to his voice and keep his

commandments, and through that man's descendants, God wanted to bring blessing to the entire world.

2. God told Moses to give the people of Israel this message: "You yourselves have seen what I did to Egypt, and how I carried you on eagles' wings and brought you to myself. Now if you obey me fully and keep my covenant, then out of all nations you will be my treasured possession. Although the whole earth is mine, you will be for me *a kingdom of priests and a holy nation*" (Exod. 19:4–6, emphasis added). Priests served as mediators between the rest of the people and God, teaching them the ways of God. Israel was called to be a *nation of priests* who would teach the rest of the world the ways of the Lord.

3. Several times in the Book of Isaiah it is written that the servant of the Lord would be a light to the nations. (In Isaiah this servant is sometimes Israel and sometimes the Messiah, who fulfills Israel's mission.) "Here is my servant, whom I uphold, my chosen one in whom I delight; I will put my Spirit on him and he will bring *justice to the nations*. . . . I, the LORD, have called you in righteousness; I will take hold of your hand. I will keep you and will make you to be a covenant for the people and *a light for the Gentiles*, to open eyes that are blind, to free captives from prison and to release from the dungeon those who sit in darkness" (Isa. 42:1, 6–7, emphasis added). "It is too small a thing for you to be my servant to restore the tribes of Jacob and bring back those of Israel I have kept. I will also make you *a light for the Gentiles*, that you may bring my salvation to *the ends of the earth*" (Isa. 49:6, emphasis added).

In keeping with Israel's calling to be a light to the nations, the Psalms are filled with exhortations to declare God's praises to the ends of the earth along with declarations of individual Israelites who determined to do that very thing, with the result that the Gentiles would turn to the God of Israel:

> Therefore I will praise you among the nations, O LORD; I will sing praises to your name.
>
> —PSALM 18:49

> I will perpetuate your memory through all generations; therefore the nations will praise you forever and ever.
>
> —PSALM 45:17

> I will praise you, O LORD, among the nations; I will sing of you among the peoples.
>
> —PSALM 108:3 (SEE ALSO Ps. 57:9)

> May God be gracious to us and bless us and make his face shine upon us...that your ways may be known on earth, your salvation among all nations. May the peoples praise you, O God; may all the peoples praise you. May the nations be glad and sing for joy, for you rule the peoples justly and guide the nations of the earth. May the peoples praise you, O God; may all the peoples praise you. Then the land will yield its harvest, and God, our God, will bless us. God will bless us, and all the ends of the earth will fear him.
>
> —PSALM 67:1–7

> All the ends of the earth will remember and turn to the LORD, and all the families of the nations will bow down before him, for dominion belongs to the LORD and he rules over the nations.
>
> —PSALM 22:27–28

> All the nations you have made will come and worship before you, O Lord; they will bring glory to your name.
>
> —PSALM 86:9

The Jewish people do not fulfill these verses simply by praying communal prayers to God (even prayers for the nations) or singing communal praises about God in synagogues while scattered among the nations, or even by living by the Torah in the sight of the nations (although this is certainly part of the biblical Jewish calling).[3] The command is to *declare God's praises among the peoples, to make him known to the nations*:

> *Declare his glory among the nations*, his marvelous deeds among all peoples.
> —Psalm 96:3, emphasis added

> Worship the Lord in the splendor of his holiness; tremble before him, all the earth. *Say among the nations*, "The Lord reigns." The world is firmly established, it cannot be moved; he will judge the peoples with equity.
> —Psalm 96:9–10, emphasis added

> Sing praises to the Lord, enthroned in Zion; *proclaim among the nations what he has done*.
> —Psalm 9:11, emphasis added

Did you realize that this was part of the sacred calling of the Jewish people—to proclaim among the nations what God has done, and in that sense, to be a "missionary" religion? Paul understood this mandate, and that's a big key to the controversy surrounding him.

Paul's Influence Can't Be Ignored

At the beginning of the last chapter I mentioned that Paul was listed as the sixth most influential Jew who ever lived by the author of *The Jewish 100*. Well, Michael Hart, the author of a book listing the 100 most influential people of all time (meaning, Jews and non-Jews) also listed Paul as #6—ahead of Einstein (#10), Moses (#15), Karl Marx (#27), and Sigmund Freud (#69).[4]

How fascinating! Paul, the Jew, was one of the most influential men who ever lived. And it was *as a Jew* that he had that influence. He was doing what Jews were supposed to do, being a light to the nations, taking the message of the God of Israel and the Messiah of Israel to the nations. And that is one of the reasons he has been criticized and attacked.

The Book of Acts preserves a very revealing account. Paul had been falsely accused of bringing Gentiles into the Temple, causing a large Jewish crowd to gather there in protest.[5] A Roman soldier allowed Paul to address the crowd (a riot had almost broken out, in fact), and as he spoke to them in Aramaic (or Hebrew), they listened attentively to his story, even when he shared how he was involved in the martyrdom of a Jewish follower of Yeshua named Stephen.

Paul then reached the conclusion of his testimony: "'Then the Lord said to me, "Go; I will send you far away to the Gentiles."' The crowd listened to Paul until he said this. Then they raised their voices and shouted, 'Rid the earth of him! He's not fit to live!'" (Acts 22:21–22). *This* was more than they could tolerate. There was something about his calling to the Gentiles that infuriated his fellow Jews. What was it?

It's important to understand the historical context, as explained by Prof. Craig Keener, an expert in the historical and cultural background to the New Testament:

> Jerusalem is not what it had been in Acts 2 [meaning, twenty-five to thirty years earlier]; tensions are rising, and in the temple *sicarii*, or assassins, are murdering aristocrats suspected of collaborating with the Gentiles. Jewish nationalism is on the rise, and nationalism's exclusivity makes it intolerant of supposedly faithful members of its people who have fellowship with members of other peoples. Thus it is incumbent on Paul to prove the integrity of his Jewishness.[6]

As we noted, Paul had just been falsely accused of bringing Gentiles into the Temple, and now, against this tense backdrop, he claims that God himself sent him to the Gentiles. How can this be? According to Acts commentator Joseph Fitzmyer, "Those who listen to Paul cannot bear to hear him say that he has been commissioned by heaven to preach a message of salvation to people who would not have to observe the Mosaic law."[7] No!

As explained more fully by another Acts commentator, Prof. Richard Longenecker, the Jewish crowd listened to Paul "with a certain respect, for he had spoken mostly of Israel's messianic hope and done so in a thoroughly Jewish context."

> When, however, Paul spoke of being directed by divine revelation to leave Jerusalem and go far away to the Gentiles who no relation to Judaism, that was "the last straw." In effect, Paul was saying that Gentiles can be approached directly with the message of salvation without first being related to the nation and its institutions. This was tantamount to placing Jews and Gentiles on an equal footing before God and for Judaism was the height of apostasy indeed![8]

Now we are getting to the heart of the matter. Is that why Paul was (and is) so controversial, because he claimed that Jew and Gentile could have equal standing before God through faith in the Messiah, without the Gentiles having to observe the Law of Moses and without having to become Jews?[9]

BUT WHO WAS PAUL, REALLY?

But before we go any further, let's remember who this Saul-Paul actually was. The comments of Prof. Jaroslav Pelikan, perhaps the world's foremost authority on church history, are relevant. He writes that, in contrast with past scholarly views that often saw Paul as "the one chiefly responsible for the de-Judaization of the gospel and even for the transmutation of the person of Jesus from a rabbi in the Jewish sense to a divine being in the Greek sense," studies in the last few decades are seeing things much differently. Thus, "scholars have not only put the picture of Jesus back into the setting of first-century Judaism; they have also rediscovered the Jewishness of the New Testament, *and particularly of the apostle Paul*, and specifically of his Epistle to the Romans."[10] Yes, scholars are rediscovering the Jewishness of Paul,[11] and yet popular misconceptions abound, even among Christians.

I've tested this out with Bible-believing Christians, asking them,

"What comes to mind when you think about the names Saul and Paul?" The prevalent thinking goes something like this: Saul of Tarsus was a Jewish leader who persecuted the Christians, and then he got converted and changed his name to Paul, a Christian leader. In other words, Saul = Jewish = bad; Paul = Christian = good. Is that correct?

Not at all. Saul of Tarsus was a Jewish leader who, from birth, also had the name Paul. (One was a Hebrew name, the other a Greek name, and this was commonplace among Jews born in Greek cities.[12]) At one point in his life he persecuted fellow Jews who believed that Yeshua was the Jewish Messiah (and this was well before they were first called "Christians"). Then he had a visionary encounter with Jesus the Messiah, he repented of his sinful opposition to the Lord, and, to the delightful surprise of those he once opposed so vehemently, he became a faithful emissary of Yeshua. He never persecuted members of a different religion, nor did he convert to another religion, nor did he take on a new name after his supposed conversion, and he identified as Jew until his last recorded moments. (See chapter 7 for more on Paul's Jewish heritage.)

For Paul, going to the Gentiles was part of Israel's priestly ministry, which included making God and his Messiah known. He described his own calling in these very words: "to be a servant of the Messiah Yeshua for the Gentiles, with the *priestly duty* of presenting the Good News of God, *so that the Gentiles may be an acceptable offering*, made holy by the [Holy Spirit]" (Rom. 15:16, cjb, emphasis added).

As explained by Joseph Shulam, a pioneering Messianic Jewish leader in Israel, and his coauthor, researcher Hillary LeCornu, "Paul is part of the people of Israel, whom God has chosen to be a 'kingdom of priests and a holy nation' before Him (cf. Ex. 19:6)." Paul's "offering" of the Gentiles "fulfills the prophetic passages in Isaiah 61:6 and 66:18–24. The nations are Israel's offering to God when His people return to their God and the land, in fulfillment of her priestly task to serve the nations."[13]

Isaiah the prophet spoke of the day when the Lord would send a remnant of the Jewish people into the nations, to those "that have never heard My fame nor beheld My glory. They shall declare My glory among these nations" (Isa. 66:19, njv). Paul understood that he was doing that very thing! As a result, the people of those nations would be brought to

Jerusalem "as an offering to the LORD—just as the Israelites bring an offering in a pure vessel to the House of the LORD. And from them likewise I will take some to be levitical priests, said the LORD" (vv. 20–21, NJV).

Gentile believers serving as levitical priests to the Lord? The Gentile nations serving as an offering to the Lord? Isaiah prophesied that this would happen in the Messianic age, but Paul understood that the Messianic era had already begun (see chapter 14, "The Secret of the Six Thousand Years"), and so, as a Jew—and therefore a member of the priestly nation—it was his sacred duty to take this Messianic message to the foreign nations. To repeat: he saw this as part of his Jewish calling.

Revealing the Mystery

Paul also recognized that there was a "mystery"—meaning a truth contained within the Hebrew Scriptures that was being revealed now that the Messiah had come—concerning Jews and Gentiles being one in Jesus, without either of them losing their identity or distinctives. He described it as "the revelation of the mystery hidden for long ages past" but was "now revealed and made known through the prophetic writings [of the Tanakh] by the command of the eternal God, *so that all nations might believe and obey him*" (Rom. 16:25–26).

More fully, he wrote:

> For I say that the Messiah became a servant of the Jewish people in order to show God's truthfulness by making good his promises to the Patriarchs, and in order to show his mercy by causing the Gentiles to glorify God—as it is written in the *Tanakh*, "Because of this I will acknowledge you among the Gentiles and sing praise to your name." [He is citing Ps. 18:49.] And again it says, "Gentiles, rejoice with his people." [Citing Deut. 32:43.] And again, "Praise ADONAI [the Lord], all Gentiles! Let all peoples praise him!" [Citing Ps. 117:1.] And again, Yesha'yahu [Isaiah] says, "The root of Yishai [Jesse] will come, he who arises to rule Gentiles; Gentiles will put their hope in him."
> —ROMANS 15:8–12, CJB

Did you follow that? Paul is citing verses from the Hebrew Bible, which speak of Gentiles worshiping God together with the Jewish people, a "mystery" others had failed to see. But there it was, written clear as day in the Jewish Bible, and here it was, happening before his eyes. You can readily imagine, though, that not everyone was happy with this teaching, with many criticizing Paul for his methods and his message. Thankfully, this Jewish genius named Saul/Paul knew exactly what he was doing, fulfilling his priestly duty as a Jew.

Ironically, Jewish journalist David Klinghoffer got this totally wrong, saying that it was good that the Jews rejected Jesus, because it led to men such as Paul (whom Klinghoffer regards as a convert to Judaism who lied about his pedigree)[14] bringing the message to the Gentiles, which resulted in Christianity becoming a powerful religion, ultimately improving the world in many important ways. Otherwise, Klinghoffer reasoned, if Jews had accepted Jesus, they would have required the whole world to observe all the commandments of the Torah, and that would have been too much for the Gentiles to bear, and so they would never had developed this wonderful religion called Christianity.[15]

The precise opposite is true: God never intended to require Gentiles to become Jews in order to follow the Messiah, and it is only because Jewish leaders such as Saul-Paul embraced this truth that the message of the one true God and the Messiah of Israel could be brought to the Gentiles without requiring them to take on the Law of Moses.

"Neither Jew nor Gentile"

In Paul's view, Jews who came to faith in Jesus should not become Gentiles, and Gentiles who came to faith in Jesus should not become Jews. "Each one should remain in the situation which he was in when God called him" (1 Cor. 7:20; see also vv. 17–19).[16] He also made clear that circumcision, in and of itself, was nothing—meaning that one's status in God was not affected by being circumcised or uncircumcised. "Keeping God's commands," he wrote, "is what counts" (1 Cor. 7:19). He even went so far as to call those teachers who insisted that Gentiles had to be circumcised "mutilators of the flesh" (Phil. 3:2), claiming that the circumcision that mattered most in God's sight was the "circumcision of the heart." (See Philippians 3:3; Romans 2:28–29.)[17]

Statements like this could certainly stir up controversy, and this is one of the reasons that some of the early Jewish groups who followed a modified Messianic faith (such as the Ebionites, who apparently denied other fundamental doctrines about Yeshua) also had a problem with Paul.[18] And yet Paul didn't hesitate to have one of his colleagues named Timothy circumcised, since people questioned Timothy's Jewish status (he had a Jewish mother and a Gentile father; see Acts 16:1–3).[19] At the same time Paul stood with another coworker named Titus who refused to be circumcised, because Titus was a Gentile. (See Galatians 2:3.) Now that Messiah had come, Gentiles had equal access to God, without having to become Jews. Not everyone was happy with this!

Then there is Paul's famous statement that "there is neither Jew nor Gentile, neither slave nor freeman, neither male nor female; for in union with the Messiah Yeshua, you are all one" (Gal. 3:28, CJB). How could he say such a thing? Actually, in his letters, he often made distinctions between Jew and Gentile, between slave and free, and between men and women, so he was not saying that such distinctions did not exist on a practical level. Rather, he was countering a mind-set of spiritual superiority, one that is reflected in the daily prayer recited by a Jewish male when he wakes up in the morning, thanking God that he is not a Gentile, a slave, or a woman.[20]

Paul made clear that, in the Messiah, there were no such spiritual "class" distinctions. He even wrote that, in terms of salvation from sin, "there is no distinction between Jew and Greek; for the same Lord is Lord of all, bestowing his riches on all who call on him. For 'everyone who calls on the name of the Lord will be saved'" (Rom. 10:12–13, ESV, quoting Joel 2:32).

Statements like this cut to the heart of ethnic pride and spiritual elitism. At the same time they could give the impression that Paul no longer cared about Jewish-Gentile distinctives. To the contrary, everywhere Paul went among the Gentile congregations, he collected money to bring back to Jerusalem to help the poor Jewish believers there,[21] making it clear to these Gentile Christians that helping the Jerusalem disciples financially was the least they could do (Rom. 15:27), and sharing without shame the constant burden he carried for his own Jewish people, to the point of wishing that he himself could be cursed so that they would be blessed, if it were possible. (See Romans 9:1–5.)

KEEPING THE LAW?

Paul also reduced the Law to bottom-line principles, emphasizing that if we walked in harmony with God, empowered by his Spirit, we would automatically be law-keepers as opposed to lawbreakers. He explained that "the fruit of the Spirit is love, joy, peace, patience, kindness, goodness, faithfulness, gentleness and self-control. Against such things there is no law" (Gal. 5:22–23). He also exhorted:

> Let no debt remain outstanding, except the continuing debt to love one another, for he who loves his fellowman has fulfilled the law. The commandments, "Do not commit adultery," "Do not murder," "Do not steal," "Do not covet," and whatever other commandment there may be, are summed up in this one rule: "Love your neighbor as yourself." Love does no harm to its neighbor. Therefore love is the fulfillment of the law.
>
> —ROMANS 13:8–10

It's obvious that verses such as these could be easily misunderstood, as if Paul was saying that specific laws no longer had any meaning. Instead, he was saying that the Law functioned as a divine scaffolding of sorts, helping the building to become erected and stable. But once the building was completed, the scaffolding would no longer be necessary. (See Galatians 3:24–25.)

In the verse cited, Paul was teaching that once the law of love is written on our hearts, by nature, we will not sin against our fellow man, thereby fulfilling the commandment to love our neighbors as ourselves and thereby stopping us from breaking many other commandments. That was part of the Messianic promise of the new covenant, spoken of by Jeremiah the prophet (Jer. 31:31–34), a covenant in which God would write his laws on our hearts and minds.

Paul believed that followers of Jesus could already experience the firstfruits of that covenant, not abolishing the Law but internalizing it. Put another way, we were no longer to relate to God primarily as servants but more so as sons, walking with God as Father (in the deepest, most intimate sense of the word) more than as Master, doing his will based on love more than fear. (See Galatians 4:1–7.)

> Paul has also been criticized for writing, Obviously, the law applies to those to whom it was given, for its purpose is to keep people from having excuses, and to show that the entire world is guilty before God. For no one can ever be made right with God by doing what the law commands. The law simply shows us how sinful we are.
>
> —Romans 3:19–20, nlt

Is he kidding? How could the Torah—God's perfect Law in which we are to delight (Ps. 19:8), on which we are to meditate day and night (Josh. 1:8; Ps. 1:2–3), and which should be more precious to us than thousands of pieces of silver and gold (Ps. 119:72)—be God's vehicle to show us how sinful we were? Surely, some have argued, a real Jew, let alone a Pharisee, could never write such things.[22] I beg to differ, based on the testimony of the Tanakh (the Hebrew Bible) that reveals in painful chapter after painful chapter that God's Law is perfect and holy but that his people are not.

Just think: God brought the people of Israel out of Egypt with the greatest display of power the world has ever seen, bringing ten plagues on the Egyptians and splitting the sea so that the Israelites could pass through. He then spoke the Ten Commandments to the Israelites on Mount Sinai with thunder and lightning and a terrifying voice, yet *within days* the Israelites had broken the first commandment and made a graven image, with the result that three thousand of them were killed. The Torah actually lists multiplied thousands of Israelite casualties during the wilderness wanderings, all the result of divine judgment,[23] and ultimately, out of the entire generation that was delivered from Egypt, only *two men* made it into the Promised Land. The Law was good, but God's people were not.

That is really the story of the Hebrew Scriptures, which speak of spiritual anarchy in the centuries following the conquest of Canaan, followed by failed kings, the destruction and dispersion of most of the ten northern tribes of Israel, the destruction of the Temple in Jerusalem, the exiling of tens of thousands of Jews, then all kinds of sins and disobedience once the exiles returned and rebuilt the Temple.

The children of Israel kept breaking God's Law, thereby revealing their sinfulness, which explains Paul's words in Romans 7: "What shall we say, then? Is the law sin? Certainly not! Indeed I would not have known what sin was except through the law. For I would not have known what coveting really was if the law had not said, 'Do not covet'" (v. 7).

By telling the children of Israel, "Thou shalt not," the commandment revealed the sinful desires of their hearts, exposing their guilt before God and their need for a Savior. And this was God's plan: having revealed his people's need and their inability to save themselves no matter how they tried, he pointed them to a solution. God sent the Messiah as an atoning sacrifice on our behalf, and by faith in his name, we would be granted forgiveness and given a brand-new start.

Yes, Paul understood the biblical, Jewish doctrine of the atoning power of the death of the righteous (see chapter 11), and he knew that what the Law could not do—because of human weakness—the Messiah could. As God said through the prophet Isaiah, *"Turn to me and be saved,* all you ends of the earth; for I am God, and there is no other" (Isa. 45:22, emphasis added). Paul believed it was that simple, and through repentance toward God and faith in the Messiah's shed blood (Acts 17:30; 20:21), both Jew and Gentile could be "saved."

Did this mean that faith nullified the Law? To the contrary, Paul taught that faith established the Law (Rom. 3:31). Did this mean that good works were not important, since we are saved by faith, not by our own works? To the contrary, Paul called for people to prove their faith by their works (Acts 26:20).[24] Did this mean that the more we sinned, the more God would shower us with his grace? To the contrary, Paul considered this attitude to be terribly dangerous: "What shall we say, then? Shall we go on sinning so that grace may increase? By no means! We died to sin; how can we live in it any longer?" (Rom. 6:1–2).

As for Paul allegedly teaching that the Law had come to an end, it all comes down to how one Greek word, *telos*, was to be translated in one specific verse—Romans 10:4. Did it mean "end"? This would be keeping with English translations such as the ESV: "For Christ is the end of the law for righteousness to everyone who believes." Or did it mean "goal," as reflected in David Stern's *Jewish New Testament*: "For the goal at which the Torah aims is the Messiah, who offers righteousness to everyone who trusts." Or, as rendered in the NLT, "For Christ has already accomplished the purpose for which the law was given. As a result, all who believe in him are made right with God." What a big difference a little word makes!

Becoming "Unkosher"

There are many other statements in Paul's letters that have been misunderstood—remember that this is even mentioned in the New Testament itself (see 2 Peter 3:15–16)—but this is because of his brilliance and depth, not because of his ignorance.[25] The man who could pen the most concise and at the same time comprehensive description of love ever written (see 1 Corinthians 13:1–8), the man who could show how both Jew and Gentile could become equal partners within the same spiritual family without losing their distinct identities, the man who understood the importance of cultural sensitivity, becoming "all things to all men" without compromising his core convictions (see 1 Corinthians 9:20–22),[26] the man whose letters written from prison have inspired and instructed hundreds of millions people was certainly no ignorant (or conniving) impostor (or "mythmaker"!).[27]

Paul was a devoted Jewish man who once hated the Jesus movement, fighting against his fellow Jews who believed in Jesus until he encountered the risen Messiah for himself. It was this Jewish man who led the mission to the Gentiles, always reminding them of their spiritual debt to the Jewish people (Rom. 15:27), urging them not to forget their roots (Rom. 11:17–25).[28]

Unfortunately, by the fourth century, after Gentile Christians had all but squeezed out the Jewish believers in Jesus, and after Constantine had "Christianized" Rome, the church had all but forgotten Paul's words of warning and exhortation. And so, the Jewish-birthed Jesus movement became "unkosher" only when it *departed* from Paul's words, not when it heeded them.[29]

But history is still being written, and since Jerusalem was restored to Jewish control in 1967, more and more Jewish believers in Jesus are recovering their roots, reading Paul afresh, and seeing how living as faithful Jews and believing in Yeshua go hand in hand. And more and more Gentile believers in Jesus are recognizing their debt to Israel and how, through faith in Jesus, rather than displacing Israel from God's plan, they are working with him to see Israel fulfill God's plan.

And most exciting of all, every Jew and every Gentile who becomes a follower of Yeshua the Messiah brings us closer to the day when, in Paul's words, "the fullness of the Gentiles" will come in and "all Israel will be saved" (Rom. 11:25–26, ESV). As it is written, "The deliverer will come from Zion; he will turn godlessness away from Jacob. And this is my covenant with them when I take away their sins" (vv. 26–27).[30]

Paul grasped how amazing this whole process was, as God sent the Messiah to Israel, which rejected him, opening the door of mercy to the Gentile world, and then the Gentile Christians in turn were called to have mercy on Israel. As he explained to the Gentile believers in Rome:

> Just as you who were at one time disobedient to God have now received mercy as a result of their disobedience, so they too have now become disobedient in order that they too may now receive mercy as a result of God's mercy to you. For God has bound all men over to disobedience so that he may have mercy on them all.
>
> —ROMANS 11:30–32

And when he finished writing these words, it's as if he had to stop writing (actually, dictating to a scribe) and just stop and praise God for his amazing wisdom and grace:

Oh, the depth of the riches of the wisdom and knowledge of God! How unsearchable his judgments, and his paths beyond tracing out! "Who has known the mind of the Lord? Or who has been his counselor?" "Who has ever given to God, that God should repay him?" For from him and through him and to him are all things. To him be the glory forever! Amen.

—Romans 11:33–36[31]

That's why I say that Paul was the Jewish genius who brought the God of Israel and the Messiah of Israel to the nations. Now those nations are bringing the message of Israel's Messiah back to the Messiah's own people. The climax of history is at hand.

Let us now unfold the secrets that will give us deeper insights into the Messiah's identity and mission.

Section III

THE HIDDEN MESSIAH
OF ISRAEL

9

THE SECRET OF THE INVISIBLE GOD WHO CAN BE SEEN

C AN JEWS BELIEVE that "Jesus is God"? If by that is meant can Jews believe that God ceased to be God in heaven and came down to earth in human form like one of the ancient mythological incarnations of Zeus, then the answer is categorically no, since God is not a man, as explicitly stated in Numbers 23:19 and 1 Samuel 15:29.

If by the question is meant that when people saw Jesus, they literally saw God—in his very form and essence—then again, the answer is categorically no, since Moses in Deuteronomy 4 stated to the people that when God appeared on Mount Sinai, they saw no form or image, and therefore they were forbidden from making a form or image of the Lord, be it animal or human. This would be an explicit violation of the Ten Commandments.[1]

But if by the question is meant could God, who is complex in his unity, sit enthroned in heaven, filling the universe with his presence, infinite and uncontainable in his majesty, and yet at one and the same time manifest his glory among us in the tent of a human body, then the answer is categorically yes, and there is nothing idolatrous about this belief at all. It is in harmony with the Hebrew Scriptures—it even explains some of the mysteries found on the pages of the Tanakh—and on some level, it has parallels with rabbinic concepts. In fact, in the midrash (the homiletical commentary) to Psalm 91 it is written:

> At [the moment that Moses finished building the Tabernacle], a great question arose: How could a Tabernacle with walls and curtains contain the Presence of the Almighty? The Master of the Universe Himself explained, "The entire world cannot contain My glory, yet when I wish, I can concentrate My entire essence into one small spot. Indeed, I am Most High, yet I sit in a [limited, constricted] refuge—in the shadow of the Tabernacle."[2]

And so, rather than being some crass religious notion that is hardly worthy of the Jewish people, this is an extraordinarily rich and deep spiritual concept, explaining how the uncontainable God—the *En Sof*, the One without beginning or end—could walk among us in intimate fellowship, being transcendent and immanent at one and the same time, untouchable and yet touchable, invisible and yet, in a sense, visible. To quote the midrash again, "The entire world cannot contain My glory, yet when I wish, I can concentrate My entire essence into one small spot."

So the real question before us is this: How does the infinite and eternal God make himself known to man? Put another way, How does the invisible God become visible?

Seeing God?

Before we look at the evidence of the Tanakh, the Hebrew Scriptures, I want to share with you some explicit statements from the New Testament writers, Jewish men who opposed idolatry with every fiber of their being and yet who clearly affirmed Yeshua's divine nature. This way we can understand what the New Testament does and does not say, putting away common misconceptions and focusing on issues of substance instead.

According to John 1:18, "No one has ever seen God" (see also 1 John 4:12); in John 5:37, Jesus said to some Jewish leaders, "You have never heard his voice nor seen his form" (see also John 6:46); and Paul wrote in 1 Timothy 6:16, "[God] lives in unapproachable light, whom no one has seen or can see"; Paul also referred to God as "invisible" in 1 Timothy 1:17. Yet Yeshua also said in John 14:9, "Anyone who has seen me has seen the Father." What exactly does that mean?

Let's open up these amazing spiritual truths, deep and profound truths befitting of the eternal God, beginning our journey in the Torah. On several occasions God emphatically reminded his people that when he spoke to them on Mount Sinai, they saw no form or image; hence it would be a grave sin to make any kind of wood or stone representation of him, be that representation animal or human.[3] In keeping with this, the Lord told Moses that "no one may see me and live" (Exod. 33:20). Yet in Exodus 24, immediately following the Sinai revelation, the Torah states:

> Moses and Aaron, Nadab and Abihu, and the seventy elders of Israel went up [Mount Sinai] and saw the God of Israel. Under his feet was something like a pavement made of sapphire, clear as the sky itself. But God did not raise his hand against these leaders of the Israelites; they saw God, and they ate and drank.
> —EXODUS 24:9–11

How can this be explained? The text speaks of seventy-four people who "saw God."

Abraham Ibn Ezra, one of the most revered Jewish biblical commentators, interpreted the text to mean that they saw God in a prophetic vision. But why, then, did God tell them in Exodus 24:1 to actually go up the mountain to the Lord, remaining at a distance from him while Moses alone drew near? And why does the text point out that God did not lift his hand against them, as would have been expected? Obviously this was far more than a prophetic vision.

As Messianic Jewish leader Asher Intrater points out:

> This is an unprecedented event. The elders see God in a bodily human form but also in glorified power. Such closeness to divine power was dangerous. It is clear that they were aware of the danger, because they took special note of the fact that God did not "lay His hand upon them."[4]

The *Targum*, the Aramaic translation-paraphrase read in the synagogues two thousand years ago, also had a problem with these verses and could not translate them directly, rendering instead, "They saw the glory of the God of Israel...they saw the glory of the Lord..." Yet the text says, "They saw the God of Israel...they saw God..." What is the answer? Let's keep looking at the texts.

There are also numerous biblical accounts where "the angel of the Lord" seems to bear the very presence of God, and people fear for their lives after encountering him, because they have "seen God." (See, e.g., Exodus 3:1–6; Judges 13:15–23.) Some Jewish traditions even refer to this angel as a "little YHWH."[5] What are we to make of these accounts?

Abraham Saw God

Genesis 18 provides a fascinating narrative, telling us that Yahweh— meaning the God of Israel—literally appeared to Abraham, engaging in a conversation with him and with his wife Sarah, and eating and drinking with them. The text begins: "The Lord [Hebrew, YHWH] appeared to him by the terebinths of Mamre; he was sitting at the entrance of the tent as the day grew hot. Looking up, he saw three men standing near him" (Gen. 18:1–2, njv).

Who were these three men? According to the Talmud, they were three angels, each with a specific mission. Yet the Talmud also states in b. Baba Mesia 86b that Abraham **"saw the Holy One, blessed be He, standing at the door** of his tent."[6]

What unfolds next is extraordinary, making clear that one of these three men was *God himself*, visiting Abraham with two angels. Notice carefully: One of them promises to return next year so that Sarah will have a son; she laughs out loud when she hears this seemingly impossible promise; the Lord then addresses Abraham, asking him why his wife laughed, doubting his promise that he would graciously visit her the coming year; Sarah heard what he said, denying that she laughed; then he replied to her. There is absolutely no way around it. Abraham, Sarah, and the Lord were all there together.

But things get even clearer. Verse 16 states that, "The men set out from there and looked down from Sodom, Abraham walking with them to see them off" (NJV) explaining in the next verses that the Lord then filled Abraham in on what he was about to do. This brings us to verse 22, "The men went on from there to Sodom, while Abraham remained standing before the LORD" (NJV), to whom he intercedes on behalf of Sodom through verse 32. So, the men went on to Sodom while the LORD remained with Abraham.

Now let's look at the last verse of chapter 18 and the first verse of chapter 19: "When the LORD had finished speaking to Abraham, he departed; and Abraham returned to his place. The two angels arrived in Sodom in the evening, as Lot was sitting in the gate of Sodom" (NJV).

There you have it! The Scripture tells us that the Lord appeared to Abraham, then it says that Abraham saw three men by his tent, then it identifies one of those three as the Lord, who holds a conversation with Abraham and Sarah. The Bible then says that Abraham walked with the men as they went on their way to Sodom, that the Lord then informed Abraham of his intentions to destroy Sodom and Gomorrah, that the men (i.e., the other two men) continued on to Sodom while Abraham stayed and talked with the Lord, and that when they were done, the Lord left and Abraham went home, and that two angels then arrived in Sodom. I'll say it again: one of those three men was YHWH, the Lord.

The awesome and exciting thing about this text is that it explicitly tells us that Abraham and Sarah talked with the Lord, that he appeared in human form to them, dusty feet and all (Gen. 18:4), and that he even sat down and ate their food. Yet all the while he remained God in heaven.

An honest and straightforward reading of the text indicates clearly that God can come to earth in human form for a period of time if he so desires. And notice: I have not quoted the New Testament to support this but instead have simply looked at the Torah. Are we willing to receive what is written there?

Did the Lord cease to be God in heaven? Certainly not. Did he cease to be a spirit? Obviously not. But did this infinite Spirit walk among us in fleshly form for a season? Absolutely yes! And did he allow himself to be seen by various people at certain times, although not in his full glory? Without a doubt—if we believe the Jewish Scriptures.[7]

The Word Made Flesh

The New Testament teaching of what is called the Incarnation is simply the fullest explanation of this divine mystery, the greatest example of divine disclosure—but it is as different from pagan idolatry as the light is different from darkness, and I believe those who will look at this with spiritual eyes will be able to understand.

Of course, all traditional Jews know the formulation of Maimonides who stated that God has no form of any kind.[8] But it's fascinating to see that the same Torah that states that the Israelites saw no *temunah*—form or image—when God appeared on Mount Sinai also says of Moses, "He saw the form—*temunah*—of YHWH" (Num. 12:8). And David said in Psalm 17:15 that after death, he would be satisfied with seeing God's *temunah*. How do we put these seemingly contradictory truths together?[9] Yeshua, the divine Son, provides the answer.

Before focusing on Jesus the Messiah, the ultimate revelation of God to humankind, let's look at how rabbinic Judaism answered some of these questions concerning divine disclosure—the hidden God making himself known—beginning with the concept of the *Memra'*, the divine Word.[10] If we look in the Tanakh, we find that God's word is sometimes an extension of himself, as in Psalm 107:20, "He sent forth his word and healed them," or Isaiah 55:10–12, which speaks of God's word going forth from his mouth, accomplishing its mission, and then returning to him. And remember that in the Creation account, God created by *speaking*.

This concept of the divine word became greatly developed in the Aramaic Targums, spoken and read in the synagogues where Hebrew was not understood.[11] In the Targums, when reference was made to God drawing near to man or interacting directly with man, very often it was not God who did these things but rather his *Memra'*, his Word (or, word).

To give just a few examples, take a look at the following chart. It compares the Hebrew text, which comes first, with its rendering in the Targums.[12]

Genesis 1:27	God created man.
	The Word of the LORD created man (Targum Pseudo-Jonathan).
Genesis 15:6	And Abraham believed in the LORD.
	And Abraham believed in the Word of the LORD.
Genesis 31:49	May the LORD keep watch between you and me.
	May the Word of the LORD keep watch between you and me.
Exodus 20:1	And the LORD spoke all these words.
	And the Word of the LORD spoke all these words.
Exodus 25:22	And I will meet with you there.
	And I will appoint my Word for you there.
Numbers 10:35	Rise up, O LORD!
	Rise up, O Word of the LORD!
Numbers 10:35	Return, O LORD!
	Return, O Word of the LORD!
Deuteronomy 1:30	The LORD your God who goes before you, he himself will fight for you.
	The LORD your God who leads before you, his Word will fight for you.
Isaiah 45:17	Israel will be saved by the LORD.
	Israel will be saved by the Word of the LORD.

Let's also look at Genesis 28:20–21, Jacob's vow. In Hebrew, it reads: "If *God* will be with me...then *the* LORD *will be my God.*" The Targum says, "If the *Word of the* LORD will be with me...then *the Word of the* LORD *will be my God.*" The Word of the Lord will be Jacob's God! And these Targums were read in the synagogues for decades, if not centuries. Week in and week out, the people heard about this walking, talking, creating, saving, delivering Word, this Word who was Jacob's God. In fact, according to Targum Neofiti, man was created in the image of the *Memra'* of the Lord.

Targum Pseudo-Jonathan to Deuteronomy 4:7 is also fascinating. The Hebrew reads, "What other nation is so great as to have their gods near them the way the LORD our God is near us whenever we pray to him?"

The Targum instead says: "The *Memra'* of Yahweh sits upon his throne high and lifted up and hears our prayer whenever we pray before him and make our petitions." That is just some of the Targumic concept of "the Word."

Now, let's go back to the New Testament and start reading in John 1, substituting the Aramaic *Memra'* when John speaks of the divine Word, which is an extension of the Lord Himself and yet not God in his entirety: "In the beginning was the *Memra'*, and the *Memra'* was with God, and the *Memra'* was God. He was with God in the beginning. Through him all things were made; without him nothing was made that has been made. In him was life, and that life was the light of men" (John 1:1–4).

This is now sounding quite Jewish! The miracle that took place through Yeshua is that this divine Word—this self-disclosure of God himself—pitched his tent among us for thirty-three years: "The *Memra'* became flesh and made his dwelling among us. We have seen his glory, the glory of the One and Only, who came from the Father, full of grace and truth" (John 1:14). And note carefully the phrase, "made his dwelling among us." The Greek word *skēnoō* means "to pitch a tent, to tabernacle," and so, just as the Lord pitched his tent among us in ancient Israel, filling it with his glory (I'm referring to the Tabernacle, which was actually a tent) while remaining God in heaven, so also he pitched a human tent among us, filling it with his glory, while remaining God in heaven. He is complex in his unity!

Related to this Aramaic concept of the *Memra'* is the Jewish Greek concept of the *logos*, the very word that John uses when writing about Yeshua, and it was Philo who famously characterized this *logos*. As explained in *The Oxford Dictionary of Jewish Religion*:

> Although in a sense an aspect of the Divine, the Logos often appears as a separate entity, namely, a half-personal emanation of God. The concept was appropriated by Philo in order to bridge the gap between the transcendent God of Judaism and the divine principle experienced by human beings. This view of the Logos as a mediating principle between God and material

creation could link up with biblical references to the creative "Word of God," by which the heavens were made (Ps. 33:6) and with the concept of *meimra* (Aram.; "word") in Targum literature (especially as it appears in Targum Onkelos).[13]

I repeat: God is complex in His unity.

You might say, "But what about the *Shema*, found in Deuteronomy 6:4, the central confession in Judaism, declaring God's absolute unity?"

Actually, the best translation, as noted by the New Jewish Version and some classical rabbinic commentators, is, "The LORD is our God, the LORD alone."[14] But even if we follow the more common rendering, "Hear O Israel, the LORD our God, the LORD is one," it's important to understand that the word *'echad* does not point to absolute unity; it simply means *one*, as in one day, consisting of night and day (Gen. 1:5); or man and woman coming together and becoming one (Gen. 2:24); or all the pieces of the Tabernacle making one unit (Exod. 36:13). In the same way, God is one—a truth explicitly affirmed in the New Testament by Yeshua and Paul and others—but he is complex in his unity, and later Christian theologians, reflecting on these biblical truths, recognized that God revealed himself to us as a tri-unity, Father, Son, and Spirit.

What is fascinating is that Menachem Mendel Schneerson (1902–1994), the man known as the Lubavitcher Rebbe and hailed by many of his followers as the Messiah, noted that the word *'echad* did not pertain to unique singularity:

> *Echad* means "one." The Shema proclaims the oneness and unity of G-d, which the people of Israel are charged to reveal in the world, and which will be fully manifest in the era of Moshiach. But is *echad* the ideal word to express the divine unity? Like its English equivalent, the word does not preclude the existence of other objects (as in the sequence "one, two, three..."), nor does it preclude its object being composed of parts (we speak of "one nation," "one forest," "one person" and "one tree," despite the fact that each of these consists of many units or components). It would seem that the term *yachid*, which means "singular" and "only one," more clearly expresses the "perfect simplicity"

of G-d (which Maimonides states to be the most fundamental principle of the Jewish faith) and the axiom that "there is none else besides Him" (Deuteronomy 4:35).

Chassidic teaching explains that, on the contrary, *echad* represents a deeper unity than *yachid*. *Yachid* is a oneness that cannot tolerate plurality—if another being or element is introduced into the equation, the *yachid* is no longer *yachid*. *Echad*, on the other hand, represents the fusion of diverse elements into a harmonious whole. The oneness of *echad* is not undermined by plurality; indeed, it employs plurality as the ingredients of unity.[15]

And this is from the lips of perhaps the most influential Hasidic rabbi of our times.

The Sefirot and the Shekhinah

Now there are other interesting rabbinic concepts (along with the *memra'*) that help bridge the gap between the hidden and the revealed God, such as the mystical Jewish concept of the ten *sefirot*, which the *Encyclopedia of Hasidism* explains as "intermediaries or graded links between the completely spiritual and unknowable Creator and the material sub-lunar world."[16]

The encyclopedia article on the *sefirot* further notes that, "God is an organic whole but with different manifestations of power—just as the life of the soul is one, though manifested variously in the eyes, hands, and other limbs." God and his sefirot are just like a man and his body: "His limbs are many but he is one."[17] This too is a fascinating concept, but it has no grounding in the Hebrew Scriptures and, to be candid, is nowhere as sublime and personal as God's self-disclosure through Jesus the Messiah, his Son.

There is also the concept of the *shekhinah*, the divine presence on earth, corresponding also to the feminine, motherly aspects of God. The rabbis taught that the *shekhinah* went into exile with the Jewish people, suffering with "her" children in foreign lands. According to this concept,

God cannot be "whole" again until his people return from their physical and spiritual wanderings and the Temple is rebuilt.

This means that there is not a simple answer to the question, "Was the *shekhinah* God?" As noted by Benjamin Sommer, a professor at Jewish Theological Seminary, "God is the same as the *shekhinah*, but the *shekhinah* does not exhaust God, so one can refer easily to 'God' and subsequently to 'God and the *shekhinah*.'"[18]

In light of these comments—that "God is the same as the *shekhinah*, but the *shekhinah* does not exhaust God," it's understandable why a Conservative rabbi once said to me, "So, from what you're saying, Jesus is like a walking *shekhinah*!" Exactly.[19]

In light of the combined evidence of the Tanakh and Jewish tradition, Prof. Sommer, who, I remind you, is a Jewish scholar teaching at one of the most prestigious Jewish institutes of higher learning, makes this important observation:

> Some Jews regard Christianity's claim to be a monotheistic religion with grave suspicion, both because of the doctrine of the trinity (how can three equal one?) and because of Christianity's core belief that God took bodily form. . . . No Jew sensitive to Judaism's own classical sources, however, can fault the theological model Christianity employs when it avows belief in a God who has an earthly body as well as a Holy Spirit and a heavenly manifestation, for that model, we have seen, is a perfectly Jewish one. A religion whose scripture contains the fluidity traditions [meaning God appearing in bodily form at different times and places], whose teachings emphasize the multiplicity of the *shekhinah*, and whose thinkers speak of the *sephirot* does not differ in its theological essentials from a religion that adores the triune God.[20]

So, for Sommer, the differences between "Judaism" and "Christianity" do *not* boil down to questions concerning the nature of God or the claim that God can appear in bodily form or be a complex unity (to use my own term).[21]

There are some other biblical texts that we have not yet examined, including the famous Messianic prophecy of Isaiah 9:6, where the promised child is called *'el gibbor*, Mighty God, among other titles. Interestingly, the most obvious reading of the Hebrew text is that the titles are descriptive of the king himself, including "mighty God" (*'el gibbor*). This view is even found in the Talmud (b. Sanhedrin 94a) and later rabbinic writings, while it is expressly supported by Abraham Ibn Ezra.[22] But how can a human being be called "mighty God"? Yeshua alone provides the answer.

Also noteworthy is Psalm 45:7, where the Davidic king, a prototype of the Messiah, is not only anointed by God (*'elohim*) but is also called God (*'elohim*), a divine one himself. How can this? Once again, only Yeshua explains it.[23]

AN EXTRAORDINARY DIVINE MYSTERY

The New Testament writers understood that God's self-disclosure was a profound mystery, and therefore they never said, "God became a human being." That would have given a false and misleading impression, as if the Lord was no longer filling the universe or reigning in heaven, as if he abandoned his throne to take up residence here. Instead, John tells us that it was the divine Word who became a human being, and through the Word we know God personally. That's why John could write, "No one has ever seen God. But the unique One, who is himself God, is near to the Father's heart. He has revealed God to us" (John 1:18, NLT).[24]

That is also why Jesus, who was born a little more than two thousand years ago, could say to his contemporaries, "I tell you the truth . . . before Abraham was born, I am!" (John 8:58). And note that he didn't say, "Before Abraham was born, *I was*" (which would have been striking enough, since Abraham was born two thousand years before Jesus!). He said, "Before Abraham was, *I am*"—associating himself with Yahweh himself, known to Israel as "I am."[25]

That is also why, after his resurrection, Thomas, one of his core disciples who refused to believe the reports of the resurrection until he saw Yeshua with his own eyes, said to him, "My Lord and my God!" In other words, he recognized that in a unique and unprecedented way, God was visiting Israel in the person of the Messiah Jesus. And yet it was just a few verses earlier that Jesus said to another core disciple, named Miriam, "I am returning to my Father and your Father, to my God and your God" (John 20:17). So, Thomas calls Jesus his God, and yet Jesus calls the heavenly Father *his* God.

As I said, this is a profound and wonderful mystery, but one that meets us right where we are: the infinite and eternal God, who sits enthroned in heaven, who fills the universe, who moves throughout the earth by his Spirit, also visited us in the person of his Son, born into this world and given the name Yeshua. And when we see him, we see God.

As Paul wrote about Jesus, "He is the image of the invisible God.... He is before all things, and in him all things hold together.... For in [Messiah] all the fullness of the Deity lives in bodily form" (Col. 1:15, 17; 2:9). Paul also wrote: "For even if there are so-called gods, whether in heaven or on earth (as indeed there are many 'gods' and many 'lords'), yet for us there is but *one God*, the Father, from whom all things came and for whom we live; and there is but *one Lord*, Jesus Christ, through whom all things came and through whom we live" (1 Cor. 8:5–6, emphasis added).[26] As stated in Hebrews 1:3, "The Son is the radiance of God's glory and the exact representation of his being..."

This is a glorious revelation, and there is nothing idolatrous about it. It unfolds the mystery of the self-disclosure of the one and only God, hidden and yet revealed, invisible and yet seen, untouchable and yet touched by flesh and blood.

How It All Ends

In the last chapter of the Book of Revelation, which is the last book of the New Testament, we are told that in the New Jerusalem, which comes down from heaven to earth, "The throne of God and of the Lamb [meaning, Jesus] will be in the city, and *his* servants will serve *him* [not *their* servants will serve *them*]. They will see *his face* [not *their faces*], and *his name* [not *their names*] will be on their foreheads" (Rev. 22:3–4, emphasis added).

One God, one throne, one face. The Son is not a separate deity or a competing God.[27] He is the one through whom the Father revealed himself, and as we see this glorious divine Son come into our fallen world and die for our sins, then and only then can we understand just how great God's love for us is.

The secret is now revealed.

10

THE SECRET OF THE
SUFFERING MESSIAH

D ID YOU KNOW that there are ancient Jewish traditions that speak of two Messiahs? And did you know that many Jews today still believe there will be two Messiahs? And did you know that there are Jewish traditions that speak of the sufferings of these Messianic figures?

The Dead Sea Scrolls make reference to the Messiahs of Aaron and Israel (meaning, a priestly Messiah and a royal Messiah),[1] but the concept of a priestly Messiah has been all but lost in traditional Judaism. (See chapter 12, "The Secret of the Priestly Messiah," for more information.) What has been preserved, though, is a teaching going back to the Talmud that there will be two Messiahs, the Messiah son of Joseph (or, Ephraim) and the Messiah son of David. And there are important rabbinic traditions that speak of the sufferings that both of them must endure, although for the most part it is the Messiah son of Joseph who is seen as the suffering Messiah, dying in the last great war before the Messiah son of David raises him from the dead. (See b. Sukkah 52a.)

THE MESSIAH TEXTS

The great Jewish anthropologist Raphael Patai devoted an entire chapter to the subject of the "Suffering Messiah" in his unparalleled collection entitled *The Messiah Texts*.[2] More than fifty years earlier Gustaf Dalman, a Christian scholar of Judaica whose reference works are used by Jewish scholars to this day, devoted an entire volume to the subject of the suffering Messiah in Jewish tradition.[3] And the texts describing the Messiah's suffering are not obscure, little-known texts representing the views and opinions of some peripheral Jewish groups. Rather, they are found in the most important branches of rabbinic literature, including the Talmud, the midrashic writings, and the medieval and modern commentaries on the Bible.[4]

Patai makes this startling statement regarding the Messiah's sufferings:

> The sufferings Israel must face in the days of the Messiah are temporary and transitory. They will last, according to the Talmudic view...seven years; a later Aggada...reduces this period to a mere forty-five days. The Messiah himself, on the other hand, must spend his entire life, from the moment of his creation until the time of his advent many centuries or even millennia later, in a state of constant and acute suffering.[5]

Summarizing the key rabbinic teachings on the sufferings and afflictions of the Messiah, Patai writes:

> Despised and afflicted with unhealing wounds, he sits in the gates of Great Rome and winds and unwinds the bandages of his festering sores; as a Midrash expresses it, "pains have adopted him." According to one of the most moving, and at the same time psychologically most meaningful, of all Messiah legends, God, when He created the Messiah, gave him the choice of whether or not to accept the sufferings for the sins of Israel. And the Messiah answered: "I accept it with joy, so that not a single soul of Israel should perish."...In the later, Zoharic [i.e., mystical] formulation of this legend, the Messiah himself summons all the diseases, pains, and sufferings of Israel to come upon him, in order thus to ease the anguish of Israel, which otherwise would be unbearable.[6]

Later Jewish traditions expanded on the sufferings of the Messiah. This midrash, describing one of the houses in heavenly Paradise (a Jewish concept), is typical:

...there sit Messiah ben David and Elijah and Messiah ben Ephraim. And there is a canopy of incense trees as in the Sanctuary which Moses made in the desert. And all its vessels and pillars are of silver, its covering is gold, its seat is purple. And in it is Messiah ben David who loves Jerusalem. Elijah of blessed memory takes hold of his head, places it in his lap and holds it, and says to him, "Endure the sufferings and the sentence of your Master who makes you suffer because of the sin of Israel." And thus it is written: *He was wounded because of our transgressions, he was crushed because of our iniquities* (Isa. 53:5)—until the time when the end comes.

And every Monday and Thursday, and every Sabbath and holiday, the Fathers of the World [i.e. Abraham, Isaac, and Jacob] and Moses and Aaron, David and Solomon, and the prophets, and the pious come and visit him, and weep with him. And he weeps with them. And they give him thanks and say to him: "Endure the sentence of your Master, for the end is near to come, and the chains which are on your neck will be broken, and you will go into freedom."[7]

And note that the midrash cites Isaiah 53:5—the text most commonly used by followers of Yeshua to point to his sufferings on our behalf—to explain why the Messiah suffers. It is because of the sin of Israel! (For more on this see chapter 11, "The Secret of the Atoning Power of the Death of the Righteous.")

The Zohar, the most sacred book of Jewish mysticism, also applies Isaiah 53:5 to the Messiah's sufferings:

In the hour in which they [i.e., the souls of the righteous sufferers] tell the Messiah about the sufferings of Israel in exile, and [about] the sinful among them who seek not the knowledge of their Master, the Messiah lifts up his voice and weeps over those sinful among them. This is what is written, *He was wounded because of our transgressions, he was crushed because of our iniquities* (Isa. 53:5).[8]

The prophet Isaiah spoke of just how deeply God identified with the suffering of his people Israel, writing, "In all their affliction he was afflicted" (Isa. 63:9, ESV), or, "In all their troubles he was troubled" (CJB). *Messiah too identifies with the suffering of his people.* This is hardly a "Christian" concept; rather, it is biblical, and it is Jewish.

Here are some key texts from the Talmud and other ancient Jewish sources that speak of the sufferings of the Messiah, speaking either of the Messiah son of David (the "main" Messiah, and, for some, the only Messiah) or the Messiah son of Joseph (sometimes simply called "Ephraim").

In a well-known Talmudic passage summarized by Patai (see above), Rabbi Yehoshua ben Levi found Elijah the prophet sitting in a cave and asked him when the Messiah would come. When Elijah replied, "Go, ask him himself," Rabbi Yehoshua asked, "And where does he sit?" Elijah then explained that he sat at the entrance of the city, further clarifying that the Messiah had these distinctive marks: "...he sits among the poor who suffer of diseases, and while all of them unwind and rewind [the bandages of all their wounds] at once, he unwinds and rewinds them one by one, for he says, 'Should I be summoned, there must be no delay'" (b. Sanhedrin 98a).

How this conveys the heart of the Messiah, eager and ready to be revealed to his people, yet suffering with them in pain and sickness. The account concludes with this poignant narrative. Rabbi Yehoshua went and found the Messiah, asking him, "When will the Master [meaning the Messiah] come?" The Messiah answered, "Today," a reply that Rabbi Yehoshua found dishonest, later saying to Elijah, "The Messiah lied to me, for he said, 'Today I shall come,' and he did not come." Elijah said, "This is what he told you: '*Today, if you but hearken to his voice*' (Ps. 95:7)."[9]

The Schottenstein Talmud, an extensive Orthodox commentary being published by Artscroll-Mesorah, offers this explanation of the passage:

> They [namely, those sitting with Messiah] were afflicted with *tzaraas*—a disease whose symptoms include discolored patches on the skin (see *Leviticus* ch. 13). The Messiah himself is likewise

afflicted, as stated in *Isaiah* (53:4): ... *Indeed, it was our diseases that he bore and our pains that he endured, whereas we considered him plagued* (i.e. suffering *tzaraas* [see 98b, note 39], *smitten by God, and afflicted.* This verse teaches that the diseases that the people ought to have suffered because of their sins are borne instead by the Messiah.[10]

Where did this idea of a suffering Messiah arise from? According to Patai:

There can be little doubt that psychologically the Suffering Messiah is but a projection and personification of Suffering Israel. ... Similarly, the Leper Messiah and the Beggar Messiah [spoken of in the Talmud] ... are but variants on the theme of Suffering Israel personified in the Suffering Messiah figure. And it is undoubtedly true in the psychological sense that, as the Zohar states, the acceptance of Israel's sufferings by the Messiah (read: their projection onto the Messiah) eases that suffering which otherwise could not be endured.[11]

THE SUFFERING MESSIAH IN THE HEBREW SCRIPTURES

But there's more: the concept of a suffering Messiah comes first and foremost from the Hebrew Scriptures, where an innocent and righteous servant of the Lord makes himself a guilt offering and dies for the sins of the people (see Isaiah 52:13–53:12), where this servant is beaten and mocked yet unbowed (see Isaiah 50:4–10), where many of the prophets suffered hardship and rejection for their obedience to the Lord (see chapter 4), and where lengthy passages such as Psalm 22 describe the intense suffering of a righteous individual who is ultimately delivered from the jaws of death and whose deliverance is so great that as a result, people from all the nations of the earth turn to the Lord.[12] It is not surprising, then, that the first followers of Jesus saw him depicted in many of these very passages from the Tanakh, drawing attention to them in the New Testament.[13] The Tanakh foretold the Messiah's suffering and pain.

Psalm 22 seemed especially applicable to Yeshua's crucifixion and resurrection, with the psalmist saying things such as, "All who see me mock me; they hurl insults, shaking their heads," and, "Roaring lions tearing their prey open their mouths wide against me," and "I am poured out like water, and all my bones are out of joint," and "My strength is dried up like a potsherd, and my tongue sticks to the roof of my mouth; you lay me in the dust of death," and "Dogs have surrounded me; a band of evil men has encircled me, they have pierced my hands and my feet" (or, "like a lion they are at my hands and feet"),[14] and, "I can count all my bones; people stare and gloat over me," and, "They divide my garments among them and cast lots for my clothing" (Ps. 22:7, 13–18).[15] What a detailed picture of public mockery and physical and emotional agony, and how strikingly it parallels the sufferings of the victim of crucifixion.

The end of the psalm is also quite remarkable, where, as a result of the psalmist being delivered from death:

> All the ends of the earth will remember and turn to the LORD, and all the families of the nations will bow down before him.... All the rich of the earth will feast and worship; all who go down to the dust will kneel before him—those who cannot keep themselves alive. Posterity will serve him; future generations will be told about the Lord. They will proclaim his righteousness to a people yet unborn—for he has done it.
>
> —PSALM 22:27–31

What a rousing response! And it is fair to ask, if this text is not ultimately prefiguring the Messiah's deliverance from death, resulting in worldwide praise to God, whose deliverance *is* it prefiguring?

Psalm 22 was, therefore, quite relevant to the writers of the New Testament.[16] But it was also cited several times in the most extensive depiction of the Messiah's sufferings in rabbinic literature, found in chapters 34, 36, and 37 of the eighth- and ninth-century midrash known as Pesikta Rabbati.[17] So, here is a rabbinic text prized by traditional Jews that outlines in graphic detail the vicarious sufferings of the Messiah.

As translated by Patai (and quoted here only in part):

They said: In the septenary [i.e., seven year period] in which the Son of David comes they will bring iron beams and put them upon his neck until his body bends and he cries and weeps, and his voice rises up into the Heights, and he says before Him: "Master of the World! How much can my strength suffer? How much my spirit? How much my soul? And how much my limbs? Am I not but flesh and blood? ... "

In that hour the Holy One, blessed be He, says to him: "Ephraim, My True Messiah, you have already accepted [this suffering] from the six days of Creation. Now your suffering shall be like My suffering. For ever since the day on which wicked Nebuchadnezzar came up and destroyed My Temple and burnt My sanctuary, and I exiled My children among the nations of the world, by your life and the life of your head, I have not sat on My Throne. And if you do not believe, see the dew that is upon my head ... "

In that hour he says before Him: "Master of the World! Now my mind is at rest, for it is sufficient for the servant to be like his Master!"[18]

Were you aware that Judaism believed in a suffering Messiah like this? The midrash continues:

The Fathers of the World [Abraham, Isaac, and Jacob] will in the future rise up in the month of Nissan and will speak to him: "Ephraim, our True Messiah! Even though we are your fathers, you are greater than we, for you suffered because of the sins of our children, and cruel punishments have come upon you the like of which have not come upon the early and the later generations, and you were put to ridicule and held in contempt by the nations of the world because of Israel, and you sat in darkness and blackness and your eyes saw no light, and your skin cleft to your bones, and your body dried out was like wood, and your eyes grew dim from fasting, and your strength became like a potsherd. All this because of the sins of our children. Do you want that our children should enjoy the happiness that the

Holy One, blessed be He, allotted to Israel, or perhaps, because
of the great sufferings that have come upon you on their account,
and because they imprisoned you in the jailhouse, your mind is
not reconciled with them?"

And the Messiah answers them: "Fathers of the World!
Everything I did, I did only for you and for your children, and
for your honor and for the honor of your children, so that they
should enjoy this happiness the Holy One, blessed be He, has
allotted to Israel."

Then the Fathers of the World say to him: "Ephraim, our
True Messiah, let your mind be at ease, for you put at ease our
minds and the mind of your Creator!"[19]

And it is Psalm 22, the psalm of the agonies of the righteous sufferer
who is delivered from the jaws of death, that is cited a number of times
in these chapters, especially chapter 36 and the beginning of chapter
37.[20] Notice also how the Messiah here willingly suffers because of (or,
for the sake of) the sins of his people, having to endure rejection, scorn,
and mockery, after which he is highly exalted.

But the point is not that this midrash is speaking about Jesus.
Obviously not. The rabbis who composed it really had no true concep-
tion of who Yeshua was, and whatever they knew of him through the
church of their day, they rejected. My point instead is that *the concept
of a suffering Messiah is well known in Jewish tradition,* and Jews have no
basis for rejecting Yeshua's Messianic claims because he suffered before
he was exalted. To the contrary, this is a pattern laid out clearly in the
Hebrew Scriptures, and it is reflecting some later rabbinic traditions
as well.

A SUFFERING MESSIAH FOR A SUFFERING PEOPLE

And so it is that the Messiah—Jesus-Yeshua—reached out to us in our
pain, becoming like us in our weakness and laying down his life as
an atoning sacrifice on our behalf. (See chapter 11, "The Secret of the
Atoning Power of the Death of the Righteous.") And it is this same Jesus,
the Jew, who was beaten, flogged, humiliated, and nailed to a cross.

As a Jew, he understands Jewish suffering, and as the Messiah, he is someone with whom his fellow Jews can identify. And because he has reached down to us where we are, he can also lift us up to where he is: Yeshua is the suffering Messiah who brings life, deliverance, and lasting victory to all who put their trust in him. As Peter (Shimon Kefa) wrote, "He himself bore our sins in his body on the tree, so that we might die to sins and live for righteousness; by his wounds you have been healed. For you were like sheep going astray, but now you have returned to the Shepherd and Overseer of your souls" (1 Pet. 2:24–25).

And herein lies a truth of great importance. There will not be two Messiahs, one who suffers and another who rules and reigns, but there will be and can only be one Messiah, he who is abased before he is exalted and disfigured before he is glorified. Isaiah expressed it wonderfully in just three short verses:

> Indeed, My servant shall prosper,
> Be exalted and raised to great heights.
>
> Just as the many were appalled at him—
> So marred was his appearance, unlike that of man,
> His form, beyond human semblance
>
> Just so he shall startle many nations.
> Kings shall be silenced because of him,
> For they shall see what has not been told them,
> Shall behold what they never have heard.
> —Isaiah 52:13–15, njv

And as we look at Jesus the Messiah, we realize that no one ever went down to such horrific depths, bearing the sins of the entire human race on his own shoulders and being mocked and crucified by the people he and his heavenly Father had created. But as low as he went, to that degree he has been exalted. As Paul explained:

> And when he appeared as a human being, he humbled himself still more by becoming obedient even to death—death on a

stake as a criminal! Therefore God raised him to the highest place and gave him the name above every name; that in honor of the name given Yeshua, every knee will bow—in heaven, on earth and under the earth—and every tongue will acknowledge that Yeshua the Messiah is ADONAI [Lord]—to the glory of God the Father.

—PHILIPPIANS 2:7–11, CJB

This, then, is the secret of the suffering Messiah. He is also the Messiah who will rule and reign.

11

THE SECRET OF THE ATONING POWER OF THE DEATH OF THE RIGHTEOUS

ECAUSE I DIDN'T grow up in an Orthodox Jewish home, I learned about many of the traditional beliefs of my people studying as an adult, and so for me, it was a real discovery to find out that traditional Judaism believed in the atoning power of the death of the righteous. I had thought that only Christians believed such things! After all, Christians are the ones who preach that Jesus the Messiah, the perfectly righteous one, took our place on the cross, dying for sins of the world. Yet there are significant parallels to this concept in ancient Jewish tradition, ultimately back to the Hebrew Scriptures.

Listen to the words of Rabbi Berel Wein, a respected Orthodox Jewish historian as he explains how the Jewish people survived the horrors of the massacres in Eastern Europe in the seventeenth century. According to Rabbi Wein:

> Another consideration tinged the Jewish response to the slaughter of its people. It was an old Jewish tradition dating back to Biblical times that the death of the righteous and innocent served as an expiation for the sins of the nation or the world. The stories of Isaac and of Nadav and Avihu, the prophetic description of Israel as the long-suffering servant of the Lord, the sacrificial service in the Temple—all served to reinforce this basic concept of the death of the righteous as an atonement for the sins of other men.
>
> Jews nurtured this classic idea of death as an atonement, and this attitude towards their own tragedies was their constant companion throughout their turbulent exile. Therefore, the

wholly bleak picture of unreasoning slaughter was somewhat relieved by the fact that the innocent did not die in vain and that the betterment of Israel and humankind somehow was advanced by their "stretching their neck to be slaughtered." What is amazing is that this abstract, sophisticated, theological thought should have become so ingrained in the psyche of the people that even the least educated and most simplistic of Jews understood the lesson and acted upon it, giving up precious life in a soaring act of belief and affirmation of the better tomorrow. This spirit of the Jews is truly reflected in the historical chronicle of the time:

"Would the Holy One, Blessed is He, dispense judgment without justice? But we may say that he whom God loves will be chastised. For since the day the Holy Temple was destroyed, the righteous are seized by death for the iniquities of the generation" (*Yeven Metzulah*, end of chapter 15).[1]

So, an Orthodox rabbi (who most definitely does not believe in Jesus) is telling us that, according to the Bible and Jewish tradition, the death of the righteous serves as an atonement for the sins of other men, "as an expiation for the sins of the nation or the world." And notice carefully the words of the medieval chronicle, *Yeven Metzulah*: it was *since the destruction of the Temple* that the righteous were "seized by death for the iniquities of their generation." The connection is crystal clear: since there are no more sacrifices of atonement, it is the death of the righteous that atones.

In similar fashion the Zohar states, "As long as Israel dwelt in the Holy Land, the rituals and the sacrifices they performed [in the Temple] removed all those diseases from the world; now the Messiah removes them from the children of the world."[2]

This is not some new doctrine that the "Christian church" created. It is thoroughly scriptural, it is quite Jewish, and it explains the purpose and meaning of Yeshua's death. The Talmud itself teaches that "the death of the righteous atones" (*mitatan shel tsaddiqim mekapperet*). In a well-known discussion (b. Mo'ed Qatan 28a), the Talmud asks why the

Book of Numbers records the death of Miriam immediately after the section on the red heifer. (See Numbers 19:1–20:1). The answer is that, just as the red heifer atones, so also the death of the righteous atones. (See also Rashi to Numbers 20:1).[3] And why, the Talmud asks, is the death of Aaron recorded in conjunction with the Torah's reference to the priestly garments? (See Numbers 20:25–28). The answer is: Just as the garments of the high priest atone (see Exodus 28, especially v. 38), so also the death of the righteous atones. (Some of the rabbinic texts read "atones for Israel" in all the cases just cited.)

This theme is actually fairly common in rabbinic literature. Look, for example, at Leviticus Rabbah 20:12, repeated elsewhere[4] verbatim:

> Rabbi Hiyya Bar Abba said: The sons of Aaron [i.e., Nadab and Abihu] died the first day of Nisan. Why then does the Torah mention their death in conjunction with the Day of Atonement [which occurred on the tenth of Tishrei; see Lev. 16:1]? It is to teach that just as the Day of Atonement atones, so also the death of the righteous atones.[5]

The Zohar supports this concept with a citation from Isaiah 53, the Messianic prophecy most widely quoted by followers of Jesus:

> The children of the world are members of one another, and when the Holy One desires to give healing to the world, He smites one just man amongst them, and for his sake heals all the rest. Whence do we learn this? From the saying, "He was wounded for our transgressions, bruised for our iniquities" [Isa. 53:5], i.e., by the letting of his blood—as when a man bleeds his arm—there was healing for us—for all the members of the body. In general a just person is only smitten in order to procure healing and atonement for a whole generation.[6]

A Christian evangelist couldn't have said it any better.

This is the very heart of the gospel message: The Messiah—the holy and righteous servant of the Lord—was smitten for the sins of the world, and through his death we can receive atonement for our sins and healing for our souls. He alone is the perfectly righteous one who can take the place of a sinning generation and sinning world.

A late midrash called Assereth Memrot states:

> The Messiah, in order to atone for them both [for Adam and David], will *make his soul a trespass offering*, as it is written next to this, in the Parashah [scriptural passage] *Behold my servant* [i.e., Isa. 52:13–53:12]: *'shm* [guilt offering], i.e. cabalistically [i.e., using Rabbinic Bible numerics], Menahem son of Ammiel [a title for the Messiah in the Talmud].[7]

The Messiah took our place. We sinned. He died. We were guilty. He was punished. We deserved death. He gave his life. We rejected him. He accepted us. What an incredible message! It's seems far too good to be true. But it *is* true, and it's biblical. It's Jewish too.

Rabbinic scholar Solomon Schechter summarizes the Talmudic teaching that suffering and death atone for sin, with specific reference to the death of the righteous:

> The atonement of suffering and death is not limited to the suffering person. The atoning effect extends to all the generation. This is especially the case with such sufferers as cannot either by reason of their righteous life or by their youth possibly have merited the afflictions which have come upon them. The death of the righteous atones just as well as certain sacrifices [with reference to b. Moed Katan 28a]. "They are caught (suffer) for the sins of the generation. If there are no righteous, the children of the schools (that is, the innocent young children) are caught for the sins of the generation" [b. Shabbat 32b]. There are also applied to Moses the Scriptural words, "And he bore the sins of many" (Isa. 53:12), because of his offering himself as an atonement for Israel's sin with the golden calf, being ready to sacrifice his very soul for Israel when he said, "And if not, blot me, I pray thee, out of thy book (that is, from the Book of the Living), which thou hast written" (Exod. 32:32 [b. Sotah 14a; b. Berakhot 32a]). *This readiness to sacrifice oneself for Israel is*

characteristic of all the great men of Israel, the patriarchs and the
Prophets acting in the same way, whilst also some Rabbis would, on
certain occasions, exclaim, "Behold, I am the atonement of Israel"
[Mekhilta 2a; m. Negaim 2:1].[8]

I remind you once again: this is the teaching of the Talmud, not the
New Testament, yet it is this very teaching that demonstrates to us just
how biblical and Jewish the doctrine is.

The Power of Righteous Martyrdom

Most Jews know about the Maccabees, those noble warriors who fought
against the oppressive Greek rulers in the second century BCE. It is their
victory that is celebrated at Hanukkah. But how many of us know what
the book of Fourth Maccabees (written by a Jewish author between 100
BCE and 100 CE) records about the significance of their deaths? It is
written that they prayed: "Cause our chastisement to be an expiation for
them. Make my blood their purification and take my soul as a ransom
for their souls" (4 Maccabees 6:28–29). Of these righteous martyrs it is
recorded: "They have become as a ransom for the sin of our nation, and
by the blood of these righteous men and the propitiation of their death,
Divine Providence delivered Israel" (4 Maccabees 17:22).

And where did this concept of righteous martyrdom first arise?
According to Jewish tradition, it went back to the binding of Isaac.
When Abraham was ready to offer his own son as a sacrifice to God,
this same book of Fourth Maccabees states: "Isaac offered himself for
the sake of righteousness. . . . Isaac did not shrink when he saw the knife
lifted against him by his father's hand" (4 Maccabees 13:12; 16:20).

This was the understanding of the rabbis. They believed that Isaac
was a grown man (actually, thirty-seven years old!) when God tested
Abraham, commanding him to offer Isaac on Mount Moriah (Gen. 22).
Although the biblical account emphasizes the obedience of Abraham,
the rabbis also stressed the obedience of Isaac. In fact, there is a midrash
that says at the time of Creation, when God was about to make man, the
angels asked what man's significance was. One of his answers was this:
"You shall see a father slay his son, and the son consenting to be slain, to

sanctify my Name" (Tanhuma, Vayyera, sec. 18). That was the height of sacrificial service: a father offering up his own son, and the son willingly laying down his life for the glory of God. Yes, I know that sounds like the gospel. In fact, the midrash compares Isaac, given the wood for the burnt offering (himself!) to carry on his shoulder, to "one who carries his cross on his own shoulder."[9]

And here is something truly fascinating: although Isaac was *not* sacrificed, the rabbis taught that, "Scripture credits Isaac with having died and his ashes having lain upon the altar" (Midrash HaGadol on Genesis 22:19). Yes, "God regards the ashes of Isaac as though they were piled upon the altar" (Sifra, 102c; b. Ta'anit 16a).

But there was a problem. Prof. Geza Vermes, a world-renowned specialist in early Jewish traditions (from whose study on the binding of Isaac I have cited several of the previous references), explains that the rabbis needed to take this a step further because of the biblical doctrine that there can be no atonement without the shedding of blood.[10] So the rabbis needed to teach that Isaac actually shed his blood. And they did!

One ancient source, compiled less than two hundred years after the death of Jesus, states: "The Holy One, blessed be He, said to Moses: 'I keep faith to pay the reward of Isaac son of Abraham, who gave one fourth of his blood on the altar'" (Mekhilta d'Rashbi, p. 4; Tanh. Vayerra, sec. 23).[11]

Vermes also notes that the "blood of the Binding of Isaac" is mentioned four times in the early Jewish midrash called the Mekhilta of Rabbi Ishmael. In Exodus 12:13, God promised the Israelites that when he passed through the land to destroy the firstborn sons of the Egyptians, he would pass over the houses of the Israelites who had applied the blood of the Passover lambs to the lintels and doorposts of their houses. The midrash interprets the verse to mean this: "'And when I see the blood, I will pass over you'—I see the blood of the Binding of Isaac" (I, 57). God wasn't looking at the blood of the lambs; he was looking at the blood of Isaac.

Vermes even states that:

> According to ancient Jewish theology, the atoning efficacy of the *Tamid* offering [the fixed, daily offering], of all the sacrifices

in which a lamb was immolated, and perhaps, basically, of all expiatory sacrifice irrespective of the nature of the victim, depended upon the virtue of the Akedah [the Binding of Isaac], the self-offering of that Lamb whom God had recognized as the perfect victim of the perfect burnt offering.[12]

In keeping with this, one of the Targums (the Aramaic paraphrastic translations of the Hebrew Scriptures read in the ancient synagogues) puts this prayer in the mouth of Abraham: "Now I pray for mercy before You, O Lord God, that when the children of Isaac come to a time of distress You may remember on their behalf the Binding of Isaac their father, and loose and forgive them their sins and deliver them from all distress."[13]

This tradition is reflected in the New Year prayer of the Talmudic rabbi Bibi bar Abba: "So when the children of Isaac commit sin and do evil, remember on their behalf the Binding of Isaac...and full of compassion towards them, be merciful to them."[14]

This same thought is also carried over in a prayer still included in the additional service for the Jewish New Year (Rosh Hashanah), which culminates with the words: "Remember today the Binding of Isaac with mercy to his descendants." We are forgiven through the merit of the sacrifice of Isaac! The rabbis even taught that the final resurrection of the dead would take place "through the merits of Isaac, who offered himself upon the altar" (Pesikta de Rav Kahane, 32). Growing up, I had no idea such traditions existed among my Jewish people.

As noted earlier, Solomon Schechter observed that "some [Talmudic] Rabbis would, on certain occasions, exclaim, 'Behold, I am the atonement of Israel.'" To this day, when a leading rabbi dies, it is quite common for the mourners to say, "May his death serve as an atonement!" And in a moving account from the Holocaust, Rabbi Shem Klingberg, known among his followers as the Zaloshitzer Rebbe, was led out to be slaughtered by the Nazis. In a matter of moments, after saying his last prayer, he would be gunned down. But first, he stopped, lifted his eyes to heaven, and cried out in a piercing voice: "Let me be an atonement for Israel!"[15] Yes, it is deeply ingrained in Jewish tradition that the death of the righteous atones.

Both the Bible and rabbinic tradition recognize that in some cases, death could serve as a payment for the sins of an individual,[16] while in the case of corporate sin, in certain situations, the death of representative sinners could satisfy God's judgment against the community as a whole.[17] But what about the death of the righteous? What if the most righteous leader in the community offered up his own life as a ransom payment? What if he said, "Kill me, but let them go." How much would his death be worth?

When terrorists take a hostage, they take someone of standing and prominence, and that one life serves as a huge bargaining chip, something we can easily understand in natural terms. How much weight does the life of the pope carry in the eyes of the Catholic Church? How valuable would the life of a Hasidic Rebbe be to his followers? What if the lives of all the people in a large Catholic or Hasidic community were threatened, and their pope or Rebbe *offered to die* in their place? Wouldn't that one life—and death—be considered to be of far greater worth than the lives of even millions of his followers? Without doubt. And it would be considered far more significant too.

A RANSOM FOR THE WORLD

In God's sight, the lives of his righteous servants have great value, and their deaths carry weight. In fact, there is abundant material to be found in Jewish tradition regarding the "merits of the patriarchs" or the "merits of the righteous."[18] And there is no life more valuable than that of the Messiah, the perfectly righteous one, and no death more important than his.

When he died, his death served as a ransom payment for the sins of the whole world. That was why he came into this world: not to be served, "but to serve, and to give his life as a ransom for many" (Mark 10:45).

Jesus did this as our great High Priest, an insight we can learn from Numbers 35, where we discover that the death of the high priest had atoning power. The context refers to intentional or unintentional manslaughter. In the case of willful homicide, the murderer had to be put to death, because, "Bloodshed pollutes the land, and atonement cannot be made for the land on which blood has been shed, except by the blood of the one who shed it" (Num. 35:33).

The only way to remove the pollution of bloodshed was by the blood of the one who first shed it. No other form of atonement was acceptable. But in the case of unintentional homicide, the manslayer would flee to a protected place called a city of refuge, where he would remain for the rest of his life (Num. 35:1–15, 22–25). There was only one thing that could secure his release from the city of refuge: the death of the high priest! "The accused must stay in his city of refuge until the death of the high priest; only after the death of the high priest may he return to his own property" (Num. 35:28).

This is critically important. Blood had been shed unintentionally. Someone was killed, the land was polluted, and the only acceptable ransom payment was the death of the one who killed. But he was not worthy of death. The homicide was accidental. So, the innocent manslayer was banished to the city of refuge for life, unless the high priest, the people's representative spiritual leader and the one who interceded for the nation, died. The high priest's death would release him. The death of the high priest would take the place of his own.

The Talmud[19] asks the question: Isn't it the exile of the innocent manslayer [in the city of refuge] that expiates? The answer is no: "It is not the exile that expiates, but the death of the high priest." Prof. Jacob Milgrom, an expert in priestly literature, comments: "As the High Priest atones for Israel's sins through his cultic [i.e., ritual] service in his lifetime (Exod. 28:36; Lev. 16:16, 21), so he atones for homicide through his death."[20]

There is also an extraordinary comment about the atoning power of the death of Messiah ben Joseph made by Moshe Alshekh, the influential sixteenth-century rabbi, in his commentary to Zechariah 12:10:

> I will yet do a third thing, and that is, that "they shall look unto me," for they shall lift up their eyes unto me in perfect repentance, when they see him whom they pierced, that is,

Messiah, the son of Joseph; for our Rabbis, of blessed memory, have said that he will *take upon himself all the guilt of Israel,* and shall then be slain in the war *to make atonement in such manner that it shall be accounted as if Israel had pierced him, for on account of their sin he has died; and, therefore, in order that it may be reckoned to them as a perfect atonement,* they will repent and look to the blessed One, saying that there is none beside him to forgive those that mourn on account of him *who died for their sin*: this is the meaning of "They shall look upon me."[21]

What extraordinary words—and they are the words of a greatly respected, traditional rabbi.

The Zohar also painted a vivid picture of the Messiah's sufferings on behalf of Israel. In a passage that just cited Isaiah 53:5, the Zohar relates:

The Messiah enters [the Hall of the Sons of Illness] and summons all the diseases and all the pains and all the sufferings of Israel that they should come upon him, and all of them come upon him. And would he not thus bring ease to Israel and take their sufferings upon himself, no man could endure the sufferings Israel has to undergo because they neglected the Torah.[22]

Had not the Messiah taken our place, suffering on our behalf, we would have perished long ago.

So the "Christian gospel" is actually Jewish, and the death of the truly righteous one—the Messiah, our great High Priest, the perfect sacrifice—atones. And this is not human sacrifice, an abhorrent practice condemned by God. This is our Righteous Messiah giving himself as a ransom for the entire human race, and, in the words of Isaiah the prophet, making himself "an offering for guilt" (Isa. 53:10, ESV; Hebrew *'asham*)—the guilt of all of us.

This is a secret that must be shouted to the whole Jewish world.

12

THE SECRET OF THE PRIESTLY MESSIAH

EVERYONE WHO BELIEVES in the biblical Messiah accepts the *royal* prophecies as referring to him, recognizing that he will be a king. But what about the prophecies that speak of an individual who will suffer and even die? What do these verses have to do with the Messiah? The answer is that the prophecies of suffering and death point to the priestly ministry of the Messiah, since it was the duty of the High Priest to intercede for his people and make atonement for their sins.[1]

Now, in ancient Israel, both kings and priests were anointed for service, and the word for anointed one is *mashiach*, from which we get the word Messiah (it is Christ in Greek). So in that sense, both kings and priests were "anointed ones." But the evidence for the priestly Messiah goes far beyond this, and by the first century of this era there was widespread belief in the coming of a *priestly* Messianic figure as well as a *royal* Messianic figure.

As we pointed out previously (see chapter 10), the authors of the Dead Sea Scrolls—deeply religious Jews—were looking for two Messianic figures, called the Messiahs of Aaron and Israel.[2] In addition to this, an important first-century CE document called the Testaments of the Twelve Patriarchs also spoke about this priestly Messiah (from the tribe of Levi) along with the expected royal Messiah (from the tribe of Judah), describing both in highly exalted terms.[3] And these concepts were ultimately derived from the Hebrew Bible itself, although for the most part, rabbinic Judaism has all but forgotten about the priestly Messiah.[4]

What then is the biblical background to this concept of a priestly Messiah? According to Psalm 110:4, the Lord made an emphatic oath that the Davidic king in Jerusalem was to be a priest forever after the order of Melchizedek. (Melchizedek was the ancient priest-king of Shalem—or Jerusalem—mentioned in Genesis 14.) As written in the psalm, "The Lord has sworn and will not change his mind: 'You are a priest forever, in the order of Melchizedek'" (Ps. 110:4). To repeat: the *king* was told that he would be a *priest* forever.

The problem is that the legitimate kings of Israel descended from David, who hailed from the tribe of Judah, but priests were descendants of Aaron, who hailed from the tribe of Levi. How could the king be a priest? Let's keep that question in mind as we continue to look at the biblical evidence.

According to one interpretation of Psalm 110, this divine oath was spoken to David by an inspired court poet, in which case David himself was declared to be a priest-king. According to another interpretation, the whole psalm was spoken by David about the Messiah. Thus the opening words, "The Lord says to my Lord: 'Sit at my right hand until I make your enemies a footstool for your feet'" (Ps 110:1), are understood to be those of David, declaring God's promise to the Messiah, David's lord.[5] And it is the royal Messiah who is designated a priest forever like Melchizedek, the first priest-king mentioned in the Scriptures.

In either case, it is interesting to note that David did perform priestly functions, such as offering sacrifices (see, e.g., 2 Samuel 24:25), a divine service which only priests could perform,[6] while according to 2 Samuel 8:17, David's sons were priests.[7] Thus David, the biblical prototype of the Messiah,[8] was to be a priestly king. But there's still more biblical evidence to review.

According to a prophetic vision recorded in Zechariah 3:8, the Lord said, "Hearken well, O High Priest Joshua, you and your fellow priests sitting before you! For those men are a sign that I am going to bring My servant the Branch" (NJV). And who is "the Branch"? He is none other than the Davidic Messiah, as widely recognized by biblical commentators.[9] In keeping with this, the New Jewish Version simply explains, "I.e., the future king of David's line. See 6:12; Jer. 23:5–6; 33:15–16; cf. Isa 11:1." So, the High Priest and his fellow priests are a sign that the Branch—the Davidic Messiah—is coming.

In the very next chapter of Zechariah, the prophet sees another interesting vision and asks the angel, "'And what are those two olive trees, one on the right and one on the left of the lampstand?...What are the two tops of the olive trees that feed their gold through those two golden tubes?' He asked me, 'Don't you know what they are?' And I replied, 'No, my lord'" (Zech. 4:11–13, NJV).

What did all these dual symbols stand for? "Then he explained, 'They are the two anointed dignitaries who attend the Lord of all the earth'" (v. 14). According to the New Jewish Version, this refers to "the high priest and the king...lit., 'sons of oil.'"[10] Once again these two key figures are joined together.

But the climactic text is found in Zechariah 6:11–13, where the prophet is commanded:

> Take from [some of the Jewish exiles] silver and gold, and make a crown, and set it on the head of Joshua, the son of Jehozadak, the high priest. And say to him, "Thus says the LORD of hosts, 'Behold, the man whose name is the Branch: for he shall branch out from his place, and he shall build the temple of the LORD. It is he who shall build the temple of the LORD and shall bear royal honor, and shall sit and rule on his throne. And there shall be a priest on his throne, and the counsel of peace shall be between them both.'"
>
> —ESV

Do you see what is happening here? (1) The prophet is commanded to put a *crown* on the head of the High Priest, Joshua (kings are supposed to wear crowns, not priests!); (2) the High Priest is then called the Branch, which was a symbolic name for the Messiah, who is a king; and (3) it is said of this High Priest that he will "sit and rule on his throne. And there shall be a priest on his throne." A crowned priest sitting on a throne and ruling? How can this be? The text concludes by saying that "the counsel of peace shall be between them both," meaning between the priest and the king, both of which are represented by Joshua, the High Priest, the man symbolically called the Branch, the personification of the Messianic Priest-King.

TWO MESSIAHS . . . OR ONE?

Later Jewish traditions, preserved in the Dead Sea Scrolls and the Testament of the Twelve Patriarchs, recognized the importance of this priestly figure, speaking of two Messiahs, a royal Messiah from the line of David and a priestly Messiah from the line of Aaron. In contrast, traditional Jewish literature lost sight of the priestly Messiah, speaking only of the Messiah son of David (and, in some texts, of the Messiah son of Joseph as well; see chapter 10, "The Secret of the Suffering Messiah").[11]

In reality, though, all of these traditions were missing something, since the Bible speaks of only one Messiah—a king from the line of David—but it makes clear that this Messiah was also to be a priest. So, David served as a prototype of the priestly King, and Joshua served as a prototype of the royal Priest—and Jesus-Yeshua brought these dual images to fulfillment.

But there's more. In the Hebrew Scriptures, this man Joshua (*Yehoshuah* in Hebrew), who embodied the image of the Messiah as priest and king, is normally referred to by the shorter form of his name: Yeshua![12] Yes, the man explicitly called the Branch, this High Priest who was crowned and sat on a throne, bringing royalty and priesthood together in one, this man who served as a prototype of the Messiah, was called Yeshua. How remarkable!

It was as our great High Priest that Jesus-Yeshua came to earth and suffered and died, doing what priests were expected to do: making atonement for sin, bearing our guilt, and interceding for the transgressors. As expressed in Isaiah 53:12 (NJV):

> For he exposed himself to death
> And was numbered among the sinners,
> Whereas he bore the guilt of the many
> And made intercession for sinners.

As the Messiah, son of David, he was born King of the Jews and he died King of the Jews,[13] but he was a priestly King whose first mission was to deal with the problem of sin. When the full effects of his priestly work have been felt throughout the world, he will return to establish his kingdom.

In keeping with this, the New Testament letter called Hebrews (which was written to Jewish believers) speaks about "this Jesus whom we declare to be God's messenger and High Priest." It states that "we have a great High Priest who has entered heaven, Jesus the Son of God," one "who understands our weaknesses, for he faced all of the same testings we do, yet he did not sin" (Heb. 3:1; 4:14–15, NLT). Yes, "He is the kind of high priest we need because he is holy and blameless, unstained by sin. He has been set apart from sinners and has been given the highest place of honor in heaven" (Heb. 7:26, NLT).

Consider the power of Yeshua's priestly work:

> For if sprinkling ceremonially unclean persons with the blood of goats and bulls and the ashes of a heifer restores their outward purity [according to Torah ritual]; then how much more the blood of the Messiah, who, through the eternal Spirit, offered himself to God as a sacrifice without blemish, will purify our conscience from works that lead to death, so that we can serve the living God!
> —HEBREWS 9:13–14, CJB

What an extraordinary High Priest!

To quote Hebrews once more, "Just as human beings have to die once, but after this comes judgment, so also the Messiah, having been offered once to bear the sins of many, will appear a second time, not to deal with sin, but to deliver those who are eagerly waiting for him" (Heb. 9:27–28, CJB).

The Dead Sea Scrolls did not get it entirely right, nor did the Talmud and rabbinic writings. Instead, the Hebrew Scriptures laid the groundwork and pointed the way, Yeshua the Messiah came and did the work, and the New Testament authors wrote it down for posterity, preserving these amazing insights about our great High Priest in a letter written to Jews, since they of all people would understand the significance of what they read.

The Messiah is both a King and a Priest. Why should this be a secret?

13

THE SECRET OF THE PROPHET
GREATER THAN MOSES

THE CHILDREN OF Israel faced a crisis. Moses, their mighty deliverer, the one who brought them out of Egypt by the powerful hand of the Lord, the one who declared God's will to them, was about to die. They were about to enter the land of Canaan, a land filled with pagan practices, practices they were to avoid at any cost (Deut. 18:9–14). How then could they hear God's voice and know his will? They couldn't do what the pagans did—going to fortune-tellers, witches, astrologers, or soothsayers—and Moses their prophet would not be there. What were they to do?

The Lord would not leave them alone, as Moses himself assured them, "The LORD your God will raise up for you a prophet like me from among your own brothers. You must listen to him" (Deut. 18:15). Or, in the Lord's own words, "I will raise up for them a prophet like you from among their brothers; I will put my words in his mouth, and he will tell them everything I command him" (Deut. 18:18).

Did the Lord keep his word? On the one hand he did, raising up prophets such as Joshua, Samuel, Elijah, and Isaiah over the centuries. On the other hand something was missing. Notice these words carefully: "The LORD your God will *raise up* for you *a prophet like me*...I will *raise up* for them *a prophet like you*" (Deut. 18:15, 18). Yet we read these words at the end of Deuteronomy, and they are meant to stand as a statement for the entire "Old Testament" period:

> Since then, *no prophet has risen in Israel like Moses*, whom the LORD knew face to face, who did all those miraculous signs and

wonders the LORD sent him to do in Egypt—to Pharaoh and to all his officials and to his whole land. For no one has ever shown the mighty power or performed the awesome deeds that Moses did in the sight of all Israel.

—DEUTERONOMY 34:10–12, EMPHASIS ADDED[1]

What happened to that Moses-like prophet?

Traditional Jewish thought tells us that there will never be another prophet like Moses and that the Torah only promised a prophet (or line of prophets) who would function like Moses (as God's mouthpiece to the people), rather than actually be on his level. This has actually become established as a fundamental principle of the Jewish faith. And so, the seventh of the Thirteen Principles of faith established by Moses Maimonides (1135–1204) states that Moses "was the father of all prophets that were before him and that will be after him. He was on a qualitatively different level than any other, and he is chosen from all other people before and after him of any that have any knowledge of God; for his was the greatest."[2]

Is this assessment correct? Certainly not. First, the promise in Deuteronomy 18 is too specific (God will raise up a prophet like Moses, repeated twice), standing in clear contrast with the reality recorded in Deuteronomy (no prophet like Moses was ever raised up). Over the centuries the people of Israel would have every right to say, "This current prophet is not like Moses! What happened to the promise?"

Second, by the time Jesus came on the scene, there is strong evidence that many Jews were expecting a great end-time prophet to arise, along with one or two Messianic figures.[3] I would dare say that the great majority of Jewish people living today have no idea about this, but two thousand years ago, this was believed by many of our Jewish forefathers. The Dead Sea Scrolls, along with several other ancient Jewish sources, point to this clearly, with at least one of those sources making reference to Deuteronomy 18:18–19—the promise that God would raise up a prophet like Moses.[4]

In one of the most famous Dead Sea Scrolls, called the Community Rule (also called the Manual of Discipline), it is written, "They shall depart from none of the counsels of the Law to walk in the stubbornness of their hearts, but shall be ruled by the primitive precepts in which the men of the Community were first instructed until *there shall come the Prophet* and the Messiahs of Aaron and Israel" (1 QS 9:11).[5]

According to Yale professor John J. Collins, a recognized authority on these texts, "The scriptural underpinning for this expectation was found in [another document in the Dead Sea Scrolls called] the Testimonia (4Q175), which strings together a series of biblical passages without interpretation."[6] These biblical passages include Deuteronomy 18:18–19, where God promised Israel that he would raise up a prophet like Moses for them, along with Numbers 24:15–17 (apparently pointing to the Messianic King) and Deuteronomy 33:8–11 (apparently pointing to the Messianic Priest, of whom I just spoke in the previous chapter).[7] There is also an interesting reference to this prophet in 1 Maccabees 14:41 (see also 4:46), written more than a century before the time of Yeshua. It speaks of certain Jewish leadership being in place "till there should arise a faithful prophet."

It is clear, then, that by the time of Jesus, there were Jews who were not just looking for the Messiah(s) to come. They were also looking for that last great prophet—the ultimate Prophet—a prophet like Moses. As noted by New Testament scholar Darrell Bock, "The expectation of a Moses-like figure in the end time was common in Judaism.... The Samaritans pointed to this passage [meaning Deuteronomy 18] as describing a restorer figure known as the *Taheb*."[8]

THE END-TIME PROPHET

By the time we come to the pages of the New Testament, we see that the idea of a great end-time Prophet is virtually taken for granted:

- In John 1:21, Jewish religious leaders were trying to find out who John the Baptist was. After asking him if he was the Messiah, to which he replied, No, "They asked him, 'Then who are you? Are you Elijah?' He said, 'I am not.' '*Are you the Prophet?*' He answered, 'No.'" Did you catch that? "John, are you *the* Prophet"—not *a* prophet.

- According to John 6:14, after Jesus miraculously supplied food for thousands of people, they began to say, "Surely this is *the Prophet* who is to come into the world."

- In John 7:40, after hearing him speak, some of the crowd said, "Surely this man is *the Prophet*." Others, however, thought that he might be the Messiah (v. 41).

- So also, in Luke 7:16, after Yeshua raised a widow's son from the dead, the people "were all filled with awe and praised God. '*A great prophet* has appeared among us,' they said. 'God has come to help his people.'"

Peter knew about this expectation, and so he declared to a Jewish crowd assembled at the Temple to celebrate Shavuot (Pentecost) roughly fifty days after Yeshua's resurrection:

> For Moses said, "The Lord your God will raise up for you a prophet like me from among your own people; you must listen to everything he tells you. Anyone who does not listen to him will be completely cut off from among his people." Indeed, all the prophets from Samuel on, as many as have spoken, have foretold these days.
>
> —Acts 3:22–24

But Peter knew something else. While many of his Jewish contemporaries were waiting for this last great Prophet, plus a royal Messiah, plus a priestly Messiah, Peter understood that that all these important figures were one and the same: Yeshua, the priestly Messiah and the royal Messiah, Yeshua, the Prophet like Moses. But there's more: the Bible makes clear that the Messiah would be even greater than Moses—meaning that Yeshua, our Messiah, was not only a Prophet like Moses, he was even greater than Moses.

Messianic Jewish scholar David Stern expressed this well:

Was Yeshua "a prophet like Moshe"? Yes, and more. A prophet speaks for God, which Yeshua did; but he also spoke as God. He spoke what the Father gave him to say, as did all the prophets; but he and the Father are one [John 10:31]. Moshe explained the sacrificial system for atonement; Yeshua was the final sacrifice for sin, the eternally effective atonement. Moshe established the system of *cohanim* [priests], with his brother Aaron as the first *cohen gadol* [high priest] of the Tabernacle; the resurrected Yeshua is the eternal *cohen gadol* in the heavenly Tabernacle that served as a model for the earthly one [Heb. 7–10]. At no point did Yeshua contradict what Moshe said; rather he clarified and strengthened the *Torah* [Matt. 5:17–20], made its application plainer [Matt. 5:21–7:29], and sometimes himself *was* the application.[9]

And yet there is more. I'm speaking of a famous rabbinic homily (called a midrash) to Isaiah 52:13, a verse often associated with the Messiah even in traditional Jewish thought. The verse reads, "See, my servant will act wisely; he will be high and lifted up and exceedingly lofty."[10]

Commenting on this verse, the midrash states:

> *Who art thou, O great mountain?* (Zech. iv. 7.) This refers to the King Messiah. And why does he call him "the great mountain?" because he is greater than the patriarchs, as it is said, "*My servant shall be high, and lifted up, and lofty exceedingly*"—he will be higher than Abraham, who says, "I raise *high* my hands unto the Lord" (Gen. xiv. 22); lifted up above Moses, to whom it is said, "*Lift it* up into thy bosom" (Num. xi. 12); loftier than the ministering angels, of whom it is written, "Their wheels were *lofty* and terrible" (Ez. i. 18). And out of whom does he come forth? Out of David. (Yalqut Shim'oni, 2:571)[11]

Based in part on this midrash, a number of leading rabbinic authorities actually rejected the view of Maimonides that no prophet greater than Moses would arise, recognizing that the Messiah would obtain a more perfect knowledge of God as well as operate at a higher level of prophecy.[12] Fascinating!

Let us, then, focus on King Messiah—greater than Abraham, greater than Moses, and even greater than the ministering angels. This is the secret of the prophet like Moses and yet greater than Moses: He is the Messiah himself, Yeshua the King of Israel. Let the truth be told.

14

THE SECRET OF THE SIX
THOUSAND YEARS

I want to share with you a fascinating Talmudic tradition along with an even more fascinating interpretation of that tradition from the writings of the Vilna Gaon, the greatest rabbinic scholar of the eighteenth and nineteenth centuries. The Talmud says:

> The world will exist six thousand years. Two thousand years of desolation [meaning from Adam to Abraham]; two thousand years of Torah [meaning from Abraham to somewhere around the beginning of the Common Era]; and two thousand years of the Messianic era [roughly the last two thousand years!]; but because our iniquities were many, all this has been lost (i.e., the Messiah did not come at the expected time; Sanhedrin 97a-b).

So, according to this Jewish tradition, which is actually quite well known, the Messiah was supposed to come nearly two thousand years ago (or, based on the traditional rabbinic chronology, which has a significant error, about seventeen hundred fifty years ago).[1] As explained by Rashi, the foremost Jewish Talmud and Bible commentator, "After the two thousand years of Torah, it was God's decree that the Messiah would come and the wicked kingdom would come to an end and the subjugation of Israel would be destroyed." Instead, because Israel's sins were many, "the Messiah has not come to this very day"—now two thousand years later.

Let's take a closer look at the actual dates involved. Most traditional Jews follow Rashi's dating, putting the expected time of the Messiah's arrival at roughly 250 CE. However, Rashi based his figures on a very significant chronological error in the Talmudic tradition, probably the most famous error of its kind in rabbinic literature. And it is a miscalculation of almost two hundred years![2] So, adjusting Rashi's calculations by roughly one hundred eighty years, we find ourselves in the very century in which Yeshua came. What do you know! *He* was the one who came at the time the Messiah was expected to come, and this according to a *rabbinic* tradition.[3]

To be perfectly clear, this Talmudic tradition uses rough figures—two thousand, two thousand, two thousand—and I am not trying to argue with precision that Jesus came into the world the very year (or decade) that the Messiah was expected to arrive. Rather, it is to point out that according to this respected Jewish tradition, the Messiah was supposed to arrive at least seventeen hundred fifty years ago. What happened?

Now, the Vilna Gaon examined one of the more obscure stories of the Talmud in which a famous sage, Rabbi Yehoshua ben Chananyah, was confronted by the elders of Athens. These Greek intellectuals, living at the beginning of the second century CE, asked Rabbi Yehoshua, "Where is the midpoint of the world?" In reply he raised his finger and said, "Here!" When asked to prove his point, he asked for ropes and measure (b. Bechorot 8b). What does this mean?

According to the Gaon, the Athenian elders were aware of the Talmudic tradition we just cited from Sanhedrin 97a-b and were arguing with Rabbi Yehoshua that:

> ...the present should be the midpoint between the two productive eras of the world, the eras of Torah and Mashiach. But obviously he has not come, for you Jews have certainly not been redeemed. We have crushed you and turned you into a nation of ruin, disaster, and despair. The "midpoint of the world" has manifestly passed by and the Era of Mashiach has not begun. Why, then, do you persist in hoping for his arrival? Why should he come in the future if he did not come at his appointed hour? Is it not clear that the time for his arrival has passed you by forever?[4]

The problem, according to the Vilna Gaon, was that the Athenian elders were unaware of another Talmudic tradition that stated that, "The son of David [i.e., the Messiah] will not come until all the government has turned to heresy" (b. Sanhedrin 97a), interpreted to mean that there would be a worldwide turning *away* from God before the Messiah would establish his kingdom. And so, the Gaon explains:

> When the Elders asked, "Where is the midpoint of the world?" Rabbi Yehoshua raised his finger and said, "Here!" He was saying that although the Jews had not merited Mashiach's coming by their deeds, nevertheless the Era of Mashiach had indeed arrived at its appointed time. At "the midpoint of the world" God began turning the wheels of history to insure the ultimate arrival of the scion of David.

In other words, God began a process of giving the human race over to its spiritual darkness and sin so as to eventually bring it to a place that:

> Mankind will realize that the only way to convert himself back into a true human, a God-like being filled with wisdom, love, kindness, and an exalted spirit, is by the acceptance of God's dominion. And when God demonstrates all this and man recognizes it, Mashiach will finally come.

And when did this process begin? It was "with the advent of the last third of human history: the Era of Mashiach may not be apparent, but it is 'here.'"[5] Yes, even though the Messiah himself has not come, the Messianic era began right on schedule, only not in the way that most were expecting. (Does this sound vaguely familiar?)

But what about Rabbi Yehoshua's request for ropes and measure? The Gaon interprets this with reference to 2 Samuel 8:2, where King David measured out Moabite captives with lengths of rope, putting two-thirds of them to death while only sparing the last third. (See also Zechariah 13:8–9, also cited in the discussion.) He explains that:

The ropes of King David are the measure of human history. The two-thirds of world history which did not choose to recognize God's dominion refused to choose life. But the last third will be directed towards eternal life by a Providence which will lead the Jews step by step to the recognition of God.

What is the basis of your assertion, asked the Elders, that "here," in the last third of human history, God's mercy is at work and we are in the Era of Mashiach? Answered Rabbi Yehoshua: Remember the ropes of King David and you will learn the ways by which God directs His world. They teach us that God will never abandon his world, that ultimately the good for which God created it will be realized.[6]

And note again those words: "we are in the Era of Mashiach"— spoken more than eighteen hundred years ago. Yes, according to the Vilna Gaon's interpretation of this Talmudic account, *the Messianic era began more than eighteen hundred years ago.* And when you make the adjustment for his error in chronology (as pointed out earlier with regard to Rashi's calculations), he is telling us in effect that the Messianic age began in the first century of this era.

I remind you, of course, that the Vilna Gaon did not believe in Jesus any more than he believed that Muhammad was the first pope. (Note also that, in all probability, the Gaon did not have an accurate picture at all of who Yeshua was and what he did.) But it is striking that this great Jewish scholar recognized that the Messianic era actually began at its appointed time and that this era was first a time of *transition.* Shades of "Christianity"!

The biggest differences between our positions are these: (1) The Gaon saw the present transition age as one of universal, increasing darkness and apostasy. I see it as an age of ever-increasing awareness of the Messiah in the midst of great darkness and apostasy. (2) He believed that the Messianic era began *without* the coming of the Messiah. I believe it began *with* his coming. Which position seems more reasonable to you?

Is it possible that Messiah *did* come two thousand years ago, but "because our iniquities were many" we did not recognize him? Isn't this a more logical position than that posited by the Vilna Gaon? In fact, this position is not only more logical but is actually more *biblical*, since it can be demonstrated that according to the Hebrew Bible, the Messiah was to arrive before the Second Temple was destroyed—in other words, more than nineteen hundred years ago.[7]

THE APPOINTED TIME

Interestingly, the respected Jewish scholar Abba Hillel Silver pointed out that there was great expectation among the Jewish people that the Messiah would come "about the second quarter of the first century CE, because the millennium was at hand."[8] This, of course, is when Jesus appeared on the scene, and so, according to Silver, "When Jesus came into Galilee, 'spreading the gospel of the Kingdom of God and saying the *time is fulfilled* and the kingdom of God is at hand' [Mark 1:14–15], he was voicing the opinion universally held that the year 5000 in the Creation calendar, which is to usher in the sixth millennium—the age of the Kingdom of God—was at hand."[9] But, when the Temple was destroyed in 70 CE, and when the Messianic hopes surrounding the false messiah Simeon Bar Kochba were dashed to pieces in 135 CE, some of the rabbis needed to figure out why the Messiah didn't come at the appointed time, ultimately revising their chronology.

What was the solution to which these rabbis came? Silver summarizes the rabbinic response as follows: "The Messianic age has actually begun with the destruction of the Temple [i.e., in 70 CE], but before its final denouement 365 or 400 years or more may elapse."[10] So, Silver argues that the only way for these early rabbis to reconcile their Messianic expectations with their view that he did not come at the expected time was to postulate that the Messianic era actually *did* begin on time—according to this chronology in the year 70 CE—but it could be several more centuries before its conclusion. This is strikingly similar to the Vilna Gaon's interpretation, and it is equally wrong.

Here are some related Talmudic traditions worth considering about the time and nature of the Messiah's coming.

The Talmud states, "If they [i.e., the people of Israel] are worthy [the

Messiah] will come 'with the clouds of heaven' [Dan. 7:13]; if they are not worthy, 'lowly and riding upon a donkey' [Zech. 9:9]" (b. Sanhedrin 98a).[11] Just days before he died, Yeshua entered Jerusalem riding on a donkey, with the crowds hailing him as King Messiah. But then the people turned on him. Is it possible that he came "lowly and riding on a donkey" because we were not worthy of his coming, and in the future, when we recognize him as Messiah, he will return in the clouds of heaven?

According to b. Yoma 39b, God did not accept the sacrifices that were offered on the Day of Atonement for the last forty years before the destruction of the [Second] Temple. (This was known to the people by means of a series of special signs, all of which turned up negative for those forty years; see b. Yoma 39a.) The Temple was destroyed in 70 CE, so from 30–70 CE, a period of forty years, the annual atonement sacrifices were not accepted. What great event happened in the year 30? Yeshua was rejected and nailed to a cross. Is it possible that God no longer accepted the atonement sacrifices because the Messiah had offered himself as the perfect, final sacrifice, making himself as a "guilt offering," as it is written in Isaiah 53:10?

Of course, we must remember that in the Talmud, these statements are only cited as several opinions among many, and none of them are absolutely binding or final. Yet these traditions had their origins somewhere, and it is not hard to see that they preserve an important belief: *The Messiah was expected to come twenty centuries ago, but something terrible happened.*

So every Jewish person must ask the question: If we have been waiting for thousands of years and still our expected Messiah has not come, is it possible we have been waiting for the wrong Messiah? Is it possible that twenty centuries ago the real Messiah did appear, suffering and dying and rising from the dead, in accordance with the prophetic scriptures and according to the biblical timetable?[12] And is it possible that without intending to do so, the Talmud has left us hints that point us in this very direction?

There is a Jewish joke that says, "When the Messiah comes, we'll ask him: Is this your first time here, or have you been here before?"

But is this really a joking matter? And could it be that we already have the answer? The one who completed the first act of this divine drama right on schedule is the one who will complete the second and final act at the end of this age. Yet another secret has been revealed.

15

THE SECRET OF THE HIDDEN WISDOM

THERE IS A great interest in Kabbalah (Jewish mysticism) today—especially in its popularized form—as many people, both Jews and Gentiles, are seeking spiritual enlightenment.[1] They are looking for deeper truths, for special illumination, for mystical insights.

For many of these seekers, "Christianity" is perceived to be an old, worn-out, traditional religion and for them, the Jesus of the New Testament represents the champion of Bible-bashing fundamentalists and narrow-minded people who appear to be anything but deep.

Perhaps there are some misunderstandings about what the New Testament actually teaches and about who Jesus-Yeshua really is. Perhaps there's far more than meets the eye.

Although Yeshua often made direct statements about himself—indeed, they were sometimes so direct that they provoked an outraged response from his hearers[2]—he frequently spoke in parables when addressing the crowds, waiting until he was alone with his disciples to explain the meaning. Why did he do this? He told his disciples, "The secret of the kingdom of God has been given to you. But to those on the outside everything is said in parables so that, 'they may be ever seeing but never perceiving, and ever hearing but never understanding; otherwise they might turn and be forgiven!'" (Mark 4:11–12, quoting from Isa. 6:10).

Do you know what he meant by "the secret of the kingdom of God"? Are you on the "outside" or on the "inside"?

At one time Yeshua gave thanks to his heavenly Father, saying, "I praise you, Father, Lord of heaven and earth, because you have hidden these things from the wise and learned, and revealed them to little children. Yes, Father, for this was your good pleasure" (Matt. 11:25–26).

This is no shallow religious fundamentalism. It is true spiritual mysticism, and of the highest order at that: to the humble, the "little children," God reveals himself; to the proud and haughty, caught up with their own wisdom and learning, he hides himself.[3]

Paul also understood the principle of this "hidden wisdom," writing to the Corinthians (Greeks who prized powerful rhetoric and deep philosophical thought), "We do, however, speak a message of wisdom among the mature, but not the wisdom of this age or of the rulers of this age, who are coming to nothing. No, we speak of God's secret wisdom, a wisdom that has been hidden and that God destined for our glory before time began" (1 Cor. 2:6–7). God's secret wisdom? Found on the pages of the New Testament?

To the believers in the city of Ephesus Paul wrote:

> To me, the least important of all God's holy people, was given this privilege of announcing to the Gentiles the Good News of the Messiah's *unfathomable riches*, and of letting everyone see how this *secret plan* is going to work out. This plan, *kept hidden for ages by God*, the Creator of everything, is for the rulers and authorities in heaven to learn, through the existence of the Messianic Community, how *many-sided God's wisdom is*.
> —Ephesians 3:8–10, cjb, emphasis added

This is not an easy concept to grasp. Paul is saying that God's eternal plan was to demonstrate his wisdom to the entire universe by bringing Jew and Gentile together in one spiritual family through the apparent weakness of Messiah's death on the cross.[4] What seems so weak to human eyes was of infinite power in God's sight. As Paul also wrote to the Corinthians, "This foolish plan of God is wiser than the wisest of human plans, and God's weakness is stronger than the greatest of human strength" (1 Cor. 1:25, nlt).

Yes:

> God chose things the world considers foolish in order to shame those who think they are wise. And he chose things that are powerless to shame those who are powerful. God chose things

despised by the world, things counted as nothing at all, and used them to bring to nothing what the world considers important. As a result, no one can ever boast in the presence of God.

—1 Corinthians 1:27–29, NLT

And here is the most amazing revelation of all. God hid his greatest treasure, his ultimate display of wisdom and power, in plain sight, and in the most unlikely of places at that. It would be like "hiding" the most priceless jewel in the world on the kitchen table during a Thanksgiving meal. Everyone would see it, but no one would recognize what they saw. That's exactly what our God did.

Hidden in Plain Sight

It reminds me of the words of Robert Jastrow, a famous astronomer who once had this to say about the subject of creation of the universe: "For the scientist who has lived by his faith in the power of reason, the story ends like a bad dream. He has scaled the mountains of ignorance, he is about to conquer the highest peak; as he pulls himself over the final rock, he is greeted by a band of theologians who have been sitting there for centuries."[5] How can it be? In the beginning God, not science?

And this is the story of God's hidden wisdom. It is not found in the difficult texts of the Zohar[6] or in Bible numerics like Gematria and Notarikon.[7] It is not found in the chants of Hindu holy men or in the esoteric experiences of Sufi mystics. And it is not found in the deepest philosophical treatises or the most complex thinkers.

Instead, it is found in a Jewish carpenter who grew up in an obscure village called Nazareth and never traveled more than fifty miles from where he was born, a Jew who suffered the most ignominious execution known to man, hanging naked on a cross with his flesh torn apart by whips and his hands and feet pierced with nails, slowly suffocating to death while every muscle screamed in pain, all while being mocked and ridiculed by the few who bothered to watch him die. And there, in that Jewish man hanging on the cross, was hidden the greatest treasure of all. In him—Jesus-Yeshua, the rejected Messiah—"are hidden all the treasures of wisdom and knowledge" (Col. 2:3). Yes, "*all* the treasures of wisdom and knowledge." Who expected to find such treasures there? They were hidden in plain sight!

In fact, God's very glory and power is hidden in this Jewish carpenter from Nazareth, of whom Paul could say that "all the fullness of the Deity lives in [him in] bodily form" (Col. 2:9). And when we discover Jesus-Yeshua for all he is, we discover God himself. And when we make that discovery, nothing else matters. We have found the very meaning of life.

Do you understand these words, spoken by the master Teacher two thousand years ago? "The kingdom of heaven is like treasure hidden in a field. When a man found it, he hid it again, and then in his joy went and sold all he had and bought that field. Again, the kingdom of heaven is like a merchant looking for fine pearls. When he found one of great value, he went away and sold everything he had and bought it" (Matt. 13:44–46).

Israel's hidden Messiah has been revealed. Losing everything to gain him is the greatest gain of all.

Epilogue

NOT JUST A LIGHT FOR THE GENTILES

MANY JEWISH LEADERS believe that Jesus is fine for the Gentiles and that Christianity is a beautiful world religion. Jesus is simply not for Jews. Judaism is for Jews! In other words, it's fine if Christians want to follow Jesus, but the Jewish people already have a covenant with God, made thirty-five hundred years ago at Mount Sinai. As for the Gentiles, if they revere Jesus and their lives are improved by believing in him, more power to them. Just don't try to push him on the Jews.[1]

A number of the Jewish rabbis and scholars I have cited throughout this book hold to this position. Rabbi Jacob Emden expressed it back in 1757, writing that:

> ...the Nazarene brought about a double kindness in the world. On the one hand, he strengthened the Torah of Moses majestically....And on the other hand, he did much good for the Gentiles...by doing away with idolatry and removing the images from their midst. He obligated them with the Seven Commandments so that they should not be as the beasts of the field. He also bestowed upon them ethical ways, and in this respect he was much more stringent with them than the Torah of Moses, as is well-known.[2]

According to Joseph Klausner:

> From the standpoint of general humanity he is, indeed, "a light to the Gentiles." His disciples have raised the torch of the Law of Israel (even though that Law has been put forward in a

mutilated and incomplete form) among the heathen of the four quarters of the world. No Jew can, therefore, overlook the value of Jesus and an estimate of his teaching from the viewpoint of universal history. This was a fact which neither Maimonides nor Yehuda ha-Levi ignored.[3]

And Israeli scholar Pinchas Lapide stated, "I believe that the Christ event leads to a way of salvation which God has opened up in order to bring the Gentile world into the community of God's Israel."[4] So, the Gentiles come to know the God of Israel through Jesus, but the children of Israel already knew the God of Israel.

Rabbi Shmuley Boteach, known as "America's rabbi," waxed eloquent about the virtues of Christianity, at the same time making clear that faith in the Christian Jesus cannot be for Jews:

Christianity is the most successful idea in the history of the world. No religion, philosophy or way of life has ever had more adherents.... *But the Jews have not and cannot ever accept Jesus as he exists in Christian theology.*

I say this not to offend Christian believers, nor to dissuade adherents from living a Christian life. On the contrary, I respect and applaud the achievements of Christianity, a religion that has brought billions of people to God. Christians operate the world's largest network of hospitals, orphanages, and schools. The scale of their good deeds in contemporary society is staggering. It is a religion that, as the great Jewish philosopher Maimonides said, has brought the knowledge of God to distant shores and distant lands [citing the Mishneh Torah, Melachim 11:4]. Christianity has an incredible power to engender compassionate and pious followers.[5]

Is this, then, an acceptable option? Jesus is for the Gentiles but not for the Jews? Absolutely not. In fact, if he is not for the Jews, then he is not for anyone. This is something he made perfectly clear, and it is a central and foundational truth of the entire New Testament.

In short, Jesus did not come into the world to establish a lovely new

Gentile religion called Christianity. He came to fulfill what was written in Moses and the Prophets. He came as the Messiah of Israel. And if he is the Messiah of Israel, then he is the Savior of the world; if he is not the Messiah of Israel, then he and/or his disciples were miserably deceived and in reality, he is the Savior of no one. As stated by Prof. Walter Riggans, "If Jesus was a charlatan, then everyone needs to know this, Jew and non-Jew alike. But, on the other hand, this means that if Jesus *is* the Messiah, then everyone needs to know this too, Jew and non-Jew alike."[6]

Of course, Christians could easily be offended by the very notion that, "We Jews can't believe in him, because he's not who the New Testament claims that he is (plus, the New Testament is certainly not the Word of God). That means that Jesus didn't really die for the sins of the world, didn't rise from the dead, didn't ascend to heaven, is not going to return, and is not the Son of God—but hey, if you Gentiles want to have him along with this religion based on falsehood, lies, and deception, be our guests!"

Certainly that kind of thinking is an insult to the Gentile world. But what if there's another way of approaching this? What if Jesus was sent by God on a mission to bring the Lord's light to the ends of the earth, since the Jews already had a covenant with God but the Gentiles were lost in darkness? So he would *not* be Israel's Messiah, nor would he ever have claimed to be such, but he *would* be the Savior of the Gentile world. Is that possible?

Once again, the answer is absolutely not. That's not what he said, that's not why he came, and that's not the heart and soul of his life mission: he came as the Messiah of Israel, and because he is the Messiah of Israel, he is also the light of the world.

THE EVIDENCE IS CLEAR

The evidence of the New Testament is overwhelmingly clear, starting with the fact that he is called "Christ" (the Greek equivalent of the Hebrew word "Messiah") more than five hundred times in the New Testament documents.[7] Yes, Jesus is the Christ—or, in the more original,

Jewish terms, Yeshua is the Messiah. This is taught throughout the entire New Testament, from his birth to his death to his resurrection to his ascension to his promised return.

Simply stated, then, if is he is not the Messiah of Israel, we should throw out the New Testament and not bother either Jews or Gentiles with its message. If he is the Messiah of Israel, then he is for the Jewish people first, as well as for all the nations of the earth. Consider this tiny sampling of New Testament evidence:

- Before his birth, the angel announced that he would be called Yeshua, "because he will save his people from their sins" (Matt. 1:21).

- At his birth he was proclaimed "King of the Jews" (not "King of the Gentiles") and when he died, the inscription hanging over his head on the cross read, "Jesus of Nazareth, the King of the Jews."[8]

- He made clear that he had not come to abolish the Torah and the Prophets; rather, his mission was "to fulfill them" (Matt. 5:17).

- Some of his first Jewish followers were drawn to him because, they said, "We have found the Messiah" (John 1:41). Another one of his first disciples, named Nathaniel, recognized who he was immediately, proclaiming, "Rabbi, you are the Son of God; you are the King of Israel" (v. 49).

- When Jesus questioned his disciples some time later as to who they believed he was, Shimon Kepha (Peter), immediately declared, "You are the Messiah, the Son of the living God" (Matt. 16:16, NLT).

- After his resurrection, Jesus encountered two Jewish men who were despondent. They had hoped that he was going to be the one who redeemed Israel, but now he was dead, and all hope was lost. Without revealing his identity to them, he rebuked them in very strong terms: "'Foolish people! So unwilling to put your trust in everything the prophets spoke! Didn't the Messiah have to die like this before entering his glory?' Then, starting with Moshe and all the prophets, he explained to them the things that can be found throughout the Tanakh [the Scriptures] concerning himself" (Luke 24:25–27, CJB).

- Shortly after this, he took his eleven disciples aside and instructed them, preparing them for their mission of declaring to Israel and the nations that the Messiah had come. He said to them, "This is what I meant when I was still with you and told you that everything written about me in the Torah of Moshe, the Prophets and the Psalms had to be fulfilled" (Luke 24:44, CJB).

- After the Messiah ascended to heaven in accordance with the words of Psalm 110:1 (where the Lord said to his anointed one, "Sit at my right hand until I make your enemies a footstool for your feet"), Shimon Kefa (Peter) declared to thousands of Jews who had gathered at the Temple in Jerusalem for the Feast of Shavu'ot (Pentecost, or Weeks) that this same Jesus who had been given over to the Romans to be crucified, had been declared by God to be "both Lord and Messiah" (Acts 2:36, NLT).

- This same message is repeated over and over again by all of Yeshua's emissaries: He is the promised Messiah, the one spoken of by Moses and the prophets.[9] As summed up in Acts 5:42, "And not for a single day, either in the Temple court or in private homes, did they stop teaching and proclaiming the Good News that Yeshua is the Messiah" (CJB).

It is no exaggeration to say that the entire New Testament message is that the Messiah has come to die for the sins of the world, to save his people Israel, and to be a light to the nations. And so, to repeat once more, if he is Israel's Messiah, then he is the Savior of the world. If he is not, he is the Savior of no one. You cannot have it both ways and claim that he's fine for the Gentiles but not for the Jews. That simply is not an option.

Luke records this fascinating account that took place a few weeks after Yeshua was born.

> There was in Yerushalayim a man named Shim'on. This man was a *tzaddik* [righteous man], he was devout, he waited eagerly for God to comfort Isra'el, and the *Ruach HaKodesh* [Holy Spirit] was upon him. It had been revealed to him by the *Ruach HaKodesh* that he would not die before he had seen the Messiah of ADONAI [the Lord]. Prompted by the Spirit, he went into the Temple courts; and when the parents brought in the child Yeshua to do for him what the Torah required, Shim'on took him in his arms, made a *b'rakhah* [blessing] to God, and said, "Now, ADONAI [Lord], according to your word, your servant is at peace as you let him go; for I have seen with my own eyes your *yeshu'ah* [salvation], which you prepared in the presence of all peoples—a light that will bring revelation to the *Goyim* [Gentiles] and glory to your people Isra'el."
>
> —Luke 2:25–32, cjb

Here was an old Jewish man named Simeon (*Shimon* in Hebrew), an extremely righteous man, who had been longing for the Messiah to come, and the Holy Spirit had revealed to him that he would not die before the Messiah was revealed. And then one day, after decades of waiting, he was moved by the Spirit to go the Temple, and it was on that very day that Miriam (Mary) and Joseph came there to offer the sacrifices of purification, according to the Law. This was it! Simeon could now die in peace because he had seen the Messiah with his own eyes—just a tiny baby—and he recognized him as the glory of his people Israel and as the light of the nations.

This is just what Isaiah had prophesied, predicting that the Servant of the Lord, an individual Israelite who fulfilled the destiny of the nation of Israel, would appear to have failed in his mission, saying to himself, "'I have labored to no purpose; I have spent my strength in vain and for nothing. Yet what is due me is in the Lord's hand, and my reward is with my God'" (Isa. 49:4).

This was the Lord's response:

> And now the Lord says—he who formed me in the womb to be his servant to bring Jacob back to him and gather Israel to himself, for I am honored in the eyes of the Lord and my God has been my strength—he says: "It is too small a thing for you to be my servant to restore the tribes of Jacob and bring back those of Israel I have kept. I will also make you a light for the Gentiles, that you may bring my salvation to the ends of the earth."
>
> —Isaiah 49:5–6

The Real Kosher Jesus

Yes, it could appear that Jesus failed in his mission to Israel, as the national leadership rejected him and, over the centuries, the vast majority of his Jewish people did not believe in him. But the prophets declared that this would happen, with the Lord giving this word of assurance: "Not only will you ultimately succeed in your mission to your people Israel, but you also will be a light to the nations, bringing my salvation to the ends of the earth."

Yes, the reason that "Jesus is for the Gentiles" is because "Jesus is for the Jews." The real kosher Jesus is the Messiah of Israel and the Savior of the world. In fact, it is *because* he appeared to fail in his mission to Israel and then became Redeemer of the nations that we can be sure that he *is* the Messiah of the Jewish people. That's exactly the sequence the prophets predicted! As it is written in Psalm 118:22–23, "The stone that the builders rejected has become the chief cornerstone. This is the Lord's doing; it is marvelous in our sight" (njv).

And in one of the most moving passages in the Bible, Isaiah declared what would happen on the day that his people—the Messiah's own people, the Jews—would recognize that when Jesus died, he was not dying for his sins but rather for theirs (Isa. 53:3–6).

Speaking with great clarity about Yeshua's suffering and death, Isaiah said, "He was despised and rejected by men, a man of sorrows, and familiar with suffering. Like one from whom men hide their faces he was despised, and we esteemed him not" (Isa. 53:3). The Messiah was rejected and cast out, but we—the Jewish people—thought nothing of it, not understanding who he was or why he was suffering. "Surely he took up our infirmities and carried our sorrows, yet we considered him stricken by God, smitten by him, and afflicted" (v. 4). We thought that he must have deserved a cruel and miserable death. He must have been a real sinner, guilty of some heinous crime.

And then, something happened. The light went on, and, looking back, we understood what was really taking place. We saw things in a brand-new light! "But he was pierced for our transgressions, he was crushed for our iniquities; the punishment that brought us peace was upon him, and by his wounds we are healed" (v. 5). He wasn't dying for his sins; he was dying for our sins. We were guilty, but he paid the price. Now we see how great was the Messiah's love for us.

"We all, like sheep, have gone astray, each of us has turned to his own way; and the LORD has laid on him the iniquity of us all" (v. 6). We were the guilty sinners, each one of us. We had committed the heinous crimes in God's sight. Yet the Lord laid our punishment on him, and because of his death in our stead, we can now live.

This is why the story of Yeshua is called the "Good News" (Gospel)— the Good News that the Messiah came at the appointed time, dying for our sins, rising from the dead, and ascending to heaven, first rejected by his own nation, then received by the nations of the world, before the day would come when Israel would rediscover their hidden Messiah, just as the prophets declared. And in keeping with the prophetic promises, he will return one day in the clouds of heaven and establish his Messianic kingdom on the earth. On that day the Lord says, "They will neither harm nor destroy on all my holy mountain [meaning, Jerusalem], for the earth will be full of the knowledge of the LORD as the waters cover the sea" (Isa. 11:9).

Jesus, the Messiah of Israel, the Savior of the world. What truly wonderful news!

Appendix A

THE NEW TESTAMENT: AN UNRELIABLE, ANTI-SEMITIC BOOK?

N VOLUME ONE of my series *Answering Jewish Objections to Jesus*, I devoted thirty-one pages to addressing the claim that, "The origins of anti-Semitism can be traced to the pages of the New Testament. From the negative depiction of the Pharisees to the charge of deicide, anti-Semitism is a Christian plague."[1] In my detailed response, which cited many top Jewish and Christian scholars, I emphasized three main points:

1. Anti-Semitism existed in various forms in the ancient world centuries before a single page of the New Testament was written, so there's no truth to the claim that "the origins of anti-Semitism can be traced to the pages of the New Testament." This is hardly in dispute and has been documented by respected scholars like Dr. Peter Schäfer, Professor of Religion and the Ronald O. Perelman Professor of Judaic Studies at Princeton University.[2]

2. The religious conflicts recorded in the Gospels reflect friction between Jewish groups—differences between Jewish followers of Yeshua and other Jews (most prominently Pharisees and Sadducees)—just like the Dead Sea Scrolls reflect legal and religious arguments between different Jewish groups. It is a mistake to read the later history of "Christian" anti-Semitism back into the New Testament.

Many scholars, both Jewish and Christian, have recognized this.[3]

3. As for passages in the New Testament that have helped fuel anti-Semitism in the church, when properly translated and understood, they are not anti-Semitic at all, nor can they be used to justify hatred or persecution of the Jews. That's one of the reasons why Israel's greatest support today comes from Christians who read the New Testament as the literal Word of God. For them, it is the source of philo-Semitism not anti-Semitism.[4] Readers who are looking for an in-depth treatment should study the relevant sections of *Answering Jewish Objections to Jesus*, volume one, where I also deal with the question of anti-Semitism in church history and provide scores of further references.[5]

I'm aware, however, that some of you reading this present book might be wondering, "But doesn't the New Testament portray Jews as children of the devil and Christ-killers?" It will be worthwhile, then, to take a few minutes and address these concerns with honesty and candor.

The New Testament Is a Jewish Book!

Before getting into some of the specific questions, let me first share with you the story of Yechiel Lichtenstein, a nineteenth-century Hungarian rabbi who despised Christianity, believing—to cite his own words—that "Christ himself was the plague and curse of the Jews, the origin and promoter of our sorrows and persecutions." With his own eyes he witnessed so-called Christians committing murderous acts against his people, acts committed in the name of Christ. Yet he also read passionate defenses of the Jewish people by others who called themselves Christians and who utterly renounced anti-Semitism, also in the name of Christ.

This led him to pick up a copy of the New Testament that forty years earlier he had angrily hurled into the corner of his study, where it lay on the ground, covered with dust. He was in for the shock of his life. He wrote:

> I had thought the New Testament to be impure, a source of pride, of selfishness, of hatred, and of the worst kind of violence, but as I opened it I felt myself peculiarly and wonderfully taken possession of. A sudden glory, a light flashed through my soul. I looked for thorns and found roses; I discovered pearls instead of pebbles; instead of hatred love; instead of vengeance forgiveness; instead of bondage freedom; instead of pride humility; conciliation instead of enmity; instead of death life, salvation, resurrection, heavenly treasure.[6]

And what of the *Jewishness* of the New Testament? Listen once more to this rabbi's articulate description:

> From every line in the New Testament, from every word, the Jewish spirit streamed forth light, life, power, endurance, faith, hope, love, charity, limitless and indestructible faith in God, kindness to prodigality, moderation to self-denial, content to the exclusion of all sense of need, consideration for others, with extreme strictness as regards self, all these things were found pervading the book.[7]

It is little wonder that this noble rabbi became an outspoken follower of Yeshua the Messiah, despite persistent persecution inflicted on him by his fellow Jews. It is also no wonder that this rabbi recognized at once just how Jewish the New Testament writings were. As we noted in chapter 2, "What's So New About Jews Reclaiming Jesus?", an increasing number of Jewish scholars are involved in rediscovering the Jewish roots of Jesus and the New Testament, arguing that Yeshua and his followers can be understood properly only when placed in their first-century Jewish context.

Does the New Testament Say That All
Jews Are Children of the Devil?

My debating partner Rabbi Shmuley Boteach writes in *Kosher Jesus*:

> At one point, Jesus goes so far as to call the Jews Satan's spawn: "You belong to your father, the devil, and you want to carry out your father's desires. He was a murderer from the beginning." [John 8:44] Jesus likewise declares that the Jews don't know God: "Then they asked him, 'Where is your father?' 'You do not know me or my Father,' Jesus replied." [John 8:19] Jesus curses the Jews, informing them they are destined to die in sin: "I am going away, and you will look for me, and you will die in your sin. Where I go, you cannot come." [John 8:21]
>
> These verses constitute some of the most poisonous attacks on Jews ever written. They would later be used throughout the centuries to justify the most grisly crimes against the Jews. In one of the great ironies and tragedies of history, the editors of the New Testament took a Jewish sage and lover of his people, put a white hood on his head and a swastika on his arm, and sent him out spewing vitriol against his people. The result was a Jesus so altered that he was no longer recognizable as a prince of peace.[8]

Were the editors of the New Testament guilty as charged? God forbid. In fact, as a devoted Jewish follower of Jesus for the last forty years, and as a careful student of the New Testament, I find Rabbi Shmuley's claim that "the editors of the New Testament took a Jewish sage and lover of his people, put a white hood on his head and a swastika on his arm, and sent him out spewing vitriol against his people" to be downright offensive. It is also highly ironic that my colleague can argue that "The result was a Jesus so altered that he was no longer recognizable as a prince of peace" when a major thesis of his book was that Jesus was *not* the Prince of Peace that Christians believe in but rather a deluded Rabbi Rambo.[9]

What about the charge that professing Christians *misused* certain statements in the New Testament as a justification for the persecution of the Jews? Without a doubt, professing Christians *have* been guilty of this, and I wrote about this tragic history in my 1992 book, *Our Hands Are Stained With Blood*, a book that has never gone out of print and that has been translated into more languages than anything I have written. But I underscore the word *misused*, since it is only by misusing these verses that so-called Christians found an alleged justification for persecuting Jews, just as they misused verses in the Hebrew Scriptures where God called his people Israel stiff-necked, hardhearted, and rebellious.[10] And let's remember that in the very same Gospel of John, where Jesus allegedly said that "all Jews were children of the devil," he taught that "salvation is from the Jews" (John 4:22).

How then should we understand the verses cited by Rabbi Shmuley? First, in context, Yeshua was addressing his fellow Jews who either rejected him as Messiah or who claimed to follow him but were not true disciples. As we saw in chapter 4, "A Threat to the Establishment," the prophets of Israel addressed their contemporaries with much harsher words when they were disobeying the Lord and living in religious hypocrisy. For example, within *the first chapter* of the Book of Isaiah, the prophet called the Jewish leaders in Jerusalem the "rulers of Sodom," while he called his own people the "people of Gomorrah" (Isa. 1:10), describing them as a "sinful nation, a people loaded with guilt, a brood of evildoers, children given to corruption! They have forsaken the LORD," he claimed. "They have spurned the Holy One of Israel and turned their backs on him" (Isa. 1:4). Can you imagine what critics would do if *those* words were in John's Gospel? And Isaiah claimed to be speaking for God himself.

Isaiah also said of his Jewish contemporaries, "They hatch the eggs of vipers and spin a spider's web" (Isa. 59:5), and he called our ancestors "sons of a sorceress...offspring of adulterers and prostitutes...a brood of rebels, the offspring of liars" (Isa. 57:3–4). He even said, "But your iniquities have separated you from your God; your sins have hidden his face from you, so that he will not hear. For your hands are stained with blood, your fingers with guilt. Your lips have spoken lies, and your tongue mutters wicked things" (Isa. 59:2–3). The words of Jesus, cited by Rabbi Shmuley, are quite tame in comparison.

Catholic scholar Urban C. von Wahlde pointed out that the Greek word translated "Jews" in the New Testament sometimes means "Judeans" (meaning, Jews living in a particular area) or "Jewish leaders."[11] He also noted that, "Even the instances with the most hostile connotations are used in a way that is intended to refer to religious authorities rather than the entire nation."[12] He points out that such language was typical of inter-Jewish debates in the first century of this era. In fact, he finds almost identical parallels between the rhetoric in John's Gospel—where Jesus tells the hostile Jewish authorities that they are walking in darkness, are blind, and have the devil as their father (see especially John 8:44)— and the rhetoric of the Dead Sea Scrolls, where rival Jewish groups are characterized as "sons of darkness" and "sons of the pit" who are under the dominion of Satan and do his works![13] In this light he rightly reminds us that "we must learn to listen to [the polemical statements in John] with first-century ears and not with twentieth-century ones."[14]

Professor Craig Evans, a respected New Testament and Aramaic scholar, after comparing the language and tone of the Dead Sea Scrolls with that of the New Testament, offers some food for thought:

> The polemic found in the writings of Qumran surpasses in intensity that of the New Testament. In contrast to Qumran's esoteric and exclusive posture, the early church proclaimed its message and invited all believers to join its fellowship. Never does the New Testament enjoin Christians to curse unbelievers or opponents. Never does the New Testament petition God to damn the enemies of the church. But Qumran did. If this group had survived and had its membership gradually become gentile over the centuries and had its distinctive writings become the group's Bible, I suspect that most of the passages cited above would be viewed as expressions of anti-Semitism. But the group did not survive, nor did it become a gentile religion, and so its criticisms have never been thought of as anti-Semitic. There is no subsequent history of the Qumran community to muddy the waters. We interpret Qumran as we should. We interpret it in

its Jewish context, for it never existed in any other context, and thus no one ever describes its polemic as anti-Semitic.[15]

Evans also makes reference to the writings of the most famous Jewish historian of the first century, Flavius Josephus, noting that "Josephus's polemic against fellow Jews outstrips anything found in the New Testament."[16] So, not only did this great historian slanderously attack Gentiles who had slandered the Jews (calling them "frivolous and utterly senseless specimens of humanity...filled with envy...folly and narrowmindedness"), he also maligned his own people. Speaking of the Zealots he writes: "In rapine and murder you vie with one another...the Temple has become the sink of all, and native hands have polluted these divine precincts." And of the Sicarii he states: They are "imposters and brigands...slaves, the dregs of society, and the bastard scum of the nation." Such quotes could be easily multiplied, yet no one would ever accuse of Josephus of anti-Semitism.

The verdict of the respected Jewish historian Professor Ellis Rivkin put things in their proper perspective:

> As a historian who has spent a lifetime seeking to understand the interaction of the religious realm with the human realm and who has been especially concerned with the how and the why of anti-Semitism, I must conclude that however much the Gospel of John lent itself to anti-Semitic uses in later times, it cannot be considered anti-Semitic within its historical frame unless we are willing to apply the same measure to other intrareligious controversies. Did Josephus deride polytheism because he was anti-Thucydides, or anti-Plato, or ant-Stoic? Or did he mock polytheism because he considered its claims to be patently false? Did Jews and Muslims or Christians and Muslims tangle with each other because the former were anti-Arab or anti-Persian or because the latter espoused what Jews and Christians believed to be false teachings about God and his revelations? It is sad indeed that intrareligious and interreligious controversies mar the history of even the most liberating religions, but there is a difference between interreligious controversy that is sincerely

generated, however unseemly, and the phenonemon of anti-Semitism, which, in my book, is a *deliberate manipulation of sacred texts to cause harm to the Jews so as to solve economic, social, political, and ecclesiastical problems.*[17]

Let's also remember that, according to the New Testament, every human being who is not in right relationship with God (this applies to Gentile and Jew alike), is walking in darkness and, in some real way, under the power of Satan.[18] In short, Jesus did *not* say that all Jews were children of the devil (remember that his only followers were Jews!). Instead, he reaffirmed that God had uniquely chosen the Jewish people to be the bearers of salvation to the world, and it is only by tearing his words out of their historical and cultural context that they can be misconstrued as "anti-Semitic."

There are other verses in the New Testament that critics claim are anti-Semitic, including 1 Thessalonians 2:14–16, written by Paul, and cited by Rabbi Shmuley with the serious charge that, "Paul's words drip with animosity toward Jews."[19] Readers interested in a detailed discussion of these controversial verses can consult volume 1 of *Answering Jewish Objections.*[20]

DOES THE NEW TESTAMENT TEACH THAT "THE JEWS KILLED CHRIST?"

Before Mel Gibson's movie *The Passion of the Christ* was released in 2004, there was great concern in the Jewish community that Jews would again be branded as "Christ-killers," provoking the American equivalent of pogroms, or even worse. Of course, no such thing happened, and regardless of the merits or demerits of the film itself, contemporary American Jews were reminded of something that all true Christians know: Real followers of Jesus do not blame Jews or Romans or anyone else for Yeshua's death on the cross. Rather, they thank God for his sacrificial death and confess that "it was our sins that nailed him to the cross."

In short:

(1) The primary emphasis on the New Testament is that *God sent his Son to die for our sins as an act of love.* As stated in the most famous verse

in the Bible, John 3:16, "For God so loved the world that he gave his one and only Son, that whoever believes in him shall not perish but have eternal life." To repeat: true Christians don't blame certain people for killing Jesus; they thank God for sending him to die in our place.

(2) In keeping with this, the New Testament emphasizes that *no one took Jesus' life from him; he laid it down volitionally, as the Good Shepherd laying down his life for his sheep.* As expressed in 1 John 3:16, "This is how we know what love is: Jesus [the Messiah] laid down his life for us." As Yeshua himself said, "Greater love has no one than this, that he lay down his life for his friends" (John 15:13; see also John 10:11, 17–18).

(3) A central message of the gospel (the good news about the Messiah) is that *Jesus died for our sins,* meaning that, in a sense, all human beings are responsible for his death. As expressed by John Newton, most famous for his hymn "Amazing Grace":

> My conscience felt and owned its guilt,
> And plunged me in despair;
> I saw my sins His blood had spilt
> And helped to nail Him there.

This means, once again, that Christians are profoundly grateful for Jesus' death, not blaming those who participated in his crucifixion but rather recognizing their guilt before a holy God and, consequently, just how incredible his forgiveness is through Jesus. As Paul wrote, "Very rarely will anyone die for a righteous man, though for a good man someone might possibly dare to die. But God demonstrates his own love for us in this: While we were still sinners, Christ died for us" (Rom 5:7–8). Or, in the grateful words of the Messiah's Jewish people after they recognize that he died for their sins, not for his own:

> But he was wounded because of our sins,
> Crushed because of our iniquities.
> He bore the chastisement that made us whole,
> And by his bruises we were healed.
> We all went astray like sheep,
> Each going his own way;

And the LORD visited upon him
The guilt of all of us.

—ISAIAH 53:5–6, NJV

(4) The attitude that Jesus had toward the people who nailed him to the cross—expressed directly toward the Roman soldiers who crucified him—was one of *forgiveness.* As Luke records, Jesus said, "Father, forgive them, for they do not know what they are doing" (Luke 23:34). Following in his footsteps, the Jewish disciple named Stephen, while being stoned to death by his fellow Jews (just as Israel killed some of its prophets in the past; see again chapter 4, "A Threat to the Establishment"), "fell on his knees and cried out, 'Lord, do not hold this sin against them'" (Acts 7:60). So, *even if* the New Testament taught that the Jews killed Christ, the natural reaction for a follower of Jesus would be, "Father, forgive them!"

(5) Immediately after Jesus' death and resurrection, Peter (*Shimon Kefa*), the leader of the core disciples (every one of them Jews), called his fellow Jews to account, in particular the Jewish leadership who had been complicit in his death, saying to them, "God has made this Jesus, whom you crucified, both Lord and [Messiah]" (Acts 2:36); and, "You handed him over to be killed, and you disowned him before Pilate, though he had decided to let him go. You disowned the Holy and Righteous One and asked that a murderer be released to you. You killed the author of life, but God raised him from the dead. We are witnesses of this" (Acts 3:13–15).[21]

But that's not all Peter said. He continued, "Now, brothers, *I know that you acted in ignorance, as did your leaders.* But this is how God fulfilled what he had foretold through all the prophets, saying that his Messiah would suffer. Repent, then, and turn to God, so that your sins may be wiped out, that times of refreshing may come from the Lord" (Acts 3:17–19, emphasis added). And Peter emphasized repeatedly in his preaching that God raised Jesus from the dead—so his death was not the end of the story but the beginning—and that God wanted to bless his people Israel as they turned to him.

It is true that the New Testament authors state that some of the religious leaders conspired against Jesus, turning him over to the Roman authorities, but that should not surprise us in the least, since the people of Israel often rejected the prophetic messengers sent to them, and it was often the religious authorities who led the opposition. (Once more, see chapter 4.) Even radical reconstructionists like Rabbi Shmuley speak of the anti-Jesus attitude of "the Jewish high priest," writing that, "His minions are corrupt priests and other traitors ever on the alert for troublemakers seeking to agitate against their Roman overlords. The chief enforcer of Rome among the Jews, the high priest serves as the emperor's muscle and can scarcely afford a rebellion in Jerusalem for which he will be held accountable."[22] Shmuley even claims—in a statement that could easily be labeled anti-Semitic, since the Sadducees were also Jews who revered the Torah—"the differences between Pharisees and Sadducees seem fairly clear-cut. The Pharisees were loyal to Jewish tradition, the Sadducees loyal to their Roman masters."[23]

When the New Testament writers do speak of Jewish involvement in Yeshua's death, they are quite accurate and careful in their description, saying this in a prayer to God, to whom they ultimately attribute the death of Jesus: "Indeed Herod and Pontius Pilate met together with the Gentiles and the people of Israel in this city to conspire against your holy servant Jesus, whom you anointed. They did what your power and will had decided beforehand should happen" (Acts 4:27–28; these verses also emphasize what is called "corporate solidarity," in which the sins of the leaders are referred to as the sins of Israel).[24]

It is also very important to remember that the same Gospels that hold some of the Jewish leadership responsible for turning Jesus over to the Romans consistently remind us that he was very popular with the Jewish masses. (According to Mark 15:10, even Pilate knew that it was "out of envy that the chief priests had handed Jesus over to him.") Even in Acts—meaning after Yeshua's resurrection—one reason Jesus' followers were persecuted was because the Sadducees were jealous of them, since large crowds were attracted to their message and miracles. (See Acts 5:12–17.)

The bottom line, though, is this, and it cannot be underscored too strongly: when the Jewish people are blamed for the Messiah's death (by their fellow Jews) in the New Testament, they are also told that they acted in ignorance, that God raised Jesus from the dead, that his death provides redemption for Israel and the world, and that God wants to bless them—not curse them!—with complete forgiveness of sins. The message is even called "good news."[25]

It is only apostate, pseudo-Christians who would persecute Jewish people and call them Christ-killers, and the fact that this has happened through the centuries is perhaps the most shameful chapter in the history of the professing church.[26]

Is the New Testament Historically Unreliable?

This is not the place to engage in a detailed defense of the reliability of the New Testament documents, as many learned and brilliant scholars have done through the years, but for those unfamiliar with the subject, let me make four important observations:

1. The New Testament is the best preserved document in the ancient Greco-Roman world, with nothing even remotely close to it.[27] It is also preserved in ancient translations (such as Syriac and Latin) as well as quoted thousands of times in Christian writings of the first several centuries of this era. Again, no other ancient document—historical, philosophical, religious, or poetical—is attested on a scale anywhere near this.[28]

2. Of the many variants that exist in the more than five thousand ancient manuscripts of part or all of the Greek New Testament, the vast majority are extremely minor, affecting virtually nothing of doctrinal or historical significance.[29] And such minor variations are to be expected when there are so many manuscript copies. In fact, although most Jewish readers are probably unaware of this, there are thousands of minor variations in the medieval Masoretic manuscripts of the Hebrew Bible (the standard text of the *Tanakh* is called the Masoretic Text).[30]

3. There are more apparent contradictions in the Hebrew Scriptures than there are in the New Testament, and they are resolved the same way, namely, by giving the authors and editors the benefit of the doubt (meaning that we assume they were not so dumb as to preserve and pass on blatantly contradictory accounts) and by looking for realistic ways to put the accounts together. In fact, it is well known that several eyewitnesses reporting on the same event will often give reports that appear to be contradictory, but upon further investigation, it becomes clear that they were actually giving accurate reports from different vantage points.[31] Critical Jewish readers wanting to attack the reliability of the New Testament documents should remember that, using this same methodology, they can even more readily attack the Hebrew Bible, not to mention the rabbinic writings.[32]

4. Top historians and archeologists have confirmed many of the details of the New Testament, while three recent volumes, covering almost twenty-five hundred closely argued pages between them, have reconfirmed the essential historical reliability of the Gospels.[33] F. F. Bruce, one of the true academic polymaths of the last century, noted that, "The earliest propagators of Christianity welcomed the fullest examination of the credentials of their message. The events which they proclaimed were, as Paul said to King Agrippa, not done in a corner, and were well able to bear all the light that could be thrown on them."[34]

In keeping with this, E. M. Blaiklock, professor of classics, Auckland University, stated, "I claim to be an historian. My approach to Classics is historical. And I tell you that the evidence for the life, the death, and the resurrection of Christ is better authenticated than most of the facts of ancient history."[35] Or, in the words of Bruce, "If the New Testament were a collection of secular writings, their authenticity would generally be regarded as beyond all doubt."[36]

I would encourage each of you to get a copy of the New Testament if you don't already have one as part of your Bible, to read it at face value, asking God to give you insight as you read, to guide you into the truth and to keep you from error, and to ask yourself, "Is this true? And if it is, how should I respond?"

Jesus actually gave this invitation to his Jewish contemporaries, and it has proven to be sound advice for the last two millennia: "If you continue to follow my teaching, you are really my disciples and you will know the truth, and the truth will set you free" (John 8:31–32, NET).

Appendix B

KOSHER JESUS AND "WHY THE JEWS CANNOT ACCEPT JESUS"

ONE OF THE main goals of Rabbi Shmuley's *Kosher Jesus* book was to present a new and different Jesus to the Jewish people, one they could accept, admire, and even revere, an Orthodox Jewish rabbi, a freedom fighter against Rome, and a great religious teacher. At the same time, Rabbi Shmuley argued that Jews cannot accept the Jesus of the New Testament.

Indeed, he makes the very bold claim that, in contrast to the writings of the New Testament, which are received as God's Word by hundreds of millions of Christians worldwide, "My image of Jesus...makes [him] a far more praiseworthy figure."[1] Consequently, my esteemed colleague must argue that the Jesus of the New Testament is not the Jesus of history, claiming that the Jesus he has created—whom I have dubbed Rabbi Rambo—is the real Jesus-Yeshua.

I have addressed his extreme reconstructions of Jesus and the New Testament documents in this book, in particular in chapters 5 and 6. I also addressed his claim that Paul was a Gentile convert to Judaism who broke away from the real Jesus movement and founded a new religion called Christianity. (See especially chapters 7 and 8.) In this appendix I will provide references to rebut the arguments Rabbi Shmuley brings in Part IV of his book, "Why the Jews Cannot Accept Jesus."

Needless to say, the first followers of Jesus were all Jews, and throughout the centuries, there has been a small but steady stream of Jews who have followed him, with approximately two hundred thousand Jewish believers in Yeshua today.[2] It is therefore fair to ask: Why *do* so many Jews accept Jesus as Messiah?

According to Rabbi Shmuley, however, there are a number of reasons that preclude Jews from believing in Jesus as Messiah, in particular as the divine Messiah. Since I have devoted five volumes (more than fifteen hundred pages in total) to addressing these objections (and many more), along with one volume chronicling the tragic story of the professing church and the Jewish people, I will simply reference the relevant sections of these books below.

Although Shmuley states in Part IV of his book that his intention "is not to disparage Christianity but to encourage an understanding of why worship of a man as deity, or belief in a messiah who did not fulfill the messianic prophecies, is anathema to us Jews,"[3] he must realize that if his arguments are true, then "Christianity" is false and no one should follow Jesus. On the other hand, if his arguments are false, then there are actually no good reasons why a Jew should reject Jesus as Messiah.[4]

REFUTING RABBI SHMULEY'S OBJECTIONS TO THE JESUS OF THE NEW TESTAMENT

1. For the objection that Jews cannot believe in the deity of the Messiah or that belief in his deity is incompatible with monotheism,[5] see chapter 9, "The Secret of the Invisible God Who Can Be Seen." More fully, see *Answering Jewish Objections to Jesus, Vol. 2: Theological Objections*, 3.1–3.4 and 3.22.[6]

2. For the objection that the virgin birth is a pagan-based myth without scriptural basis,[7] see *Answering Jewish Objections to Jesus, Vol. 4: New Testament Objections*, 5.9.

3. For the objection that the concept of original sin is unscriptural and unJewish,[8] see *Answering Jewish Objections to Jesus, Vol. 2: Theological Objections*, 3.20.

4. For the objection that the New Testament concepts of salvation, repentance, and blood atonement deviate from the teachings of the *Tanakh*,[9] see *Answering Jewish Objections to Jesus, Vol. 2: Theological Objections*, 3.8–3.18.

5. For the objection that Jesus does not qualify as the Messiah because he is not a descendant of David,[10] see *Answering Jewish Objections to Jesus, Vol. 4: New Testament Objections*, 5.10–5.12.

6. For the objection that Jesus did not fulfill the Messianic prophecies,[11] see *Answering Jewish Objections to Jesus, Vol. 3: Messianic Prophecy Objections* in its entirety.

7. For the objection that the New Testament claims that God's eternal covenant with Israel has been annulled, see *Our Hands Are Stained With Blood*, chapters 12–14 and 16. See also *Answering Jewish Objections to Jesus, Vol. 5: Traditional Jewish Objections* for the question of the Jewish people, the Oral Law, and Jewish tradition.

8. For the objection that "Missionaries often use emotional arguments, guilt trips, and even scare tactics in an effort to persuade Jews to join the ranks of Christianity,"[12] see *Answering Jewish Objections to Jesus, Vol. 1: General and Historical Objections*, 1.10–1.15.

A Closing Word of Affirmation and Hope

To end with disagreement, however, would be unfair to my courageous colleague, and so I celebrate the fact that he calls Christianity "the most successful idea in the history of the world,"[13] that he argues that Jews and Christians "will find more commonality with Jesus' Jewishness than we ever expected,"[14] and that "through a discovery of the Jewish Jesus, we strengthen America's Judeo-Christian values."[15] He even closes his book by hoping that Jews and Christians will "come together to achieve Godly goals and virtuous ends through the personality of Jesus himself, even as we both understand him in completely different ways."[16]

I commend Shmuley for these lofty goals and would like to assure him that he is on the right path, although he still has a way to go, since it is the real Jesus-Yeshua—the Messiah of Israel and the Savior of the world—who is the key to uniting Jews and Gentiles in one spiritual family, so that together we can have a powerful and positive impact on this world. As Yeshua said to a Torah teacher in his day who had answered one of his questions well, I now say to Shmuley, "You are not far from the kingdom of God" (Mark 12:34).

The endorsement that I submitted for the *Kosher Jesus* book contained one final line that was not printed, probably because of space constraints. It read, "May *Kosher Jesus* become a major step towards the worldwide Jewish reclamation of Jesus-Yeshua as one of our own!"

It is my hope and prayer that the publication of *The Real Kosher Jesus* will bring us one step closer to that goal.

NOTES

Introduction—So, When Did Jesus Become Catholic?

1. In case you're curious, my last name, Brown, was shortened from a longer Jewish name when my grandparents came to America from Russia more than one hundred years ago. (This happened to many immigrants when they arrived at Ellis Island to be processed.) No one in our family knows what the original name was, but an ultra-Orthodox rabbi from Brooklyn who sat next me on a flight from Amsterdam told me that there were many Browns on his very Jewish block.
2. Shmuley Boteach, *Kosher Jesus* (Springfield, NJ: Gefen Books, 2012), ix, www.gefenpublishing.com.
3. Ibid.
4. Ibid., x.
5. Ibid.
6. Ibid., xvii.

1—"May His Name and Memory Be Blotted Out!"

1. History.com, "Nov 9, 1938: 'The Night of the Broken Glass,'" This Day in History, http://www.history.com/this-day-in-history/the-night-of-broken-glass (accessed February 20, 2012).
2. Daniel Jonah Goldhagen, *Hitler's Willing Executioners* (New York: Vintage Books, 1997), 111.
3. Jim Walker, "Martin Luther's Dirty Little Book: On the Jews and Their Lies," http://www.nobeliefs.com/luther.htm (accessed February 20, 2012).
4. Martin Luther, *That Jesus Christ Was Born a Jew* (1523), as excerpted at Council of Centers on Jewish-Christian Relations, http://www.ccjr.us/dialogika-resources/primary-texts-from-the-history-of-the-relationship/272-luther-1523 (accessed February 20, 2012). Other translations are available online.
5. From Luther's *Of the Ineffable Name and the Generations of Christ* [Vom Schem Hamphoras und vom Geschlecht Christi], published in 1543. For the first part of the quote, see David M. Whitford, *Luther: A Guide for the Perplexed* (London: T & T Clark, 2011), 161, note 37; for the second part of the quote, see conveniently http://strateias.org/luther.htm. Perhaps the most quoted lines from the book are, "Here in Wittenberg, in our parish church, there is a sow carved into the stone under which lie young pigs and Jews who are sucking; behind the sow stands a rabbi who is lifting up the right leg of the sow, raises behind the sow, bows down and looks with great effort into the Talmud under the sow, as if he wanted to read and see something most difficult and exceptional; no doubt they

gained their Shem Hamphoras [ineffable name, referring to the unpronounceable, sacred name of the Lord] from that place." This quote can be accessed widely online.

6. Cited in Michael Brown, *Our Hands Are Stained With Blood* (Shippensburg, PA: Destiny Image, 1992), 192. This quote is readily available online.

7. Ibid., 52. This quote is readily available online.

8. Martin Luther, *On the Jews and Their Lies* (1543), Martin H. Bertram, trans. (n.p.: Fortress Press and Augsburg Press, 1971), http://www .humanitas-international.org/showcase/chronography/documents/luther -jews.htm (accessed February 20, 2012). While the text I have used can be followed here, there are numerous editions of this book in English, with many variations, none of which affect the overall counsel given by Luther. The German original was entitled *Von den Jüden und jren Lügen*. In the pre-Internet days, the only place I could find Luther's volume in English was in a neo-Nazi catalog!

9. Lutherans had either ignored or repudiated these writings for centuries, memorializing instead his 1523 pro-Jewish booklet. For details, see Michael L. Brown, *Answering Jewish Objections to Jesus, Vol. 1: General and Historical Objections* (Grand Rapids, MI: Baker, 2000), 133–135.

10. I have personally discussed this with church history professors and students at seminaries where I have taught. For an attempt to explain (but not excuse) Luther's anti-Jewish writings, see Eric W. Gritsch, "Was Luther Anti-Semitic?", *Christianity Today*, July 1, 1993, http://www .ctlibrary.com/ch/1993/issue39/3938.html (accessed February 23, 2012).

11. Edward H. Flannery, *The Anguish of the Jews* (Mahweh, NJ: Paulist Press, 2004), 1.

12. Raul Hilberg, *The Destruction of the European Jews*, 3rd ed. (New Haven, CT: Yale University Press, 2003), three volumes.

13. Dennis Prager and Joseph Telushkin, *Why the Jews? The Reason for Antisemitism* (New York: Simon & Schuster, 1983), 104.

14. Hilberg, *The Destruction of the European Jews*, 7–8.

15. Benjamin Shlomo Hamburger, *False Messiahs and Their Opposers* [in Hebrew] (B'nai Brak, Israel: Mechon Moreshet Ashkenaz, 1989), 19. The quotation at the end of the paragraph is from Rav Shimon Walbah, an Israeli Orthodox rabbi (my translation).

16. According to Herbert W. Basser, "*Avon Gilyon* (*Document of Sin*, b. Shabb. 116a) or *Euvanggeleon* (*Good News*)," 93, in Zev Garber, ed., *The Jewish Jesus: Revelation, Reflection, Reclamation* (West Lafayette, IN: Purdue University Press, 2011), "Although there were exceptions, the vast majority of Jews could not and many still cannot utter his name at all. Even when circumlocutions were used...they were generally followed by an

imprecation. While Maimonides did not detest Christianity as much as he abhorred Islam, still he could not mention the name of Jesus without cursing that his bones should rot" (with reference to Maimonides' *Epistle to Yemen*).

17. In John's Gospel, references to Yeshua being called "rabbi" precede those of Yochanan (John) being called by that title (see John 1:38, 49; 3:2, 26), but since John's ministry introduced that of Jesus, it is probably that he received that honorific title a few months earlier. For usage of the term "rabbi" in the first century, see chapter 3.

18. For the Israelites depicted as scattered sheep in the Tanakh, see, e.g., Jeremiah 23:1–5; Ezekiel 34:1–16; Zechariah 10:2–3.

19. The Samaritans considered themselves to be the true Israelites, uniquely faithful to the Torah; they were often viewed as half-breeds in rabbinic literature. See "Samaritanism," in John J. Collins and Daniel C. Harlow, eds., *The Eerdmans Dictionary of Early Judaism* (Grand Rapids, MI: Eerdmans, 2011), 1186–1188.

20. For a book-length reflection on this theme by a Hebrew-Catholic author, see Roy H. Schoeman, *Salvation Is From the Jews* (San Francisco: Ignatius Press, 2003).

21. For shocking examples, see Brown, *Our Hands Are Stained With Blood*, 95–97, excerpted from James Parkes, *The Conflict of the Church and the Synagogue* (New York: Atheneum, 1969), 394–399.

22. For discussion of Paul's quotation sources from the Hebrew text of the Tanakh, see Michael L. Brown, *Answering Jewish Objections to Jesus, Vol. 4: New Testament Objections* (Grand Rapids, MI: Baker, 2010), 16–17.

23. See John G. Gager, "Did Jewish Christians See the Rise of Islam," in Adam H. Becker and Annette Yoshiko Reed, eds., *The Ways That Never Parted: Jews and Christians in Late Antiquity and the Early Middle Ages* (Minneapolis: Fortress Press, 2007), 361–372. A number of other articles in this volume are quite relevant. See also Matt Jackson-McCabe, ed., *Jewish Christianity Reconsidered: Rethinking Ancient Groups and Texts* (Minneapolis: Fortress Press, 2007). For the most comprehensive study to date on Jewish believers in church history (part of a planned multi-volume series), see Oskar Skarsaune and Reidar Hvalvik, *Jewish Believers in Jesus: The Early Centuries* (Peabody, MA: Hendrickson Publishers, 2007).

24. In his extraordinary book *The Righteous: The Unsung Heroes of the Holocaust* (New York: Henry Holt and Company, 2003), xvi, the acclaimed Jewish historian Martin Gilbert observed, "Were a single page devoted to each person already recognized as Righteous, it would take fifty books the size of this one to tell all their stories."

25. Actually, as I have traveled to many nations and spoken on the subject of "Christian anti-Semitism," I began to realize that, to a great extent, it was an Anglo-Christian phenomenon and that believers in Asia and Africa and other continents are completely unaware of the phenomenon. A case in point was the Chinese translator of *Our Hands Are Stained With Blood*, who wrote to me amidst "wails" and "weeping" as he worked on the translation. Jewish readers might also be interested to know that the vast majority of American evangelical Christians to whom I brought this message have also been utterly shocked to hear it, so foreign is the concept of "Christian anti-Semitism" to them. Of related but indirect interest, see Philip Jenkins, *The Lost History of Christianity: The Thousand-Year Golden Age of the Church in the Middle East, Africa, and Asia—and How It Died* (New York: Harper One, 2008).

2—WHAT'S SO NEW ABOUT JEWS RECLAIMING JESUS?

1. With the exception of just a few titles, all of these books are in my personal library. This list of books cited is meant to be representative rather than comprehensive.

2. For a reliable analysis of the evidence, see Peter Schäfer, *Jesus in the Talmud* (Princeton, NJ: Princeton University Press, 2007).

3. Matthew Hoffman, *From Rebel to Rabbi: Reclaiming Jesus and the Making of Modern Jewish Culture* (Stanford, CA: Stanford University Press, 2007), 1.

4. Donald Hagner, *The Jewish Reclamation of Jesus: An Analysis and Critique of Modern Jewish Study of Jesus* (Grand Rapids, MI: Zondervan Academic Books, 1984).

5. John T. Pawlikowski, "Modern Jewish Views of Jesus," Jewish-Christian Relations, January 2, 2008, http://www.jcrelations.net/Modern+Jewish+Views+of+Jesus.3195.0.html?L=3 (accessed February 21, 2012).

6. Zev Garber, ed., *The Jewish Jesus: Revelation, Reflection, Reclamation* (West Lafayette, IN: Purdue University Press, 2011).

7. Ibid., 358–382.

8. Joseph Klausner, *Jesus of Nazareth: His Life, Times, and Teaching* (repr.; New York: Bloch Publishing, 1997), back cover. In 1925, just three years after Klausner's volume came out, Harry A. Wolfson wrote an article entitled "How the Jews Will Reclaim Jesus," but it is primarily known through its publication in the *Menorah Journal* (1962), 25–31.

9. Ibid., 363, 368, 374, 413, cited in this order at Good News for Israel, http://www.gnfi.org/important.php (accessed February 21, 2012). Note that even in 1922 Klausner could discuss other important books about Jesus penned by Jewish scholars.

10. Bloch also published the follow-up volume by Joseph Klausner, *From Jesus to Paul* (repr., New York: Bloch Publishing, 1978).

11. David Flusser, *Judaism and the Origins of Christianity* (Jerusalem: Magnes Press, 1988).

12. David Flusser, *The Sage From Galilee: Rediscovering Jesus' Genius* (Grand Rapids, MI: William B. Eerdsman Publishing, 2007). One of Flusser's Christian students was Hebrew scholar Brad H. Young, a professor at Oral Roberts University. Among his major works are *Jesus the Jewish Theologian* (Peabody, MA: Hendrickson, 1995) and *Meet the Rabbis: Rabbinic Thought and the Teachings of Jesus* (Peabody, MA: Hendrickson, 2007). For Young's work on the parables of Jesus in light of rabbinic literature, see chapter 3.

13. Yehezkel Kaufmann, *Christianity and Judaism: Two Covenants*, English trans., C. W. Efroymson (Jerusalem: Magnes Press, 1988), 49.

14. Ibid., 60.

15. Ben Zion Bokser, *Judaism and the Christian Predicament* (New York: Alfred A. Knopf, 1967), 207, cited in Trude Weiss-Rosmarin, ed., *Jewish Expressions of Jesus: An Anthology* (New York: Ktav Publishing House, 1977), 227. The anthology contains excerpts from the writings of Bokser, Haim Cohon, Jules Isaac, Walter Kaufmann, Joseph Klausner, Jacob Z. Lauterbach, Franz Rosenweig, Samuel Sandmel, Hans Joachim Schoeps, Abba Hillel Silver, and Solomon Zeitlin.

16. Published by Fortress Press, Minneapolis, MN, with the exception of *The Changing Faces of Jesus* and *The Authentic Gospel of Jesus*, both published by Penguin, New York. In *Jesus and the World of Judaism*, 87–88, Vermes called for a comprehensive "religious history of the Jews from the Maccabess to AD 500 that fully incorporates the New Testament data." In 2003 Fortress Press issued a new edition of *Jesus and the World of Judaism* under the title *Jesus in His Jewish Context*.

17. Published by Penguin, New York.

18. Geza Vermes, *The Authentic Gospel of Jesus* (New York: Penguin, 2003), vii.

19. Hyam Maccoby, *Jesus the Pharisee* (n.p.: SCM Press, 2003). See *Kosher Jesus*, xi. For my sharp critiques of Maccoby's relevant volumes, see chapters 5 and 7.

20. Harvey Falk, *Jesus the Pharisee: A New Look at the Jewishness of Jesus* (n.p.: 1985). For a review of Falk's volume, see Richard N. Ostling, "What Sort of Jew Was Jesus?," *Time*, April 12, 2005, http://www.time.com/time/magazine/article/0,9171,1048374-1,00.html (accessed February 21, 2012).

21. "Rabbi Jacob Emden's Views on Christianity and the Noahide Commandments," *Journal of Ecumenical Studies* 19, no. 1 (Winter 1982), cited in

Falk, *Jesus the Pharisee*, 14–18, and as viewed at Auburn.edu, http://www .auburn.edu/~allenkc/falk1a.html (accessed February 21, 2012).

22. Ibid., cited in Falk, *Jesus the Pharisee*, 21.

23. Cited in Fred MacDowell, "On the Original 'Kosher Jesus' by R. Chaim Volozhiner's Grandson, Universalist Dreamer," (blog), January 19, 2012, http://onthemainline.blogspot.com/2012/01/on-original-kosher-jesus-by-r-chaim.html (accessed February 21, 2012). Also referenced in Marc B. Shapiro, "Thoughts on Confrontation and Sundry Matters, Part 1," *Seforim Blog* (blog), January 25, 2009, http://seforim.blogspot.com/ 2009/09/thoughts-on-confrontation-sundry.html (accessed February 21, 2012).

24. Cf. Abraham Geiger, *Judaism and Its History in Two Parts*, Eng. trans., Charles Newburgh (New York: Bloch, 1911), 130–136, for a representative statement; reprinted in Gregory A. Barker and Stephen E. Gregg, eds., *Jesus Beyond Christianity: The Classic Texts* (Oxford: Oxford University Press, 2010), 38–43; see further Susannah Heschel, *Abraham Geiger and the Jewish Jesus* (Chicago: University of Chicago Press, 1998).

25. Sholem Asch, *The Nazarene*, Eng. trans., Maurice Samuel (repr.; New York: Carroll and Graf Publishers, Inc., 1984).

26. Gerald Friedlander, *The Jewish Sources of the Sermon on the Mount* (New York: Bloch, 1911).

27. Claude G. Montefiore, *The Synoptic Gospels, Edited With an Introduction and a Commentary*, second edition (London: Macmillan and Co., 1927).

28. Hyman Gerson Enelow, *A Jewish View of Jesus* (New York: Bloch Publishing Co., 1931).

29. Thomas T. Walker, *Jewish Views of Jesus; An Introduction and an Appreciation* (repr.; New York: Arno Press, 1973).

30. Samuel Sandmel, *A Jewish Understanding of the New Testament*, 3rd ed. (Woodstock, VT: Skylight Publishing, 2005). David Daube, *The New Testament and Rabbinic Judaism* (repr.; New York: Arno Press, 1973).

31. Schalom Ben-Chorin, *Brother Jesus: The Nazarene Through Jewish Eyes*, Eng. trans. Jared S. Klein and Max Reinhart (Athens, GA: University of Georgia Press, 2001).

32. Pinchas Lapide, *The Resurrection of Jesus* (Minneapolis: Augsburg, 1983), 13.

33. Ibid., 15.

34. Irving M. Zeitlin, *Jesus and the Judaism of His Time* (Cambridge, England: Polity Press, 1991).

35. Paula Fredriksen, *Jesus of Nazareth, King of the Jews: A Jewish Life and the Emergence of Christianity* (New York: Knopf, 1999). Fredriksen also wrote *From Jesus to Christ: The Origins of the New Testament Images of Christ*, 2nd ed. (New Haven, CT: Yale University Press, 2000).

36. Robert Kupor, *Jesus the Misunderstood Jew: What the New Testament Really Says About the Man From Nazareth* (New York: iUniverse, Inc., 2007).

37. Amy-Jill Levine, *The Misunderstood Jew: The Church and the Scandal of the Jewish Jesus* (New York: HarperOne, 2007). Levine's book is the more scholarly and better known of the two.

38. Hershel Shanks, ed., *Christianity and Rabbinic Judaism: A Parallel History of Their Origins and Early Development* (Washington DC: Biblical Archeology Society, 1992).

39. Arthur Zannoni, ed., *Jews and Christians Speak of Jesus* (Minneapolis, MN: Augsburg Fortress, 1994).

40. Beatrice Bruteau, ed., *Jesus Through Jewish Eyes: Rabbis and Scholars Engage an Ancient Brother in a New Conversation* (Maryknoll, NY: Orbis Books, 2001).

41. See, e.g., Jacob Neusner and Bruce Chilton, *Judaism in the New Testament: Practices and Beliefs* (New York: Routledge, 1995). Neusner, perhaps the most prolific author in Jewish history with roughly 1,000 books written or edited, also wrote *A Rabbi Talks With Jesus* (New York: Doubleday, 1993).

42. Michael L. Brown, "Messianic Judaism and Jewish Jesus Research," *Mishkan* 33 (2000): 36–48.

43. J. H. Charlesworth and Loren L. Johns, eds., *Hillel and Jesus: Comparative Studies of Two Major Religious Leaders* (Minneapolis, MN: Fortress, 1997).

44. Lawrence H. Schiffman, "The Jewishness of Jesus: Commandments Concerning Interpersonal Relations," in Zannoni, ed., *Jews and Christians Speak of Jesus*, 37–53.

45. Zeitlin, *Jesus and the Judaism of His Time*.

46. Philip Sigal, *The Halakah of Jesus of Nazareth According to the Gospel of Matthew* (Lanham, MD: Univ. Press of America, 1986). Unique to Sigal's approach is the fact that he accepts Matthew's picture of the Pharisees but distances them from the "proto-rabbis." In other words, these *perushim* are not the Tannaitic forerunners of the prominent Talmudic leaders.

47. For the key works of Flusser, see above; for an introduction to the work of Shmuel Safrai, see his articles in idem, ed., *The Literature of the Sages: Oral Law, Halakha, Mishna, Tosefta, Talmud, External Tractates* (Philadelphia: Fortress, 1987), 35–210. For a representative application of their methodology, cf. Young, *Jesus the Jewish Theologian*.

48. Samuel Tobias Lachs, *A Rabbinic Commentary on the New Testament: The Gospels of Matthew, Mark and Luke* (Hoboken, NJ: Ktav Pub. Inc., 1987).

49. Dan Cohn-Sherbok, *Rabbinic Perspectives on the New Testament* (n.p.: Edwin Mellen Press, 1990).

50. Michael Cook, *Modern Jews Engage the New Testament: Enhancing Jewish Well-Being in a Christian Environment* (Woodstock, VT: Jewish Light Publishing, 2008).

51. Amy-Jill Levine and Marc Z. Brettler, eds., *The Jewish Annotated New Testament* (New York: Oxford University Press, 2011). In an interview in the *Forward*, Levine stated, "The more I study the New Testament, the better a Jew I become. The New Testament informs me about Jewish history; in studying the New Testament in relation to other Jewish sources of the period—Dead Sea Scrolls, Josephus and Philo, early rabbinic literature, the Targumim, synagogue inscriptions, etc.—I can see the vibrancy of the Jewish tradition. And while I do not worship Jesus as lord and savior, I find his parables compelling stories and his ethical teachings often inspirational. I do not think one needs to worship the messenger in order to appreciate much of his (very Jewish) message of the Kingdom of Heaven." In the same interview Brettler said, "As a scholar of the Hebrew Bible, I am very partial to Matthew, since it is so infused with quotations from the Hebrew Bible and uses Hebrew Bible verses in the same way that some Dead Sea Scrolls and rabbinic texts do. It thus feels especially Jewish to me. I have also grown to like 1 Corinthians more. I find it elegant, and its poem beginning at 13:4, 'Love is patient, love is kind,' is sublime." [Jay Michaelson, "Jewish Roots of the New Testament," *Jewish Daily Forward*, February 12, 2012, http://www.forward.com/articles/151032/#ixzz1mEzPfec2 (accessed February 23, 2012).]

52. Daniel Boyarin, *The Jewish Gospels: The Story of the Jewish Christ* (New York: The New Press, 2012). An advanced excerpt of the book states, "Jesus, when he came, came in a form that many Jews were expecting, a second divine figure incarnated in a human. The argument was not: Is a divine Messiah coming, but only: Is this carpenter from Nazareth the One we are expecting? Some Jews said yes and some—not surprisingly—said no. We, today, call the first group Christians and the second group Jews, but it was not like that then, not at all."

53. James H. Charlesworth, *Jesus Within Judaism* (New York: Doubleday, 1988).

54. Bruce Chilton, *Rabbi Jesus: An Intimate Biography* (New York: Doubleday, 2000).

55. Ann Spangler and Lois Tverberg, *Sitting at the Feet of Rabbi Jesus: How the Jewishness of Jesus Can Transform Your Faith* (Grand Rapids, MI: Zondervan, 2009).

56. John P. Meier, *A Marginal Jew: Rethinking the Historical Jesus*, multi-volume (New Haven, CT: Yale University Press).

57. For an excellent sampling, see Barker and Gregg, *Jesus Beyond Christianity*.
58. This is commonly claimed among Jews reclaiming Jesus.
59. Zeitlin, *Jesus and the Judaism of His Time*, 47, building on Max Weber's term "religious virtuoso."
60. Boteach, *Kosher Jesus*, 106.
61. Vermes, *The Authentic Gospel of Jesus*, vii.
62. Albert Einstein, cited in George Sylvester Viereck, "What Life Means to Einstein," *The Saturday Evening Post*, October 26, 1929, http://www .saturdayeveningpost.com/wp-content/uploads/satevepost/what_life_ means_to_einstein.pdf (accessed February 21, 2012).
63. Daniel Matt, in Bruteau, ed., *Jesus Through Jewish Eyes*, 74–80.
64. Boteach, *Kosher Jesus*, xviii.
65. William E. Phipps, *The Wisdom and Wit of Rabbi Jesus* (Louisville, KY: Westminster/John Knox, 1993), 8–30. He understands Jesus' conflicts with some of the religious leaders in this context, as do others. See chapter 4.
66. Lewis D. Solomon, in Bruteau, ed., *Jesus Through Jewish Eyes*, 161.
67. Lance Flitter, in Bruteau, ed., *Jesus Through Jewish Eyes*, 128. He (along with others), places some of Jesus' conflicts with the legal traditions of his day in the context of him being a religious reformer. See chapters 3 and 4.
68. Stephen Wise, cited in John Fischer, "Jesus Through Jewish Eyes," Menorah Ministries, http://menorahministries.com/Scriptorium/Jesus-ThruJewishEyes.htm (accessed February 21, 2012).
69. Dan Cohn-Sherbok, in Barker and Gregg, *Jesus Beyond Christianity*, 72 (the entire quote is, "Like the prophets of the Hebrew Bible, Jesus can be seen as the conscience of Israel").
70. Cited in Jakob Jocz, *The Jewish People and Jesus Christ* (London: SPCK, 1962), referenced in John Fischer, "Jesus Through Jewish Eyes."
71. Viereck, "What Life Means to Einstein."
72. Ibid. His full response to whether he accepted the historical existence of Jesus was, "Unquestionably. No one can read the Gospels without feeling the actual presence of Jesus. His personality pulsates in every word. No myth is filled with such life. How different, for instance, is the impression which we receive from an account of legendary heroes of antiquity like Theseus. Theseus and other heroes of his type lack the authentic vitality of Jesus."
73. Martin Buber, *Two Types of Faith* (New York: Harper, 1961), 12–13, cited also by Fischer, "Jesus Through Jewish Eyes."
74. Martin Buber, "Three Talks on Judaism," translated by Paul Levertoff in "Jewish Opinions About Jesus" *Der Weg* 7, no. 1 (January–February,

1933), 8. Buber's words have become famous in Messianic Jewish circles and are frequently cited on their websites.

3—A Rabbi Like No Other

1. Julius Wellhausen, *Einleitung in die drei ersten Evangelien* (Berlin: n.p., 1905), 113. This is the standard translation of his original German that occurs in many different English sources.
2. Cited in Jonathan Bernis, *A Rabbi Looks at Jesus of Nazareth* (Bloomington, MN: Chosen, 2011), 34; Bernis is a Messianic Jewish leader, not a traditional Jewish rabbi.
3. For Yeshua wearing the fringes (or tassels) on the four corners of his outer garment, as required by the Torah (see Numbers 15:38-39; Deuteronomy 22:12; cf. also Zechariah 8:23), see Matthew 9:20; 14:36 as translated in versions such as the CJB and ESV, among other translations. Translating the Greek word *kraspedon* as "hem" (as in, e.g., KJV and NIV), is not as accurate. For a full explanation, see Michael L. Brown, *60 Questions Christians Ask About Jewish Beliefs and Practices* (Bloomington, MN: Chosen, 2011), 88–92.
4. Defined by Dictionary.com as "a mixture of chopped nuts and apples, wine, and spices that is eaten at the Seder meal on Passover: traditionally regarded as symbolic of the mortar used by Israelite slaves in Egypt."
5. Klausner, *Jesus of Nazareth*, 364. According to Klausner (page 414), "Jesus was not a Christian, but he *became* a Christian," his emphasis.
6. Based on the word *christos*, the Greek equivalent of the Hebrew for "Messiah." One could say that the first believers (including Jews and Gentiles in Antioch; Acts 11:26) were called "Messianics," except that would imply that those who coined the term understood "Christ" to mean "Messiah," which seems not to be the case. In fact, it appears that "Christ" (*christos* in Greek) was mistaken for *chrestos* or the like, thought either to be a proper name or else related to the Greek word for "useful." Either way, it would have had no meaning to outsiders unfamiliar with the concept of "Messiah"; what stood out was that these people were devoted to someone named "Christ," hence they were "Christians." See further Darrell L. Bock, *Acts*, Baker Exegetical Commentary on the New Testament (Grand Rapids, MI: Baker Academic, 2007), 416.
7. Formal rabbinic ordination didn't begin until more than one generation after Yeshua's death. See further H. Shanks, "Is the Title 'Rabbi' Anachronistic in the Gospels?" *Jewish Quarterly Review* 53 (1962–63): 337–345.
8. John is considered by critics to be a strongly "Christianized" version of the Jesus story of the New Testament, yet Jesus is called Rabbi in John.
9. For "rabbi," see Matthew 26:25, 49; Mark 9:5; 10:51; 11:21; 14:45; John 1:38, 49; 3:2; 4:31; 6:25; 9:2; 11:8.

10. Boteach, *Kosher Jesus*, x. Note, however, that there are some anachronistic statements in Shmuley's description, such as that Jesus "wore a head covering," since that was hardly customary at that time, and, to be sure, kosher laws in Jesus' day were nowhere as developed as they became over the centuries, just to give two examples.

11. See, e.g., Matthew 4:19; 8:22; 9:9; 10:38; 16:24; 19:21. And cf. Lachs, *Rabbinic Commentary on the New Testament*, 66.

12. David H. Stern, *Jewish New Testament Commentary* (n.p.: Messianic Jewish Resources International, 1992), 23, s.v. "Matt. 5:1."

13. See, e.g., Gerald Friedlander, *The Jewish Sources of the Sermon on the Mount*, and notice the detailed discussion in Montefiore, *Synoptic Gospels*, to Matthew 5–7; more recently, see Herbert Basser, *The Mind Behind the Gospels: A Commentary on Matthew 1–14* (Boston: Academic Studies Press, 2009), 110–206; see also the substantial discussion of potential rabbinic background in Robert A. Guelich, *The Sermon on the Mount: A Foundation for Understanding* (Waco, TX: The W Publishing Group, 1982); in brief, see Boteach, *Kosher Jesus*, 106–107, for a sampling of parallels only from the Tanakh. For a concise Messianic Jewish approach, see Stern, *Jewish New Testament Commentary*, 23–34.

14. Vermes, *The Authentic Gospel of Jesus*, 173–174.

15. Brad H. Young, *Jesus and His Jewish Parables: Rediscovering the Roots of Jesus' Teaching* (New York/Mahwah: Paulist Press, 1989); see also R. Steven Notley and Ze'ev Safrai, *Parables of the Sages: Jewish Wisdom From Jesus to Rav Ashi* (Jerusalem: Carta, 2011).

16. Klausner, *Jesus of Nazareth*, 414; see also Vermes, *The Authentic Gospel of Jesus*, 114–172.

17. The preceding verses are also relevant: "The kingdom of heaven is like a mustard seed, which a man took and planted in his field. Though it is the smallest of all your seeds, yet when it grows, it is the largest of garden plants and becomes a tree, so that the birds of the air come and perch in its branches" (Matt 13:31–32). As explained in the *New Bible Commentary*, "Both the mustard seed and the yeast are parables of small beginnings. *Mustard seed* was proverbial for something minute (*cf.* 17:20), yet the full-grown plant could grow to 3 m. A handful of *yeast* eventually permeates *a large amount of flour* (lit. 'three measures', enough to make bread for 100 people!). So God's work, the *kingdom of heaven*, may appear unimpressive at first, but appearances can be deceptive, and no-one will be able to ignore it in the end. In the meantime the disciples must be patient. Human valuation misses the point; little becomes great when God is at work." [D. A. Carson, ed., *New Bible Commentary: 21st Century Edition* (4th ed.; Downers Grove, IL: InterVarsity Press, 1994).]

18. See, e.g., Matthew 25:31–46; Luke 14:12–14.

19. As noted by Craig S. Keener, *The IVP Bible Background Commentary: New Testament* (Downers Grove, IL: InterVarsity Press, 1993), to Luke 10:29, "Jewish teachers usually used 'neighbor' to mean 'fellow Israelite.' Leviticus 19:18 clearly means 'fellow Israelite' in the immediate context, but the less immediate context applies the principle also to any non-Israelite in the land (19:34)." According to John Nolland, *Luke 9:21– 18:34* (Word Biblical Commentary; Dallas: Word, 2002), 584, "There are more generous sentiments in some Jewish texts (e.g., *Ep. Arist.* 228; *T. Zeb* 5:1), but more typically the sense of group loyalty and loyalty to God found expression in firm boundaries for the reach of neighbor-love (the Qumran covenanters were to 'love the sons of light...and hate all the sons of darkness' [1QS 1:9–10; cf. 2:24; 5:25; 1QM 1:1]....Jesus' practice and teaching supported a total abolition of boundaries to love of neighbor." See also ibid., 592: "On the question of the scope of neighbor love, see at v 27. The question assumes a restricted scope for neighbor love (cf. Sir 12:1–4: 'If you do good, know to whom you do it ... and do not help the sinner')."

20. M. Gittin 9:10; see also b. Gittin 90a; m. Ketubot 7:6; m. Nedarim 11:12; b. Sanhedrin 22a.

21. Jacob Neusner, *The Mishnah: A New Translation* (New Haven: Yale University Press, 1988), 487, his emphasis. I have removed the highly useful outline format of Neusner's rendering in this instance, lest the uninitiated reader think it was part of the original text. When citing him again, below, I used his original formatting.

22. They have been preserved for us in Greek, which, at that time, was the most widely used language in the world, although it is possible that some parts of the New Testament were originally composed in Hebrew or Aramaic. For discussion and analysis, see Michael L. Brown, "Recovering the Inspired Text? An Assessment of the Work of the Jerusalem School in the Light of *Understanding the Difficult Words of Jesus*," *Mishkan* 17/18 (1992): 38–64; idem, "The Issue of the Inspired Text: A Rejoinder to David Bivin," *Mishkan* 20 (1994), 53–63, where I also cite relevant studies seeking to reconstruct the purported Hebrew or Aramaic original.

23. There are scores of books addressing the identities and distinctives of these various Jewish groups; for a representative sampling of current scholarly views, see *The Eerdmans Dictionary of Early Judaism*. For in-depth treatment by a variety of leading scholars, see Jacob Neusner, Alan Avery-Peck, and Bruce Chilton, eds., *Judaism in Late Antiquity*, three vols. (Leiden and Boston: Brill Academic Publishers, 2001).

24. Boteach, *Kosher Jesus*, 110.

25. See Klausner, *Jesus of Nazareth*; although Abraham Geiger suggested that Jesus was a Pharisee one century ago (see chapter 2), that was certainly

the minority view among Jewish scholars at the time, and it can hardly be called the dominant view today. Suffice it to say that the statement "Jesus was a Pharisee" is fraught with controversy, including the question of identifying exactly what it meant to be a Pharisee at that time. That being said, there are many Messianic Jews who do believe that Yeshua was a Pharisee and have no problem with that concept. See John Fischer, "Jesus Through Jewish Eyes."

26. Flusser, *The Sage From Galilee*, 99–100.
27. Fischer, "Jesus Through Jewish Eyes." For another perspective, cf. Arnold G. Fruchtenbaum, *Jesus Was a Jew* (San Antonio: Ariel Ministries, 2010). Fruchtenbaum is another respected Messianic Jewish scholar.
28. See note 23 above.
29. See, e.g., Luke 8:1–3; cf. further Ben Witherington III, *Women in the Ministry of Jesus: A Study of Jesus' Attitudes to Women and Their Roles as Reflected in His Earthly Life*, Society for New Testament Studies Monograph Series (New York: Cambridge University Press, 1984).
30. Scholars actually call this "the criterion of embarrassment," meaning, accounts or sayings that have been preserved by the biblical authors that are likely to be true since it would be highly unlikely that they would create such accounts or saying when they could prove embarrassing to their leaders and heroes. For a popular and practical presentation of this, see Norman L. Geisler and Frank Turek, *I Don't Have Enough Faith to Be an Atheist* (Wheaton: Crossway Books, 2004), 275–298.
31. See Rodney Stark, *The Rise of Christianity: How the Obscure, Marginal, Jesus Movement Became the Dominant Religious Force* (New York: Harper Collins, 1997). He writes that "the more favorable Christian view of women is also demonstrated in their condemnation of divorce, incest, marital infidelity, and polygamy.... Like pagans, early Christians prized female chastity, but unlike pagans they rejected the double standard that gave pagan men so much sexual license.... Should they be widowed, Christian women also enjoyed very substantial advantages" (104). He adds, "Close examination of Roman persecutions also suggests that women held positions of power and status within the Christian churches" (110).
32. For Elisha's feeding miracle, see 2 Kings 4:42–44; it is, of course, dwarfed by Jesus the Messiah's feeding miracles; see Matthew 14:14–21; 15:29–38. In both accounts in Matthew, outstanding miracles of healing also took place.
33. For Honi the Circle Drawer, see, e.g., m. Taanit 3:8; for Hanina ben Dosa, see, e.g., b. Berakhot 34b.
34. Jesus is also called rabbi in the context of the man born blind in John 9.
35. For the ritual fringe, see note 3 for this chapter.

36. See Michael L. Brown, *Israel's Divine Healer*, Studies in Old Testament Biblical Theology (Grand Rapids, MI: Zondervan, 1995), 63–66, with extensive documentation.

37. Ibid., 64–65, with reference to t. Hullin 2:22-23 and discussion of m. Sanhedrin 10:1, with further documentation.

38. On the question of miracles today, see the new major study of Craig S. Keener, *Miracles: The Credibility of the New Testament Accounts*, 2 vols. (Grand Rapids, MI: Baker Academic, 2011), with massive documentation of ancient and contemporary miracle accounts.

39. See, e.g., Mark 3:1–6; Luke 13:10–18; John 5:1–19.

40. For a wide-ranging, critical study of Jesus and Sabbath law, see John P. Meier, *A Marginal Jew: Rethinking the Historical Jesus, Volume 4: Law and Love* (New Haven: Yale University Press, 2009), 235–341. The whole volume is relevant to the question of Yeshua and *halakhah* (Jewish law), but Meier's historical methodology has rightly been called into question by other top scholars. See Donald A. Hagner, "Jesus and the Synoptic Sabbath Controversies," in Bock and Webb, *Key Events in the Life of the Historical Jesus*, 251–292, who brings valid criticism to Meier's methodology and conclusions (see 287–288), stating that the evidence for Meier's conclusion ("the historical Jesus is the halakic Jesus") is "extremely flimsy" and expressing his disappointment—as a leading New Testament scholar himself—that "Meier demeans the 'Christian depiction of Jesus,'" leaving no room for his uniqueness.

41. This is the Soncino translation.

42. Neusner, *The Mishnah*, 178–179, this time preserving Neusner's unique outline format.

43. Asher Intrater, *Who Ate Lunch With Abraham?* (Peoria, AZ: Intermedia Publishing Group, 2011), 47; more fully, 154–157.

44. Claude Montefiore, *Synoptic Gospels*, cxx, excerpted in Barker and Gregg, ed., *Jesus Beyond Christianity: The Classic Texts* (New York: Oxford University Press, 2010), 51.

45. Ibid., my emphasis.

46. Dan Cohn-Sherbok, "Closing Reflection," in Barker and Gregg, *Jesus Beyond Christianity*, 74.

47. Ibid., 72–73.

48. Montefiore, *Synoptic Gospels*, cxx, excerpted in Barker and Gregg, *Jesus Beyond Christianity*, 52.

4—A THREAT TO THE ESTABLISHMENT

1. Excerpted and reorganized from Leonard Ravenhill, "Picture of a Prophet," http://www.ravenhill.org/prophet.htm (accessed February 23, 2012). Used by permission of David Ravenhill, son. Copyright © 1994.

2. Abraham Joshua Heschel, *The Prophets* (New York: Harper & Row, 1969), 10.
3. See, e.g., the uprising of Korah and the other Israelites in Numbers 16.
4. See, e.g., Amos 5:21–27, beginning with "I hate, I despise your religious feasts; I cannot stand your assemblies."
5. See b. Yebamot 49b.
6. For the parallels between Jeremiah 7 and 26, which may reflect the same account, with ch. 26 providing chronological data, see Michael L. Brown, "Jeremiah," in Tremper Longman III and David E. Garland, eds., *The Expositor's Bible Commentary, Revised Edition* (Grand Rapids, MI: Zondervan, 2010), 338–339.
7. I do not have the original source for this quote; it is found with source unknown in Arthur Wallis, *In the Day of Thy Power* (repr.; Fort Washington, PA: CLC Publications, 2010), 279, note 7.
8. Heschel, *The Prophets*, 12.
9. Ravenhill, "Picture of a Prophet."
10. Heschel, *The Prophets*, 19.
11. I have frequently found this statement online, especially on polemical Islamic websites: "The Jewish Bible has more anti-Semitism than the Quran and Gospel combined." A Google search on February 15, 2010, yielded 454 hits for this exact phrase in quotes.
12. See Exodus Rabbah 41:7; Leviticus Rabbah 10:3; Numbers Rabbah 15:21; b. Sanhedrin 7a. According to the accounts, Hur, who was a colleague of Aaron, the high priest and the brother of Moses, rebuked his people for making a golden calf (see Exodus 32): "Hur arose and rebuked them: 'You brainless fools! Have you forgotten the miracles God performed for you?' Whereupon they rose against him and slew him" (Exodus Rabbah 41:7).
13. See b. Sanhedrin 103b; b. Yebamot 49b .
14. See Jeremiah 26:20–24; 2 Chronicles 24:17–23. For the Talmudic expansion of this, see b. Gittin 57b; see also b. Sanhedrin 96b.
15. See the commentary of Rashi to Isaiah 1:21, apparently following Ecclesiastes Rabbah 3:19. Both texts reference the murder of Zechariah son of Jehoiada as well.
16. Pesikta Rabbati 26:13.
17. In Barker and Gregg, *Jesus Beyond Christianity*, 72; Cohn-Sherbok is the author or editor of more than forty books; he also moderated the 2010 Oxford debate between Rabbi Shmuley Boteach and me.
18. Montefiore, *Synoptic Gospels*, cxx, excerpted in Barker and Gregg, *Jesus Beyond Christianity*, 51.
19. Cf. also the words of John the Immerser in Matthew 3:7–10.

20. According to Boteach, *Kosher Jesus*, 100–101, "Jeremiah repeatedly predicted the destruction of the First Temple.... Even so, Jeremiah is revered to this day as one of the greatest Jewish prophets." Apparently, Rabbi Shmuley fails to realize the irony in affirming these words of Jeremiah as authentic demonstrations of love for his Jewish people while rejecting the similar words of Jesus in the New Testament as the work of alleged anti-Semitic editors.

21. See, e.g., Jeremiah 20:1–2, where a priest has Jeremiah beaten and put in stocks, and Jeremiah 14:14, where God says the false prophets are prophesying lies in his name.

22. Cited in Craig S. Keener, *The Historical Jesus of the Gospels* (Grand Rapids, MI: William B. Eerdmans, 2009), 283.

23. See Matthew 20–22.

24. Some church leaders over the centuries have grossly misinterpreted Matthew 21:43, as if Jesus was teaching that "the church" was going to replace Israel. In point of fact, the context makes plain that the issue was the replacing of corrupt leadership with a new people: "Therefore I tell you that the kingdom of God will be taken away from you and given to a people who will produce its fruit.... When the chief priests and the Pharisees heard Jesus' parables, they knew he was talking about them. They looked for a way to arrest him, but they were afraid of the crowd because the people held that he was a prophet" (Matt. 21:43, 45–46). The "people who will produce [the vineyard's] fruit" were, in the first instance, Yeshua's Jewish disciples! Note also a common theme in the Gospels and Acts: the Jewish people, generally speaking, revered Jesus; it was some of the Jewish leadership that rejected him. (See further Appendix A.)

25. Keener, *The Historical Jesus of the Gospels*, 293–294. Keener carefully examines the evidence and concludes that the cleansing of the Temple should be accepted as a historical event. For an even more detailed treatment with ample bibliography, see Klyne R. Snodgrass, "The Temple Incident," in Darrell L. Bock and Robert L. Webb, eds., *Key Events in the Life of the Historical Jesus* (Grand Rapids: Eerdmans, 2010), 429–480. He concludes, "Whatever else is said, the temple incident shows Jesus' concern for the spiritual health of the nation Israel and the validity/purity of the center of Israelite worship, the temple.... More importantly, this act was also an unparalleled and unexpected expression of the authority of Jesus.... Although lacking priestly jurisdiction, Jesus was claiming and exercising a surprising authority over the temple and its workings, an authority which carried with it messianic expectations" (ibid., 474-475).

26. See, e.g., Isaiah 22:4; Jeremiah 9:1 (see also 20–21); 13:17; 14:17.

27. See, e.g., Jeremiah 25:1–11.

28. See, e.g., Luke 19:41–44; 21:20–24.

29. The Babylonian Talmud—normally what we refer to when we say "the Talmud"—reached its final form around 600 CE.

30. I categorically reject the charge that the Jews were guilty of "deicide," meaning, "killing God." At no point is such a charge spoken in the New Testament, and I am absolutely not hinting at the "deicide" charge in my statement here. Some of the Jewish leadership were guilty of rejecting Jesus as Messiah and Prophet, but in no way were they—let alone the people as a whole—guilty of "deicide," a terrible libel brought by professing Christians over the centuries that has been responsible for much Jewish suffering. For an honest assessment of the New Testament evidence, see Appendix A.

5—How Jesus Got Hijacked by a Well-Meaning Rabbi

1. Boteach, *Kosher Jesus*, 6. One wonders how this lines up with the Talmudic dictum that, "We don't depend on miracles" (see b. Pesachim 64b; b. Shabbat 32a).

2. This is a well-known Augustine quote, but I do not have the original source. Note also the comments of Jewish researcher Adam Gregerman in a review of *Kosher Jesus*, "One commonplace is that... reconstructions [of the 'historical Jesus'] usually end up resembling the people doing the reconstruction. Liberal Christians find a liberal Jesus; conservative Christians find a conservative Jesus.... Boteach sees a Jesus in his own image.... In this ostensibly historical portrait, Boteach affirms as accurate only that which mirrors his version of traditional Judaism. Even when he turns to Jesus' political agenda, Boteach, arguing that Jesus zealously sought 'to reestablish an independent Jewish commonwealth,' by force if necessary, makes him resemble a modern religious Zionist." [Adam Gregerman, "It's 'Kosher' to Accept Real Jesus?" *Jewish Daily Forward*, February 9, 2012, http://www.forward.com/articles/151028/#ixzz1luCEWDX9 (accessed February 22, 2012).]

3. Boteach, *Kosher Jesus*, 9. The next part of this fictional account introduces Paul, allegedly the man who invented Christianity, for which see chapters 7 and 8.

4. Flusser, *The Sage From Galilee*, 164.

5. Leah Abramowitz, "The Jewish Syndrome," Jewish Virtual Library, http://www.jewishvirtuallibrary.org/jsource/History/jersynd.html (accessed February 22, 2012).

6. Ibid. If you search YouTube for "Jerusalem syndrome" you'll find some very interesting videos!

7. See chapter 4.

8. Boteach, *Kosher Jesus*, ix. Shmuley writes, "My opinions on Jesus have been profoundly shaped by the writings of Hyam Maccoby and his

compelling insights into the historical Jesus." For this part of his study, he relied in particular on Hyam Maccoby, *Revolution in Judaea: Jesus and the Jewish Resistance* (New York: Taplinger Pub. Co., 1980; the first edition was published in 1973). For his reliance on other works by Maccoby, see chapter 7.

9. See, e.g., S. G. F. Brandon, *Jesus and the Zealots: A Study of the Political Factor in Primitive Christianity* (Manchester: Manchester University Press, 1967); more broadly, Richard A. Horsley, *Bandits, Prophets, and Messiahs: Popular Movements at the Time of Jesus* (Minneapolis: Winston Press, 1985); cf. idem, *Jesus and the Spiral of Violence: Popular Jewish Resistance in Roman Palestine* (San Francisco: Harper & Row, 1987); for strong and persuasive critiques of the "violent revolutionary" theories, see the works of Martin Hengel and Oscar Cullman cited below, note 22.

10. For those reading the Bible for the first time, you need not be concerned. We have an abundance of manuscripts for both the Hebrew and Greek Scriptures—called the Old and New Testament by Christians—and there are many excellent modern translations that do a great job of conveying what the biblical authors wanted to get across.

11. Keener, *The IVP Bible Background Commentary: New Testament*, 251, my emphasis.

12. For more on this, see chapter 6.

13. I. Howard Marshall, *The Gospel of Luke*, New International Greek Testament Commentary (Grand Rapids, MI: Eerdmans, 1978), 823–824, 825, with reference to "the decisive criticism of this view by Hahn, 167–170" (referring to Ferdinand Hahn, *Christologische Hoheitstitel* [Göttingen, Vandenhoeck & Ruprecht, 1963]; published in English as *The Titles of Jesus in Christology: Their History in Early Christianity* [New York: World, 1969]).

14. Joseph A. Fitzmyer, *The Gospel According to Luke X-XXIV*, The Anchor Bible (New York: Doubleday, 1985), 1432.

15. Ibid., 1434.

16. Marshall, *Luke*, 827; he adds, "But the words have been taken in other ways: ironically, 'Two swords will be enough...sc. to fulfill the prophecy and to make us look like brigands'...Neither of these two alternatives is at all probable."

17. Keener, *IVP Bible Background Commentary: New Testament*, 250.

18. Marshall, *Luke*, 827.

19. John Nolland, *Luke 18:35–24:53*, Word Biblical Commentary (Dallas: Word, 1993), 1076. Some scholars believe that Jesus, using urgent and hyperbolic language to underscore the dangers that lie ahead, was simply telling the disciples that they would need to defend themselves, a conclusion deduced from the text by David Flusser in Israel on the eve of

the Gulf War in 1991; see *The Sage from Galilee,* xiii. Given, however, the emphasis Jesus put on nonresistance to violent persecution, this is unlikely, even though it is far from a call for an armed revolt.

20. See Michael L. Brown, *Answering Jewish Objections to Jesus, Vol. 1: General and Historical Objections,* 123. We learn in the Torah that families often divided over the question of loyalty to the Lord, so what Jesus was saying was nothing new. In fact, it is recounted in Exodus 32 that the tribe of Levi did not join their fellow Israelites in the worship of the Golden Calf at Mount Sinai, and so Moses said to them, "Thus says the Lord, the God of Israel: Each of you put sword on thigh, go back and forth from gate to gate throughout the camp, and slay brother, neighbor, and kin" (Exod. 32:27, NJV). In the case of Moses, he actually called for the use of literal swords, with three thousand Israelites killed; in the case of Jesus, he spoke of a figurative sword, again, as the context makes perfectly clear.

21. Doron Mendels, *The Rise and Fall of Jewish Nationalism: Jewish and Christian Ethnicity in Ancient Palestine* (New York: Doubleday, 1992), 348.

22. As noted by Martin Hengel, *Was Jesus a Revolutionist?,* Eng. trans., William Klassen (Philadelphia: Fortress Press, 1971), 23, whatever Jesus was saying about his disciples needing swords (for Hengel it was meant paradoxically), "In no case can one see in it a demand for armed revolt." See also the critiques of the violent revolutionary theories in Oscar Cullman, *Jesus and the Revolutionaries,* Eng. trans., Gareth Putnam (New York: Harper & Row, 1970). According to Cullman, 50, "Certainly [Jesus] bitterly disappointed the Zealots, and this disappointment may have played a part in Judas' betrayal of him. The early Christians, however, followed in the footprints of their Master." He also noted (51–52) that the "eschatological radicalism" of Jesus led "to a rejection of resistance movements, since these divert one's attention from the kingdom of God with their setting of goals, and violate by their use of violence the command to absolute justice and absolute love."

23. For a fair summary (with refutation), see Zeitlin, *Jesus and the Judaism of His Time,* 129–151.

24. Ibid.

25. Hengel, *Was Jesus a Revolutionist?,* 9, emphasis mine.

26. Ibid., emphasis mine.

27. Ibid., 34–35.

28. Ibid., 31–32.

29. Ibid., 32.

30. Gerhard Lohfink, *Jesus and Community: The Social Dimension of Christian Faith,* Eng. trans., John P. Galvin (Philadelphia: Fortress Press, 1984),

124; it is important to bear in mind how sensitive these post-Holocaust German theologians were to calls to violent revolution.

31. This pattern is to be repeated by his followers; see 1 Corinthians 11:1, where Paul wrote, "Follow my example, as I follow the example of Christ." Or, as rendered in the CJB, "Try to imitate me, even as I myself try to imitate the Messiah." The goal was for the student to be like his teacher and the student like his master (see Matt 10:24–25a; for the Jewish background to this passage, cf. Basser, *The Mind Behind the Gospels*, 254–255). Most explicitly, see John 13:12–16, where Jesus performs the role of a lowly servant and washes his disciples' feet, setting an example for them. As stated in verses 14–15, "Now that I, your Lord and Teacher, have washed your feet, you also should wash one another's feet. I have set you an example that you should do as I have done for you." See also Philippians 2:5–11, where the self-abasing attitude of Jesus serves as a pattern for us. How different things would be if the pattern he set was one of a violent revolutionary!

32. Vernon C. Grounds, *Revolution and the Christian Faith* (Philadelphia: Lippincot, 1971), 223.

6—THE LAMB WHO WAS SLAIN

1. This verse is quoted in Acts 8:32; see also Jeremiah 11:19, "But I was like a gentle lamb led to the slaughter" (ESV).

2. Revelation 5:6, 8, 12, 13; 6:1, 16; 7:9, 10, 14, 17; 8:1; 12:11; 13:8; 14:1, 4 (2x), 10; 15:3; 17:14 (2x); 19:7, 9; 21:9, 14, 22, 23; 22:1, 3.

3. There are some scholars who question the ancient accounts of the flight to Pella but still believe that the Jewish disciples did leave Jerusalem rather than revolt against the Romans. For an assessment of the evidence, see Jonathan Bourgel, "The Jewish Christians' Move from Jerusalem as a Pragmatic Choice," in Dan Jaffé, ed., *Studies in Rabbinic Judaism and Early Christianity: Text and Context* (Leiden: E. J. Brill, 2010), 107–138.

4. For Jewish studies on the Sermon on the Mount, see above, chapter 3, note 13; as I have argued throughout this volume (and as many others would affirm), on the one hand, Jesus-Yeshua can only be rightly understood against the Jewish background of his time; on the other hand, that background only helps us to see just how unique he was.

5. For further discussion of the Jewish background, see Brown, *Answering Jewish Objections to Jesus, Vol. 4: New Testament Objections*, 141–142, where I note that, "The issue is one of legal retaliation, in this case, for being publicly shamed, which we know because of the words, If someone strikes you on the right cheek, implying a backhanded slap against the face. That is to say, a right-handed orientation is assumed in similar legal cases, and, since a right-handed slap would strike the *left* cheek and a

right-handed person would not strike with the left hand, being struck on the *right* cheek means being struck with the back of the hand," and Jewish law as recorded in the Mishnah legislated greater compensation for the public shame suffered by a backhanded slap. See further Basser, *The Mind Behind the Gospels*, 146–149.

6. H. S. Vigeveno, *Jesus the Revolutionary* (Glendale, CA: Gospel Light, 1966), 11.

7. For illustrative quotes from early Christian leaders on gladiatorial combat, see Christian-History.org, "Christian Quotes About Gladiators," http://www.christian-history.org/gladiator-christian-quotes.html (accessed February 23, 2012).

8. The most conspicuous parallels come from the Jewish prayer called the Kaddish, as noted by many commentators. See, e.g., Basser, *The Mind Behind the Gospels*, 174–181.

9. Lest you accuse Luke, the author of Luke and Acts, of being anti-Semitic by pointing out the activities of these particular Jewish troublemakers, let's not forget that in the previous chapter, Paul and his colleague Silas— heroes in the Book of Acts—were singled out *as Jews* by their accusers, and as noted by Luke. The verse in question, which I only quoted in part in the text, above, reads, "These men are throwing our city into confusion. They are Jews and are advocating customs that are not lawful for us to accept or practice, since we are Romans" (Act 16:20–21, NET). On the larger question of the alleged anti-Semitism in the New Testament, see Appendix A, with further references.

10. See chapter 5.

11. For the "criterion of embarrassment," chapter 3, note 30.

12. This account is repeated almost verbatim in Mark 8:31 and Luke 9:22.

13. For varied Jewish Messianic expectations at that time, see, e.g., James H. Charlesworth, ed., *The Messiah: Developments in Earliest Judaism and Christianity* (Minneapolis, MN: Fortress, 1992); John J. Collins, *The Scepter and the Star: The Messiahs of the Dead Sea Scrolls and Other Ancient Literature* (New York: Doubleday, 1995); Magnus Zetterholm, ed., *The Messiah in Early Judaism and Christianity* (Minneapolis, MN: Fortress, 2007); Richard S. Hess and M. Daniel Carroll R., eds., *Israel's Messiah in the Bible and the Dead Sea Scrolls* (Grand Rapids. MI: Baker Academic, 2003); cf. also Joseph A. Fitzmyer, *The One Who Is to Come* (Grand Rapids, MI: Eerdmans, 2007); "Messianism," in *The Eerdmans Dictionary of Early Judaism*, 938–942.

14. For more on Pilate, see Brown, *Answering Jewish Objections to Jesus, Vol. 4: New Testament Objections*, 53–55.

15. This also prolonged the agony, since the blood rushing to the head would make it more difficult to lose consciousness.

16. For the most part, it is impossible to verify these traditions, but the evidence clearly points to the martyrdom of a significant number of the first leaders in the Jesus movement. Some advocates of the "violent revolution" theory have pointed to Jesus calling a "Zealot" to be one of his disciples, but this is making something out of nothing since: (1) Jesus transformed those he called into his service; (2) had this Simon been a typical Zealot, he would hardly have worked side by side with a hated tax-collector like Matthew (who, presumably, was also transformed had he been corrupt in any of his practices in the past); and (3) as we have pointed out throughout chapters 5 and 6, the whole tenor of the New Testament contradicts the violent, revolutionary aspirations and methods of the Zealots.

17. In fact, when some Greek or Roman authorities accused the early followers of Jesus of things like sedition or revolt, it is clear from the charges that the Christians were completely misunderstood. See, e.g., the accusation by Celsus in the second century, "The Christians form among themselves secret societies that exist outside the system of laws...an obscure and mysterious community founded on revolt and on the advantage that accrues from it." As the Christian leader Justin Martyr (beheaded in 165 CE) stated, "We are publicly accused of being atheists [because they would not worship the emperor as a god] and criminals who are guilty of high treason." Note too that these Christians were ones whom Rabbi Shmuley Boteach would also count as followers of Jesus the Lamb rather than followers of the fictional Jesus the freedom fighter against Rome.

18. In Gandhi's words, "The example of Jesus suffering is a factor in the composition of my un-dying faith in non-violence." For background, see the foreword of Thomas Merton in *Gandhi on Non-Violence* (New York: New Directions Publishing, 1964), 4. Gandhi also said, "Jesus was the most active resister known perhaps to history. This was non-violence par excellence" (ibid., 40).

19. Transcribed from a videotape of King's speech.

20. Cited in *Gandhi on Non-Violence*, 34.

21. The revolt began in 66 CE and was completely crushed by 74 CE; for a convenient summary, with brief bibliography, see "Revolt, First Jewish," in Collins and Harlow, *The Eerdmans Dictionary of Early Judaism*, 1146–1149.

22. Ibid.

23. See "Bar Kochba Revolt," in Collins and Harlow, *The Eerdmans Dictionary of Early Judaism*, 421–425, here citing 424–425.

24. Ibid., 425.

25. The most important accounts of his martyrdom are found in b. Berakhot 61b and y. Sotah 4:5.

7—Was Paul the One Who Changed It All?

1. Michael Shapiro, *The Jewish 100: A Ranking of the Most Influential Jews of All Time* (n.p.: Citadel Press, 1994), cited in Adherents.com, "The 100 Most Influential Jews of All Time," http://www.adherents.com/largecom/ fam_jew100.html (accessed February 24, 2012).
2. See Brown, *Answering Jewish Objections to Jesus, Vol. 4: New Testament Objections*, 188–202.
3. Eugene J. Fischer, "Typical Jewish Misunderstandings of Christ, Christianity, and Jewish-Christian Relations Over the Centuries," in Garber, *The Jewish Jesus*, 240 (the article runs from 228–248). In sum, he claims, this is "what is typically taught to Jewish students," stating more fully: "Jesus was a good guy. Paul was a bad goy. The Christians got power and persecuted the Jews, always and everywhere and everywhen. The Crusades happened. Then the Inquisition, blood libels, and pogroms. Then there was the Holocaust. Then the British Christians would not let us into Palestine. But we persevered and America saved us." Fischer rightly concludes, "This is about as valid as the old joke summarizing Jewish feasts: 'They tried to kill us. They failed. Let's eat.' But not as funny. And it fails utterly to begin to explain how the Jews over the centuries within Christendom survived often enough, and often enough thrived."
4. Hyam Maccoby, *The Mythmaker: Paul and the Invention of Christianity* (New York: Harper & Row, 1986).
5. Boteach, *Kosher Jesus*, 8.
6. Ibid.
7. Ibid., 9.
8. Ibid., 10–11.
9. See chapters 2, 5, and earlier in this chapter.
10. See chapter 5, note 8.
11. David Klinghoffer, *Why the Jews Rejected Jesus: The Turning Point of Western History* (New York: Doubleday, 2005). See my review in *Mishkan* 44 (2005), 82–87. Available online at http://realmessiah.com/read/ review-david-klinghoffer-why-jews-rejected-jesus (accessed February 24, 2012). As I noted in my review, "Ironically, Maccoby also wrote a volume entitled *Jesus the Pharisee*, which undermines one of the major premises of Klinghoffer's study."
12. Most commonly Hyam Maccoby, "The Washing of Cups," *Journal of New Testament Studies* 14 (1982): 3–15.
13. G. F Hawthorne, R. P. Martin, and D. G. Reid, eds., *Dictionary of Paul and His Letters* (Downers Grove, IL: InterVarsity Press, 1993).
14. John G. Gager, review of H. Maccoby, *The Mythmaker: Paul and the Invention of Christianity*, *Jewish Quarterly Review* 79, no. 2–3 (1988–1989): 248, my emphasis. The entire review runs from 248–250.

15. James D. G. Dunn, *The Theology of Paul the Apostle* (Grand Rapids, MI: Eerdmans, 2006).

16. James D. G. Dunn, *The New Perspective on Paul*, rev. ed. (Grand Rapids, MI: Eerdmans, 2007). This volume is more than 500 pages long. See also the Paul Page, at http://www.thepaulpage.com/new-perspective/introduction-and-summary/ (accessed February 24, 2012).

17. James D. G. Dunn, *Romans 9–16*, Word Biblical Commentary (Dallas: Word, 2002), 635–636, my emphasis.

18. Maccoby's other work on Paul, *Paul and Hellenism* (London: SCM Press, 1991), has been noticed a bit more than his *Mythmaker* volume, but one of his central theses there (see 54–89) has been dismissed as "an astonishingly anachronistic connection," again, a very strong dismissal of a theory by another scholar, indicating just how far-fetched some of his views are. See *Justification and Variegated Nomism: The Paradoxes of Paul* 413, note 54. According to Gunn, *The Theology of the Apostle Paul*, 603, note 12, Maccoby's *Paul and Hellenism* is "regrettable," labeling the book a "highly tendentious and quite uncritical argument." It is not surprising, that one of the few scholars to make reference to Maccoby is Barrie A. Wilson in his book *How Jesus Became a Christian* (n.p.: Random House Canada, 2008), and he too has to make Paul into a liar (and this is just one of the many conspiratorial theories and cover-ups that Wilson advances in his sensationalistic book).

19. Alan F. Segal, *Paul the Convert: The Apostolate and Apostasy of Saul the Pharisee* (New Haven, CT: Yale University Press, 1990).

20. *Library Journal*, June 15, 1986, my emphasis.

21. Gregerman, "It's 'Kosher' to Accept Real Jesus?"

22. Cf. the discussion in Heikki Räisänen, *Paul and the Law* (Philadelphia: Fortress, 1986).

23. See, e.g., Stephen Westerholm, *Perspectives Old and New on Paul: The "Lutheran" Paul and His Critics* (Grand Rapids, MI: Eerdmans, 2003); idem, *Israel's Law and the Church's Faith: Paul and His Recent Interpreters* (1988; repr., Eugene, OR: Wipf & Stock, 1998). Presumably Maccoby's *Mythmaker* book came out in time to have been noticed in Westerholm's 1988 volume.

24. John Gager, *Reinventing Paul* (New York: Oxford University Press, 2000).

25. See Räisänen, *Paul and the Law*, 2–3, note 20, where the views of the third-century philosopher Porphyry are also cited (ibid., 2).

26. As translated in Falk, *Jesus the Pharisee*, 18, available online at Auburn .edu, http://www.auburn.edu/~allenkc/falk1a.html (accessed February 21, 2012).

27. Joseph Klausner, *From Jesus to Paul* (New York: MacMillian, 1943).

28. Ibid., 453–454, with examples on 454–458.

29. Ibid., 458.

30. Segal, *Paul the Convert: The Apostolate and Apostasy of Saul the Pharisee*, xi–xii.

31. Daniel Boyarin, *A Radical Jew: Paul and the Politics of Identity* (Berkeley, CA: University of California Press, 1994), 2.

32. In his endorsement of Brad H. Young, *Paul the Jewish Theologian* (Peabody, MA: Hendrickson, 1997).

33. Julie Galambush, *The Reluctant Parting: How the New Testament's Jewish Writers Created a Christian Book* (San Francisco: HarperSanFranciso, 2005), 115. I would agree with the final sentence in this quote if it had read, "If Paul can still be said to have founded Christianity—in terms of what it became over the centuries, severed from its Jewish roots and persecuting the Jews—it is now clear that he did so unintentionally."

34. Beginning in the thirteenth century, Catholic censors removed portions of the Talmud and other rabbinic writings they found offensive, to the point that the rabbis sometimes censored their own texts lest they offend the Catholic leaders.

35. For the actual question of Yeshua being the Son of God and what that would imply, see chapter 9.

36. Boteach, *Kosher Jesus*, 204: "The New Testament editors and Paul painted a divine figure of Jesus."

37. See, e.g., pages xviii, 9, 11, 12, 19, 116 in *Kosher Jesus*.

38. According to David Flusser, *The Sage From Galilee*, 101, "Jesus evidently did understand his divine sonship as unique and decisive." Even if we grant that there were different ideas of what "s/Son of God" meant in the first-century Jewish world, there can be no question that this theme is found throughout the New Testament, which directly contradicts Rabbi Shmuley's allegation that Paul introduced the concept of Jesus as Son of God.

39. In the next chapter, we'll address the last allegation, namely, that "[T]he stranger tells the stunned disciples that their rabbi's death brought all the laws of the Torah to completion. His execution abrogated all obligations specified in the Law."

8—The Jewish Genius Who Brought the God of Israel to the Nations

1. The Hebrew word *torah* means instruction, teaching, and law, in particular the divine Teaching/Law that God gave to Israel at Sinai.

2. For translation issues ("be blessed through you," "bless themselves through you," or "find blessing through you") see Michael L. Brown, "*b-r-k*," in Willem VanGemeren, ed., *The New International Dictionary of Old Testament Theology and Exegesis* (Grand Rapids, MI: Zondervan,

1997), 1:757– 67, specifically 759–760 (with reference to Genesis 12:3; 18:18; 28:14; 22:18; and 26:4). On any of these interpretations, Abraham's seed was destined to bring blessing to the entire world.

3. See, e.g., Deuteronomy 4:6–8.

4. Michael H. Hart, *The 100: A Ranking of the Most Influential Persons in History* (*Revised and Updated for the Nineties*) (New York: Hart Publishing Co., 1978).

5. For the gravity of this offense, see Keener, *IVP Bible Background Commentary: New Testament*, to Acts 21:28: "The barrier between the outer court, open to the Gentiles, and the Court of the Women was about four feet high, with warning signs posted at intervals in Greek and Latin: 'Any foreigner who passes this point will be responsible for his own death' (the inscriptions are reported in ancient literature and one has been found by archaeologists). This was the one offense for which Jewish authorities could execute capital punishment—even on Roman citizens—without consulting with Rome."

6. Ibid., to Acts 21:20–22.

7. *The Acts of the Apostles*, The Anchor Bible (New York: Doubleday, 1998), 711. William Neill, *The Acts of the Apostles*, New Century Bible Commentary (repr., Grand Rapids: Eerdmans, 1987), 225, takes a more radical approach, perhaps assuming too much re: Paul's alleged "notoriously heretical views." He writes, "Paul's audience had no objection to proselytizing among Gentiles; the Jews themselves practiced this. What roused them to an outburst of unbridled fury at this point was that a man who claimed to be a loyal Jew asserted that he had been divinely enjoined to propagate his notoriously heretical views in the pagan world—such as that compliance with sacred Jewish law was not obligatory for all who professed to belong to the people of God, and that uncircumcised Gentiles would be regarded as equal with Jews in the sight of God."

8. Richard N. Longenecker, "Acts," in Frank E. Gaebelein, ed., *Expositor's Bible Commentary* (Grand Rapids, MI: Zondervan, 1984), 9:526.

9. That was the position of the other core disciples; it was just that Paul's life mission was to bring the good news to the Gentiles, and he articulated the implications of Jew and Gentile being one in Jesus with radical clarity. Note that Paul and Acts confirm this as well; see Acts 15:1–31; Galatians 2:1–10.

10. Jaroslav Pelikan, *Jesus Through the Centuries: His Place in the History of Culture* (New Haven, CT: Yale University Press, 1985), 18, my emphasis.

11. See also Risto Santala, *Paul the Man and the Teacher: In Light of the Jewish Sources* (Jerusalem: Keren Ahvah Meshihit, 1995); the entire book can be accessed online at http://www.ristosantala.com/rsla/Paul/paul01 .html (accessed February 24, 2012).

12. According to Keener, *IVP Bible Background Commentary: New Testament*, to Acts 13:9, "Roman citizens had three names. As a citizen, Saul had a Roman cognomen ("Paul," meaning "small"); his other Roman names remain unknown to us. As inscriptions show was common, his Roman name sounded similar to his Jewish name (Saul, from the name of the Old Testament's most famous Benjamite). This is not a name change; now that Paul is moving in a predominantly Roman environment, he begins to go by his Roman name, and some of Luke's readers recognize for the first time that Luke is writing about someone of whom they had already heard."

13. Joseph Shulam with Hillary LeCornu, *A Commentary on the Jewish Roots of Romans* (Baltimore: Messianic Jewish Publishers, 1998), 495.

14. For refutation of this, see chapter 7, "Was Paul the One Who Changed It All?"

15. This is the fundamental thesis of Klinghoffer, *Why the Jews Rejected Jesus.*

16. Throughout Acts, Paul is described as living as a faithful Jew, ultimately confirmed in Acts 21:18–26. It is fair to ask why Luke, the author of Acts and sometimes part of Paul's ministry team, would present Paul as being pro-Torah as a Jew if Paul was actually anti-Torah.

17. David Stern points out that when Stephen accused his people of having "uncircumcised hearts and ears" (Acts 7:51), he was using the language and terminology of the Hebrew Scriptures themselves, where God indicted the children of Israel in these same terms (cf. Lev. 26:41; Deut. 10:16; 30:6; Jer. 4:4; 9:25[26]; Ezek. 44:7, 9). See Stern, *Jewish New Testament Commentary*, 245–246.

18. For a complete collection of all relevant ancient texts (in the original languages and translation) concerning these various "Jewish-Christian" groups, see A. F. J. Klijn and G. J. Reinink, *Patristic Evidence for Jewish-Christian Sects* (Leiden: E. J. Brill, 1973); for an excellent summary, see Ray Pritz, *Nazarene Jewish Christianity: From the End of the New Testament Period Until Its Disappearance in the Fourth Century* (Jerusalem: Magnes Press; Leiden: E. J. Brill, 1988).

19. Cf. Shaye D. Cohen, "Was Timothy Jewish (Acts 16:1–3)? Patristic Exegesis, Rabbinic Law, and Matrilineal Descent," *Journal of Biblical Literature* 105 (1986): 251–268.

20. The positive concept behind this prayer was that only a male Jew was required to (and therefore had the privilege to) keep all the commandments of the Torah, since each other three categories (Gentile, slaves, and women) were exempt from keeping most or some of the commandments. For the discussion of the dating of this prayer (in the context of the development of ancient Jewish liturgy), see A. Z. Idelsohn, *Jewish Liturgy and Its Development* (repr., New York: Dover Publications, 1995); see

also Joseph Heinemann, *Prayer in the Talmud* (Berlin/New York: Walter de Gruyter, 1976). See, e.g., Acts 24:17; Romans 15:25–28. These were almost certainly "the poor" that the senior Jewish disciples in Jerusalem urged Paul to care for (Gal. 2:10).

21. Klinghoffer, *Why the Jews Rejected Jesus*, 90–118.

22. As I noted in Michael L. Brown, *Answering Jewish Objections to Jesus, Vol 5: Traditional Jewish Objections* (San Francisco: Purple Pomegranate, 2010), 35: "During Israel's forty years in the desert, at least 42,000 Israelites were killed in more than ten acts of divine judgment—including: plagues (Num. 14:36–37, killing the ten spies who brought the bad report; 16:41–50, killing 14,700; Num. 25:1–9, killing 24,000; see also Exod. 32:35; Num. 11:33, which do not mention casualties); supernatural fire burning up the people (Lev. 10:1–4, killing Nadab and Abihu, Aaron's sons; Num. 11:1, killing some of the mixed multitude, according to Rashi; Num. 16:35, killing 250); the earth swallowing people up (Num. 16:1–34, killing Korah, all his leaders, and all their households); the Levites acting as God's agents of judgment (Exod. 32:19–29, killing 3,000)."

23. See further James 2:14–26.

24. There is a massive literature dealing with "Paul and the Law," and even to mention the most important studies of the last twenty-five years would be impossible in the space of a short endnote. For surveys, see above, chapter 7, note 23.

25. For positive reflections on this from a Jewish perspective, see Daube, *The New Testament and Rabbinic Judaism*, 336–337, where he writes that Paul took over his missionary methods "from Jewish teaching on the subject: the idea that you must adopt the customs and mood of the person you wish to win over, and the idea that, to be a successful maker of proselytes, you must become a servant of men and humble yourself." See further Brown, *Answering Jewish Objections to Jesus, Vol. 4: New Testament Objections*, 192.

26. With reference again to Hyam Maccoby's volume, *The Mythmaker: Paul and the Invention of Christianity*.

27. Cf. Terrance Callan, *Forgetting the Root: The Emergence of Christianity From Judaism* (New York/Mahwah: Paulist Press, 1986).

28. For the debate on when this "parting of the ways" actually began, see James D. G. Dunn, ed., *Jews and Christians: The Parting of the Ways A.D. 70 to 135* (Grand Rapids, MI: Eerdmans, 1999); Becker and Reed, *The Ways That Never Parted*; Jackson-McCabe, *Jewish Christianity Reconsidered*.

29. Quoting Isaiah 59:20–21; 27:9; Jeremiah 31:33–34; for Paul's use of these texts, see above, chapter 1, note 22.

30. Quoting Isaiah 40:13 and Job 41:11.

9—The Secret of the Invisible God Who Can Be Seen

1. See Exodus 20:2–6; Deuteronomy 5:6–10.
2. As cited and translated in *The Complete ArtScroll Siddur* (translated with an annotated commentary by Rabbi Nosson Scherman) (Brooklyn: Mesorah Publications, 1984), 381; the rendering of the words "My entire essence" by Rabbi Scherman is somewhat expansive, but reflects his traditional Jewish understanding of the text.
3. See especially Deuteronomy 4:12–28.
4. Intrater, *Who Ate Lunch With Abraham?*, 35.
5. On this phenomenon as explained in traditional Judaism, Prof. Benjamin Sommer notes, "The idea of an angel whose self to some degree overlaps with Yhwh but did not exhaust Yhwh's self is picked up in mystical texts of the rabbinic era—that is, in *merkavah* (chariot) mysticism, in *heikhalot* (palace) mysticism, and in the texts known as *Shi'ur Qomah* (measuring the height or the body [of God]). This biblical idea of the angel becomes evident in the figure variously called the 'angel of the Presence' (*mal'akh hapanim*), the 'prince of the Presence' (*sar hapanim*), Yahoel, and Metatron. Some texts identified this figure as a 'little Yhwh,' a designation that attests at once to the figure's overlap with God and the fact that this figure does not incorporate aspects of God." See Benjamin Sommer, *The Bodies of God and the World of Ancient Israel* (Cambridge: Cambridge University Press, 2009), 128.
6. The bold text here reflects the actual words of the Talmud as rendered in the Steinsaltz translation and commentary.
7. According to Intrater, *Who Ate Lunch With Abraham*, 143–145, there are more than fifty examples of divine appearances in the Tanakh.
8. See Marc B. Shapiro, *The Limits of Orthodox Theology: Maimonides' Thirteen Principles Reappraised* (Oxford: The Littman Library of Jewish Civilization, 2004), 45–70.
9. Shapiro, ibid., offers significant differences with this tenet of Maimonides culled from numerous *rabbinic* sources.
10. See Michael L. Brown, *Answering Jewish Objections to Jesus, Vol. 2: Theological Objections* (Grand Rapids: Baker, 2000), 16–22; for different approaches, see Bruce Chilton, *Judaic Approaches to the Gospels* (Atlanta: Scholars Press, 1994), 271–315; and John Ronning, *The Jewish Targums and John's Logos Theology* (Peabody, MA: Hendrickson, 2010); Robert Hayward, *Divine Name and Presence: The Memra* (Totowa, NJ: Allanheld, Osmun Publishers, 1981).
11. See "Targum, Targumim," in *The Eerdmans Dictionary of Early Judaism*, 1278–1281.
12. Where not noted, all other citations from the Torah are from Targum Onkelos.

13. R. J. Werblowsky and G. Wigoder, eds., *The Oxford Dictionary of Jewish Religion* (New York: Oxford University Press, 1997), s.v. "*logos*," 423.

14. The NJV cites Abraham Ibn Ezra and Rashbam (Rabbi Samuel Ben Meir) in support, both of them leading traditional commentators.

15. Chabad.org, "The Numerology of Redemption," http://www.chabad.org/parshah/article_cdo/aid/2741/jewish/The-Numerology-of-Redemption.htm (accessed February 24, 2012). He also stated that "[as] one chassidic thinker once put it, G-d did not have to create a world to be *yachid*. He was singularly and exclusively one before the world was created, and remains so after the fact. It was to express His *echad*-ness that He created the world, created man, granted him freedom of choice, and commanded him the Torah. He created existences that, at least in their own perception, are distinct of Him, and gave them the tools to bring their lives into utter harmony with His will. When a diverse and plural world chooses, by its own initiative, to unite with Him, the divine oneness assumes a new, deeper expression: G-d is *echad*." When I asked one of the Rebbe's emissaries what he was saying, he replied, "I read the article and what it's saying in Chassidic terms is that the world and G-d are not separate but one. In essence 'G-d is everything and everything is G-d.' That said I can appreciate how you may find this as a way of explaining what you believe. The idea of plurality not diminishing G-d's Oneness. The issue though is that this idea of finding G-d's Oneness within the plurality of creation doesn't address the Nature of G-d. It address the nature of the world and the way in which G-d wants us to perceive the truth about the world; i.e., that the world is not a contradiction to G-d; it's sole purpose is to fulfill the will of the Creator."

16. Simon Herman, "Sefirot," in Tzvi M. Rabinowicz, *The Encyclopedia of Hasidism* (Northvale, NJ: Aronson, 1996), 436.

17. Ibid., 436–437.

18. Sommer, *The Bodies of God*, 254, note 21, commenting in particular on Targum Pseudo-Jonathan to Deuteronomy 31:3.

19. Note Hebrews 1:3 as rendered in the CJB, "This Son is the radiance of the *Sh'khinah*, the very expression of God's essence, upholding all that exists by his powerful word."

20. Sommer, *The Bodies of God*, 135.

21. See Brown, *Answering Jewish Objections to Jesus, Vol. 2: Theological Objections*, 3–14.

22. In section nine of the Huppat Eliyahu in Otsar Midrashim, all of these names are given as titles of the Messiah.

23. See Brown, *Answering Jewish Objections to Jesus, Vol. 2: Theological Objections*, 14–48.

24. Ibid., 25, with note 40.

25. See especially Exodus 3:14; cf. also the Septuagint rendering of Isaiah 43:10 with *ego eimi*, "I am" as in John 8:58. (The Septuagint was the Jewish translation of the Hebrew Scriptures into Greek approximately two centuries before Jesus.)

26. For further discussion, cf. now Larry W. Hurtado, *One God, One Lord* (Philadelphia: Fortress, 1988); more fully, idem, *Lord Jesus Christ: Devotion to Jesus in Earliest Christianity* (Grand Rapids, MI: Eerdmans, 2003); Richard Bauckham, *Jesus and the God of Israel: God Crucified and Other Studies on the New Testament's Christology of Divine Identity* (Grand Rapids, MI: Eerdmans, 2008); the volume of James F. McGrath, *The Only True God: Early Christian Monotheism in Its Jewish Context* (Urbana: University of Illinois Press, 2009), does not take into account the entirety of New Testament evidence (such as Hebrews 1) and fails to recognize that Yeshua's divine identification in the Gospels goes far beyond the representative messenger role (not to mention the significance of the theophanies—divine appearances—in the Tanakh as well), which is why Jesus is identified—along with God the Father—Revelation as the "Alpha and the Omega, the Beginning and the End" (or, "First and Last"); see Revelation 1:8; 21:6; 22:13.

27. See also 1 Corinthians 15:28, "Now when everything has been subjected to the Son, then he will subject himself to God, who subjected everything to him; so that God may be everything in everyone" (CJB).

10—The Secret of the Suffering Messiah

1. The Testament of the Twelve Patriarchs also speaks of a Messiah from the tribe of Levi (again, a priestly Messiah) as well as a Messiah from the line of David, but scholars are divided over whether the work can be traced to Jewish or Christian (or, Jewish-Christian) authors.

2. Raphael Patai, *The Messiah Texts* (Detroit: Wayne State University, 1979), 104–121. There are some contemporary Jewish scholars who believe that within the Dead Sea Scrolls there are references to a Messianic figure who would suffer—and perhaps even die and rise again. (There are different texts involved, referring to different individuals.) See Michael O. Wise, *The First Messiah: Investigating the Savior Before Christ*; Israel Knohl, *The Messiah Before Jesus: The Suffering Servant of the Dead Sea Scrolls*; idem, *Messiahs and Resurrection in "The Gabriel Revelation"* (New York: Continuum, 2009); see also Matthias Henze, ed., *Hazon Gabriel: New Readings of the Gabriel Revelation* (Atlanta: Society of Biblical Literature, 2011). Although some think that the discovery of a suffering Messiah *before* Jesus would somehow detract from who Jesus is, I feel the reverse is true: It would indicate that some Jews *were* expecting a suffering Messiah.

3. G. H. Dalman, *Der leidende und der sterbende Messias der Synagoge im ersten nachchristlichen Jarhtausend* (Berlin: Reuther, 1888). Cf. also idem, *Jesaja 53: das Prophetenwort vom Sühnleiden des Gottesknechtes mit besonderer Berücksichtung der jüdischen Literatur*, 2nd ed. (Leipzig: J. C. Hinrichs', 1914). For a thorough bibliography on the subject through 1987, see Emil Schürer, *The History of the Jewish People in the Age of Jesus Christ (175 B.C.–A.D. 135)*, rev. Eng. vers. by Geza Vermes, Fergus Millar, and Matthew Black (Edinburgh: T & T Clark, 1973-1987), 2:547–549.

4. For a more complete discussion, see Brown, *Answering Jewish Objections to Jesus, Vol. 2: Theological Objections*, 220–231, where I deal with the objection that, "Jews do not believe in a suffering Messiah." Note, however, that the references on 227–228 to "Rabbi Moshe Ibn Krispin" should probably be changed to "Jewish philosopher Moshe Ibn Krispin."

5. Patai, *The Messiah Texts*, 104.

6. Ibid.

7. Midrash Konen, from Bet HaMidrash, 2:29–30, as translated by Patai, *The Messiah Texts*, 114.

8. Zohar 2:212a, as translated by Patai, *The Messiah Texts*, 116. For Isaiah 53 cited by the Zohar in the context of the atoning power of the death of the righteous, see chapter 11.

9. As translated in Patai, *The Messiah Texts*.

10. *The Schottenstein Talmud Sanhedrin 3a (Folios 84b-99a)* (Brooklyn: ArtScroll Mesorah, 1995), 98a[5], with reference to the leading Rabbinic commentaries. The actual text in the Schottenstein Talmud includes the Hebrew of Isaiah 53:4, represented here by my ellipsis. Nothing has been deleted from the text.

11. Patai, *The Messiah Texts*, 105.

12. Michael L. Brown, *Answering Jewish Objections to Jesus, Vol. 3: Messianic Prophecy Objections* (Grand Rapids, MI: Baker, 2003), 117–127.

13. Cf. G. K. Beale and D. A. Carson, eds., *Commentary on the New Testament Use of the Old Testament* (Grand Rapids, MI: Baker Academic, 2007).

14. See Brown, *Answering Jewish Objections to Jesus, Vol. 3: Messianic Prophecy Objections*, 122–127.

15. Crucifixion was not known in ancient Israel. It was invented by the Persians, then borrowed by the Greeks and then the Romans, who ultimately outlawed it as too barbaric for even their tastes.

16. See note 12.

17. Often called Ephraim in these chapters, it still appears that it is the Messiah son of David who is described, and as the Hasidic scholar Rabbi J. Immanuel Schochet notes, "The term Ephraim, though, may relate here to collective Israel, thus referring to Mashiach ben David." *Mashiach*,

(Brooklyn: S.I.E., 1991) 92–93, note 2, where he also points out some overlap in terminology in the descriptive titles of the two Messiahs.

18. Pesikta Rabbati 162a, in Patai, *The Messiah Texts*, 112–113. Cf. Yeshua's words to his disciples about suffering in Matthew 10:22–25 and John 15:18–21. For references to extensive rabbinic parallels, see above, chapter 5, note 32.

19. Excerpted from Pesikta Rabbati, chapter 36 in Patai, *The Messiah Texts*, 113.

20. See Rivka Ulmer, "Psalm 22 in Pesikta Rabbati: The Suffering of the Jewish Messiah and Jesus," in Garber, *The Jewish Jesus*, 106–128.

11—The Secret of the Atoning Power of the Death of the Righteous

1. Berel Wein, *The Triumph of Survival: The Story of the Jews in the Modern Era 1650–1990* (Brooklyn: Shaar, 1990), 14.

2. 2:212a. This is the rendering of Patai, *The Messiah Texts*, 116.

3. According to *Siftey Hakhamim*, a commentary on the commentary of Rashi, "Just as the red heifer, which is not a real sacrifice atones, so also the death of the righteous atones."

4. For example, y. Yoma 2:1, Pesikta DeRav Kahana 26:16.

5. Louis Ginzberg, *Legends of the Jews* (n.p.: Nabu Press, 2010), 3:191, cites Sifre Deuteronomy 31, "The death of the pious man is a greater misfortune to Israel than the Temple's burning to ashes." For further references to the atoning power of the death of the righteous, see ibid., 6:75, note 386; 107, note 602.

6. Cited in S. R. Driver and Adolph Neubauer, eds. and trs., *The Fifty-Third Chapter of Isaiah According to the Jewish Interpreters*, 2 Vols. (repr., New York: Ktav, 1969), 2:15; the Zohar states that this explains a verse in Ecclesiastes (7:15), "In this meaningless life of mine I have seen both of these: a righteous man perishing in his righteousness, and a wicked man living long in his wickedness." Cf. also b. Shabbat 33b, "The righteous are taken by the iniquity of the generation."

7. Driver and Nebauer, *The Fifty-Third Chapter of Isaiah According to the Jewish Interpreters*, 1:394–395 (the numeric value for guilt offering is 341, which equals the numeric value of Menahem ben Ammiel); the emphasis in the original indicates scripture citations. The midrash concludes with another citation from Isaiah 53: "And what is written after it? *He shall his seed, shall have long days, and the pleasure of the Lord shall prosper in his hand.*"

8. Solomon Schechter, *Aspects of Rabbinic Theology* (New York: MacMillan, 1909), 310–311, my emphasis.

9. See Genesis Rabbah 56:3, cited in this context by Jon D. Levenson, *The Death and Resurrection of the Beloved Son: The Transformation of Child Sacrifice in Judaism and Christianity* (New Haven, CT: Yale University Press, 1993), 105.

10. For a detailed discussion, see Brown, *Answering Jewish Objections to Jesus, Vol. 2: Theological Objections*, 103–123; Vermes believes that this was also the doctrine of the ancient rabbis.

11. See also the note of Solomon Buber in his edition of Midrash Tanhuma, to this verse.

12. Geza Vermes, "Redemption and Genesis xxii," 211. For some critical interaction with the work of Vermes—primarily relative to the dating of some of the relevant material, not the content—cf. Bruce Chilton, "Recent Discussion of the Akedah," in idem, *Targumic Approaches to the Gospels: Essays in the Mutual Definition of Judaism and Christianity* (Lanham, MD: University Press of America, 1986), 39–49.

13. See Vermes, "Redemption and Genesis xxii," 206, citing the Fragmentary Targum.

14. Leviticus Rabbah, 29:9, cited in Vermes, ibid., 213.

15. Avraham Yaakov Finkel, *Contemporary Sages* (Northvale, NJ: Aronson, 1994), 84.

16. See, e.g., Genesis 9:6; and m. Yoma 8:8; b. Yoma 85b-86a.

17. See Numbers 25:1–9; for more extensive treatment of the entire subject treated in this chapter, see Brown, *Answering Jewish Objections to Jesus, Vol. 2: Theological Objections*, 153–167.

18. Cf., e.g., Rashi to Exodus 32:7–13.

19. m. Makkot 2:6; b. Makkot 11b; see also Leviticus Rabbah 10:6.

20. Jacob Milgrom, *The JPS Torah Commentary: Numbers* (Philadelphia: The Jewish Publication Society, 1993), 294. For a response to the objection that, "Nowhere in Jewish teaching does a sacrifice pay for future sins," see Brown, *Answering Jewish Objections to Jesus, Vol. 2: Theological Objections*, 165.

21. As cited in David Baron, *The Visions and Prophecies of Zechariah* (repr., Grand Rapids, MI: Kregel, 1972), 442, but with my own minor modifications and with my emphasis.

22. See Patai, *The Messiah Texts*, 116.

12—The Secret of the Priestly Messiah

1. See, e.g., Exodus 28–29; Leviticus 16.

2. For refutation of the idea that the authors of the Scrolls expected only one Messiah of Aaron and Israel, see Collins, *The Scepter and the Star*; note also L. H. Schiffman, "Messianic Figures and Ideas in the Qumran Scrolls," in Charlesworth, *The Messiah*, 116–129. It is also noteworthy

that in several other Qumran texts there is reference to a Davidic Messiah *and* a priest (see Collins, *The Scepter and the Star*, 74–101).

3. See Patai, *The Messiah Texts*, 191–192, for important excerpts. For full editions of the Testament of the Twelve Patriarchs, see James H. Charlesworth, ed., *The Old Testament Pseudepigrapha*, Volume One (Garden City, NY: Doubleday, 1983), 775–828 (ed. and trans. by H. C. Kee, who dates the fundamental writing of the Testaments to around 100 BCE); H. F. D. Sparks, ed., *The Apocryphal Old Testament* (Oxford: Clarendon, 1984), 505–600 (trans. by M. de Jonge).

4. For a rare, related example, see Avot d'Rabbi Nathan 34:6.

5. Cf., e.g., Midrash Tehillim 2:9; 18:29. For a refutation of the midrashic interpretation that applies Psalm 110 to Abraham, see Brown, *Answering Jewish Objections to Jesus, Vol. 3: Messianic Prophecy Objections*, 139–140, where I note that the interpretation is "as fascinating as it is far-fetched."

6. It is important to remember that King Saul, David's predecessor, got into big trouble by offering a sacrifice without priestly authorization (see 1 Sam. 13:14), while a later, godly king like Uzziah was stricken by God for daring to infringe on priestly ministry (in his case, burning incense in the Temple; see 2 Chron. 26:16–26).

7. For further discussion, see Brown, *Answering Jewish Objections to Jesus, Vol. 1: General and Historical Objections*, 86, with note 35 on 226.

8. This is universally recognized by traditional Jewish and Christian scholars; for key biblical references where the Messianic king is actually called "David," cf. Jeremiah 30:8–9; Ezekiel 34:20–24; 37:24–28; Hosea 3:5. Note also verses such as Isaiah 9:5–6[6–7]; 11:1; Jeremiah 23:5; 30:20–26.

9. Targum Jonathan actually substitutes "Messiah" for "Branch."

10. Cf. the reference to Avot d'Rabbi Nathan 34:6, above, note 381, where these two "sons of oil" are interpreted to be Aaron and the Messiah.

11. It should also be remembered that during the days of the Second Temple, specifically during the Hasmonean Dynasty, the ruling king over Jewish people was actually the high priest, and from the time of Simon (143/2–135/4 BCE) the titles of high priest and prince were considered hereditary, passed on to John Hyrcanus I and II and then to Aristobulus (for the entire period in question, see Schürer, et al., *History of the Jewish People*, 1:137–242).

12. For the reports that Rabbi Yitzhaq Kaduri (Israel's most revered teacher of mysticism who died in 2006 somewhere around the age of 110) claimed to have met the Messiah and that his name was Yehoshuah, see, e.g., WND.com, "Messiah Mystery Follows Death of Mystical Rabbi," May 18, 2007, http://www.wnd.com/2007/05/41669/ (accessed February 25, 2012).

13. For references, see Appendix A, note 2.

13—The Secret of the Prophet Greater Than Moses

1. According to Prof. Jeffrey H. Tigay, *The JPS Torah Commentary: Deuteronomy* (Philadelphia: The Jewish Publication Society, 2003), "As 34:10 indicates, no future prophet would ever be enough 'like' Moses to be his equal. The comparison refers only to the prophetic *role* that Moses played as God's spokesman." The language, however, is too similar, each time using *qwm*, raise up, and "like [Moses]," and so it would only be logical that the Jewish people would begin to look for *that* prophet. See Michael Rydelnik, *The Messianic Hope: Is the Hebrew Bible Really Messianic* (Nashville: B&H Academic), 58–64. Whenever the verse was written, its significance was clear once the Old Testament canon was closed. Had such a prophet been raised up during OT times, the verse would have had no meaning. According to Tigay, *Deuteronomy*, 338, "The verse [Deut 34:10] contrasts Joshua to Moses: although Joshua succeeded Moses, neither he nor any subsequent prophet was Moses' equal."

2. Cf. Shapiro, *The Limits of Orthodox Theology*, 87–90.

3. See chapter 12, note 2.

4. See also 1 Maccabees 4:46; 14:41.

5. As rendered in Collins, *The Scepter and the Star*, 79.

6. Ibid.; see also Fitzmyer, *The One Who Is to Come*, 89, "*a prophet* (undoubtedly a prophet like Moses, an allusion to Deut. 18:15, 18) . . ."

7. Collins, *The Scepter and the Star*, 79-80; see further 128–131.

8. See Bock, *Acts* 178-179, with references. See also Howard M. Teeple, *The Mosaic Eschatological Prophet* (Philadelphia: Society of Biblical Literature, 1957).

9. *Jewish New Testament Commentary*, 231.

10. This is my translation of the Hebrew that corresponds more with the following English translation of the midrash. The Hebrew in both texts is identical.

11. As translated in Driver and Neubauer, *The Fifty-Third Chapter of Isaiah According to the Jewish Interpreters*, 2:9. Why did the midrash attribute such prominence to the Messiah here, based on Isaiah 52:13? It could be that elsewhere in Isaiah, such terms of exaltation (raised, lifted up, highly exalted) were rightly applied only to God. In fact, you could argue that nowhere in the entire book of Isaiah is anyone—including the Lord himself—described in such exalted terms, and so it was only natural that this would catch the attention of the midrashic preachers and writers. God promises to judge everyone who is high and lofty (see Isa. 2:12–14) whereas he deserves to be called the high and lofty one (see Isa. 6:1; 57:15; cf. also Isa. 33:10; 5:16).

12. See Shapiro, *The Limits of Orthodox Theology*, 87–91, who references Nachmanides, Gersonides, Joseph Albo, and R. Tsevi Hirsch Chajes.

14—THE SECRET OF THE SIX THOUSAND YEARS

1. See Mitchell First, *Jewish History in Conflict: A Study of the Major Discrepancy Between Rabbinic and Conventional Chronology* (Northvale, NJ: Aronson, 1997); cf. also Judah M. Rosenthal, "Seder Olam," *Encyclopedia Judaica* 14:1091–1093. For the Hebrew text with translation and commentary, cf. Heinrich W. Guggenheimer, *Seder Olam: The Rabbinic View of Biblical Chronology* (Northvale, NJ: Aronson, 1998).
2. See note 1, immediately above.
3. Again, my point is not that rabbinic tradition expected the Messiah to appear the exact years that Jesus appeared on the scene but rather to that general era of time, more than nineteen centuries ago once the chronological error is adjusted.
4. This is the expanded rendering of the Hebrew text by Aharon Feldman in *The Juggler and the King: The Jew and the Conquest of Evil. An Elaboration of the Vilna Gaon's Insights Into the Hidden Wisdom of the Sages* (Jerusalem/New York: Feldheim), 146.
5. Ibid., 149–150.
6. Ibid., 151–152.
7. I have built this case in more detail in Brown, *Answering Jewish Objections to Jesus, Vol. 1: General and Historical Objections*, 75–80. See ibid., 80–84, for the prophetic significance of the Torah calendar.
8. Abba Hillel Silver, *A History of Messianic Speculation in Israel* (New York: MacMillan, 1927), 7.
9. Ibid., 6, his emphasis.
10. Ibid., 19.
11. See also the commentary to Daniel 7:13–14 attributed to Saadiah Gaon, where these verses are once again interpreted messianically, and see Rashi to the verses cited in Daniel and Zechariah.
12. See note 7 above.

15—THE SECRET OF THE HIDDEN WISDOM

1. See, conveniently, Rav Michael Laitman with Collin Canright, *The Complete Idiot's Guide to Kabbalah* (New York: Alpha, 2007), with comments on the modern, pop-Kabbalah phenomenon.
2. See, e.g., John 8:56–59; 10:27–31.
3. See also Matthew 18:1–4: "At that time the disciples came to Jesus and asked, 'Who is the greatest in the kingdom of heaven?' He called a little child and had him stand among them. And he said: 'I tell you the truth,

unless you change and become like little children, you will never enter the kingdom of heaven. Therefore, whoever humbles himself like this child is the greatest in the kingdom of heaven.'"

4. See chapter 8.
5. See Robert Jastrow, *God and the Astronomers* (New York: Norton, 1978).
6. See note 1 for further references.
7. See, concisely, Erich Bischoff, *Kabbala: An Introduction to Jewish Mysticism and Its Secret Doctrine* (New York Beach, ME: S. Weiser, 1985), 11–13.

Epilogue—Not Just a Light for the Gentiles

1. See Walter Riggans, *Yeshua Ben David* (Crowborough: MARC, 1995), 79–93.
2. As translated in Falk, *Jesus the Pharisee*, 21.
3. Klausner, *Jesus of Nazareth*, 413.
4. See above, note 15.
5. Boteach, *Kosher Jesus*, 142, my emphasis.
6. Riggans, *Yeshua Ben David*, 93.
7. On Paul's extensive use of the term, see Martin Hengel, *Between Jesus and Paul* (Eng. trans., John Bowden; Philadelphia: Fortress Press, 1983), 65–77. He notes that this usage "expressed the fact that the crucified Jesus and no other is the eschatological bringer of salvation. *yešūᵃ mᶜšīhā* was already the most important missionary confession in the earliest Palestinian community, which even in the Aramaic form demonstrated the tendency towards making this a double name. The historical basis for it can be found in the crucifixion of Jesus as a messianic pretender" (ibid., 77).
8. See Matthew 2:2–3; John 19:19; see also Matthew 27:37; Mark 15:26; Luke 23:38.
9. See, e.g., Acts 3:18, 20; 4:26; 7:52; 8:5; 9:22; 17:3; 18:5, 28; 26:23.

Appendix A—The New Testament: An Unreliable, Anti-Semitic Book?

1. Brown, *Answering Jewish Objections to Jesus, Vol. 1: General and Historical Objections*, 145–175.
2. See especially Peter Schäfer, *Judeophobia: Attitudes Toward the Jews in the Ancient World* (Cambridge, MA: Harvard University Press, 1997).
3. See again the relevant material cited above, note 1.
4. It is actually this evangelical Christian love that provided some of the impetus for Rabbi Shmuley to write *Kosher Jesus*, saying that there is a new day in Jewish-Christian relations.

5. See also Brown, *Our Hands Are Stained With Blood*.
6. See Jacob Gartenhaus, *Famous Jewish Christians* (Grand Rapids, MI: Baker, 1979), 124.
7. Ibid., 125.
8. Boteach, *Kosher Jesus*, 128.
9. See chapter 5.
10. If you skipped over chapter 4, "A Threat to the Establishment," please go back and read it carefully. You will see there that if the words of Jesus can be called anti-Semitic, then God himself, along with Moses and the prophets of Israel, can be called anti-Semitic.
11. Urban C. von Wahlde, "The Gospel of John and the Presentation of Jews and Judaism," in David Efroymson, Eugene J. Fischer, and Leon Klenicki, eds., *Within Context: Essays on Jews and Judaism in the New Testament* (Collegeville, MN: Liturgical Press, 1993), 74.
12. Ibid., 81.
13. Cf. ibid., 80 (with references also to the Testament of Levi); cf. Lawrence H. Schiffman, *Reclaiming the Dead Sea Scrolls* (Philadelphia: Jewish Publication Society, 1994), 249–252.
14. Von Wahlde, ibid., 82.
15. Craig A. Evans in idem and Donald A. Hagner, eds., *Anti-Semitism and Early Christianity* (Minneapolis: Fortress, 1993), 8.
16. Ibid., with reference to Johnson, "The New Testament's Anti-Jewish Slander and the Conventions of Ancient Polemic," *Journal of Biblical Literature* 108 (1989), 419–441. Remember also that Josephus wrote for both Roman readers and Jewish readers, and therefore the argument cannot be raised that he was a Jew writing only to Jews about Jewish matters. Rather, both Josephus and John wrote for both a Jewish and Gentile audience, the main difference being that John wrote first and foremost to believers in the Messiah, be they Jew or Gentile.
17. See Ellis Rivkin, "Anti-Semitism in the New Testament," in idem, Ellis Rivkin, "A Jew Look at the New Testament," in idem, *What Crucified Jesus: Messianism, Pharisaism, and the Development of Christianity* (New York: UAHC Press, 1997), 124 (see in full, 107–129), his emphasis; for the references to Josephus, see Johnson, "Anti-Jewish Slander," 434–436.
18. See, e.g., Ephesians 2:1–3; 2 Corinthians 4:6; Colossians 3:13; 1 John 5:19.
19. Boteach, *Kosher Jesus*, 116. He even claims, with both inaccuracy and hyperbole, that "Jesus wanted to deliver the Jews from Rome. Paul wanted only to deliver them from Judaism. Furthermore, Jesus was exclusively interested in the Jewish people, while Paul was obsessed with proselytizing gentiles." Every statement here is patently false, as we have seen. In short, Jesus was not a freedom fighter against Rome (that, instead, is

the fictional Rabbi Rambo); Paul taught that Jewish followers of Jesus should continue to live as Jews; after his resurrection, Jesus commissioned his disciples to take his message to all nations, making clear while he was alive that he was dying for the sins of the world; and Paul, who loved the Gentiles and felt they were worthy of his love and hard work, never stopped praying for his Jewish people, carrying a deep burden for them throughout his life.

20. See note 1 for details.

21. See also Acts 4:25–28; 5:27–31; 13:26–30, 32, 38–39.

22. Boteach, *Kosher Jesus*, 7.

23. Ibid., 18.

24. For an excellent and concise discussion, see Walter C. Kaiser Jr., *Toward Old Testament Ethics* (Grand Rapids, MI: Zondervan, 1993), 67–72.

25. For the DVD of my 2004 debate with Rabbi Shmuley, where these issues were discussed with great passion on both sides, see http://tinyurl .com/7ajjvlh.

26. See further Brown, *Answering Jewish Objections to Jesus, Vol. 1: General and Historical Objections*, 101–145, 175–176, with extensive references.

27. More broadly, see Brown, *Answering Jewish Objections to Jesus, Vol. 4: New Testament Objections*, 41–59.

28. F. F. Bruce, *The New Testament Documents: Are They Reliable?*, 6th ed. (Downers Grove, IL: InterVarsity, 2001) remains very helpful. For relevant excerpts, see Brown, *Answering Jewish Objections to Jesus, Vol. 4: New Testament Objections*, 42–47.

29. See, e.g., Daniel B. Wallace, ed., *Revisiting the Corruption of the New Testament: Manuscript, Patristic, and Apocryphal Evidence* (Grand Rapids, MI: Kregel, 2011).

30. See the Prolegomenon of Harry M. Orlinsky to the reprint of Christian D. Ginsburg, *Introduction to the Massoretico-critical Edition of the Hebrew Bible* (New York: Ktav, 1966).

31. See Richard Bauckham, *Jesus and the Eyewitnesses: The Gospels as Eyewitness Testimony* (Grand Rapids, MI: Eerdmans, 2006).

32. Cf. Michael L. Brown, "Unequal Weights and Measures: A Critique of the Methodology of the Anti-Missionaries," printed as the Appendix to idem, *Answering Jewish Objections to Jesus, Vol. 5: Traditional Jewish Objections*, 269–277; it is also available online at http://realmessiah.ask drbrown.org/read/unequal-weights-and-measures (accessed February 25, 2012).

33. See Keener, *The Historical Jesus of the Gospels*; Bock and Webb, *Key Events in the Life of the Historical Jesus*; Paul Rhodes Eddy and Gregory A. Boyd, *The Jesus Legend: A Case for the Historical Reliability of the Synoptic Jesus Tradition* (Grand Rapids, MI: Baker Academic, 2007); cf. also Bauckham,

Jesus and the Eyewitnesses; Craig L. Blomberg, *The Historical Reliability of the Gospels*, 2nd ed. (Downers Grove, IL: IVP Academic, 2007); idem, *The Historical Reliability of John's Gospel: Issues and Commentary* (Downers Grove, IL: InterVarsity, 2001).

34. Bruce, *The New Testament Documents*, 122.
35. Quoted in Josh McDowell, *Skeptics Who Demanded a Verdict* (Wheaton, IL: Tyndale House, 1989), 85.
36. Bruce, *The New Testament Documents*, 15.

Appendix B—*Kosher Jesus* and "Why the Jews Cannot Accept Jesus"

1. Boteach, *Kosher Jesus*, 139.
2. This is a conservative estimate. According to Schoeman, *Salvation Is from the Jews*, 351, "By the mid 1970s, *Time* magazine placed the number of Messianic Jews in the U.S. at over 50,000; by 1993 this number had grown to 160,000 in the U.S. and about 350,000 worldwide (1989 estimate)....There are currently over 400 Messianic synagogues worldwide, with at least 150 in the U.S."
3. Boteach, *Kosher Jesus*, 150.
4. See epilogue, "Not Just a Light for the Gentiles."
5. Boteach, *Kosher Jesus*, chapters 23–25, 27.
6. This numbering refers to the objections answered rather than to page numbers.
7. Boteach, *Kosher Jesus*, chapter 23.
8. Ibid., chapter 28.
9. Ibid., chapter 29.
10. Ibid., chapter 30.
11. Ibid., chapter 31.
12. Ibid., chapter 33 (citing 185 here).
13. Ibid., 149.
14. Ibid., 207.
15. Ibid., 212.
16. Ibid., 218.